AMERICA'S
TEST KITCHEN

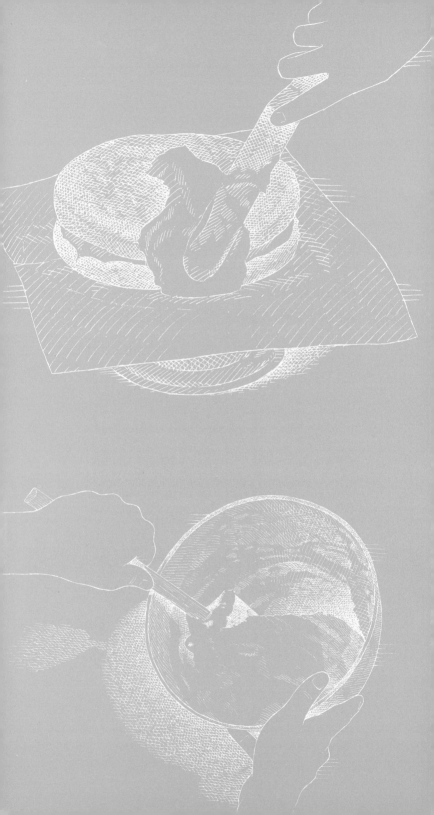

Kitchen
Smarts

Questions and Answers
to Boost Your Cooking IQ

THE EDITORS AT
AMERICA'S TEST KITCHEN

ILLUSTRATIONS BY
JOHN BURGOYNE

America's Test Kitchen
21 Drydock, Suite 210E, Boston, MA 02210

Library of Congress Cataloging-in-Publication Data

Names: Burgoyne, John (Illustrator), illustrator. | America's Test Kitchen (Firm)
Title: Kitchen smarts : questions and answers to boost your cooking IQ / the editors at America's Test Kitchen ; illustrations by John Burgoyne.
Description: Boston, MA : America's Test Kitchen, [2017] | Includes index.
Identifiers: LCCN 2017021876 | ISBN 9781940352718 (pbk.)
Subjects: LCSH: Cooking--Technique. | Cooking.
Classification: LCC TX651 .K58 2017 | DDC 641.5--dc23
LC record available at https://lccn.loc.gov/2017021876
Manufactured in Canada
10 9 8 7 6 5 4 3 2 1

Distributed by Penguin Random House Publisher Services
Tel: 800.733.3000

Chief Creative Officer
Jack Bishop

Editorial Director, Books
Elizabeth Carduff

Executive Editor
Adam Kowit

Project Editor
Rachel Greenhaus

Editorial Assistant
Alyssa Langer

Design Director, Books
Carole Goodman

Deputy Art Director, Books
Jen Kanavos Hoffman

Illustration
John Burgoyne

Cover Illustration
Michael Klein

Production Director
Guy Rochford

Senior Production Manager
Jessica Lindheimer Quirk

Production Manager
Christine Walsh

Imaging Manager
Lauren Robbins

Production and Imaging Specialists
Heather Dube, Dennis Noble, Jessica Voas

Copy Editor
Karen Wise

Proofreader
Pat Jalbert-Levine

Indexer
Ken DellaPenta

Contents

Where Do I Start?

A Thematic Table of Contents

YOU HAVE QUESTIONS AND WE HAVE ANSWERS . . . BUT IF YOU need some help figuring out where to begin, pick a topic that piques your interest and jump to the pages listed below.

Poultry
10, 11, 12, 59, 157,
173, 177, 179, 278, 279, 280

Eggs

18, 19, 84, 203, 261

Dairy
85, 86, 87, 88, 89, 90,
91, 95, 162, 216, 224,
228, 231, 240, 267

Fruit
33, 34, 37, 105, 106, 126,
152, 153, 222, 232

Vegetables
28, 29, 30, 31, 32, 35,
36, 37, 97, 98, 99, 100,
101, 102, 103, 104, 112,
113, 114, 115, 116, 117,
141, 154, 155, 156, 163,
168, 174, 191, 192,
234, 269

Herbs and Spices

107, 108, 109, 110, 111,
118, 119, 120, 121,
193, 213, 261, 262

Salt
23, 24, 25, 122,
150, 151, 214, 244

Storage
26, 27, 35, 45, 220,
221, 222, 225, 268

Equipment
47, 48, 49, 50, 128, 129,
130, 131, 132, 133, 134, 135,
136, 137, 138, 139, 140, 141,
142, 143, 160, 161, 164, 165,
166, 167, 168, 169, 170, 180,
181, 182, 190, 193, 194, 195,
237, 238

Welcome to America's Test Kitchen

This book has been tested, written, and edited by the folks at America's Test Kitchen. Located in Boston's Seaport District in the historic Innovation and Design Building, it features 15,000 square feet of kitchen space including photography and video studios. It is the home of *Cook's Illustrated* magazine and *Cook's Country* magazine and is the Monday-through-Friday destination for more than 60 test cooks, editors, and cookware specialists. Our mission is to test recipes over and over again until we understand how and why they work and until we arrive at the "best" version. As we like to say, "We make the mistakes so you don't have to."

All of this would not be possible without a belief that good cooking is based on a foundation of objective technique. Some people like spicy foods and others don't, but there is a right way to sauté, there is a best way to cook a pot roast, and there are measurable scientific principles involved in producing perfectly beaten, stable egg whites. Our ultimate goal is to investigate the fundamental principles of cooking to give you the tools you need to become a better cook.

To see what goes on behind the scenes at America's Test Kitchen, check out our social media channels. You can watch us work (in our actual test kitchen) by tuning in to *America's Test Kitchen* or *Cook's Country from America's Test Kitchen* on public television or on our websites. Listen to test kitchen experts on public radio (SplendidTable.org) to hear insights that illuminate the truth about real home cooking. Want to hone your cooking skills or finally learn how to bake—with an America's Test Kitchen test cook? Enroll in one of our online cooking classes. However you choose to visit us, we welcome you into our kitchen, where you can stand by our side as we test our way to the best recipes in America.

facebook.com/AmericasTestKitchen

twitter.com/TestKitchen

youtube.com/AmericasTestKitchen

instagram.com/TestKitchen

pinterest.com/TestKitchen

google.com/+AmericasTestKitchen

AmericasTestKitchen.com

CooksIllustrated.com

CooksCountry.com

OnlineCookingSchool.com

Introduction

In the decades since *Cook's Illustrated* magazine was first published, we've received thousands of letters from curious, clever, and just plain confused home cooks who have come up against stumpers in the kitchen. The questions range from basic, practical queries about how to cook fried chicken without making a hot mess (page 183) to highly scientific investigations into the chemistry behind why the starchy batter on that chicken crisps up in the hot oil (page 243). Readers also turn to us for a gut-check on common food and cooking myths, and we're happy to go toe-to-toe with traditional wisdom to figure out the truth: Do you really need to rinse off chicken before you cook it (page 12)?

Today, with the ubiquity of tablets, computers, and smartphones, most of us simply run an Internet search any time we have a kitchen question, no matter how strange that question might be. But when you search online, you end up with a cacophony of answers, and it's a real challenge to figure out who truly knows what they're talking about. Luckily, in this book we've packed together hundreds of definitive, researched, kitchen-tested answers to questions large and small, common and bizarre. As the saying goes, there are no dumb questions, but we would add that there are dumb—and wrong!—answers. We've been in the answer business for many years and here, for the first time ever, we've collected all that hard-earned wisdom in one place. We've done the equipment testing, ingredient tasting, and recipe development required to get to the bottom of your kitchen conundrums. We're even here for the questions you didn't know you had: For instance, have you ever noticed that stews taste better the day after you make them? Want to know why? Turn to page 210!

Whether you're playing fast and loose with recipe substitutions, dying to understand the physics behind how a whisk works (page 182), or just want to make sure you know how to pronounce *mirepoix* without embarrassing yourself (page 284; it's meer-PWAH), we're here to give you all the answers you need to become a better, more confident cook.

Kitchen Mythbusters

What If Grandma Was Wrong?

Cooking knowledge and kitchen skills are often handed down from one generation to the next. But sometimes what gets passed down is more than a classic lasagna recipe or a secret trick for making pie dough; it's traditional wisdom about ingredients and techniques that may or may not be accurate, as much as we hate to admit it. We'll be the first to credit our parents and grandparents for our love of cooking and food, and maybe even our famous peach pie with the perfect crust, but they also taught us more than a few "facts" that turned out to be not exactly true. And over time, many of these inherited ideas have become widely held and largely unquestioned beliefs. In this chapter, we fact-check some of the most common and enduring pieces of kitchen mythology to see what's really worth passing on and what needs to be debunked once and for all— sorry, Grandma and Grandpa.

WHICH OF THESE COMMON COOKING "FACTS" ARE ACTUALLY TRUE and which are just myths?

1
Covering a pot will make the water boil faster.

2
Slamming the oven door or stomping your feet in the kitchen while a cake is baking will cause the cake to fall.

3
You can safely eat oysters only in months whose names contain the letter *R*.

4
You should never wash fresh mushrooms.

5
The thin white lines on the skin of a chile pepper indicate how spicy the pepper will be.

6 Adding oil to pasta cooking water will keep the pasta from sticking.

7 Cocktails taste better the longer they're stirred.

9 You can regrow scallions by putting the roots in a glass of water, even if you've used up the green parts.

8 Searing meat over high heat is the best way to seal in the meat's juices.

10 When you cook with wine, liquor, or beer, all the alcohol evaporates and burns off.

Answers

1 True (page 21)
2 Myth (page 17)
3 Myth (page 13)
4 Myth (page 31)
5 Myth (page 30)
6 Myth (page 22)
7 True (page 41)
8 Myth (page 6)
9 True (page 37)
10 Myth (page 39)

Searing meat at the start of cooking seals in the juices.

⚭

As far as we can tell, searing has no effect on how much moisture meat retains during cooking.

Cooking a steak usually occurs in two stages: a quick sear in a hot skillet to brown the surface, followed by gentler cooking to finish. Many people believe that searing the raw steak "seals in" the moisture in the meat, resulting in a juicier finished product than meat browned at the end of cooking. Yet we've all seen that well-seared steaks exude juices as they rest. So is this just a kitchen myth?

We weighed eight rib-eye steaks and divided them into two batches. We seared the first batch in a skillet over high heat, then cooked them in a 250-degree oven until they reached an internal temperature of 125 degrees. For the second batch we reversed the order, first placing the steaks in a 250-degree oven until they reached approximately 110 degrees, then searing them until their interiors hit 125 degrees. We weighed the steaks after cooking and averaged the results, then compared that with the average weight of the steaks before cooking. Both batches of steaks lost nearly an identical amount of liquid: around 22 percent of their weight. If searing truly seals in juices, the steaks seared first would have had more moisture trapped inside than those seared after cooking in the oven.

One thing that does make a difference in how juicy meat will be is resting it after cooking. Resting allows the juices, which are driven to the center of the meat during cooking, to redistribute themselves more evenly. As a result, meat that has rested sheds less juice than meat sliced straight from the grill, skillet, or oven. For more information, see page 227.

Cutting into meat while it's cooking to check its doneness will cause it to lose its juices.

⫷

This is an acceptable method for some cuts of meat but should be avoided with others.

For precision, and also to prevent moisture loss, it's better to use a thermometer to check doneness. When cooking a particularly thin piece of meat, however, it's difficult to use a thermometer, so our recommended alternative is the "nick-and-peek" method of making a small cut into the meat with a paring knife to check doneness. However, widespread belief holds that cutting into meat while it's cooking should be avoided since it allegedly allows precious juices to escape.

To put this theory to the test, we prepared two samples each of 1¼-inch-thick pan-fried strip steaks (cooked to medium-rare, or 130 degrees), pan-seared oven-roasted pork tenderloins (cooked to medium, or 140 degrees), and pan-roasted chicken breasts (cooked until well-done, or 160 degrees). We used both methods—thermometer and paring knife—to test for doneness and measured the amount of liquid expelled after each sample had rested for about 10 minutes. Both strip steaks exuded equal amounts of liquid (2 teaspoons), while the pork tenderloin checked using the nick-and-peek method lost ¼ teaspoon more juice, and the nicked chicken breast lost ¾ teaspoon more. Why the difference? Because the pork and the chicken were more fully cooked than the medium-rare steaks, it was necessary to make a relatively deep cut to determine doneness. In these cases, then, there is more moisture loss, so we recommend the thermometer method. Save nicking and peeking for fish and thin cuts of meat where a shallow slash will work just fine.

You should always fully thaw steaks before you start cooking them.

Actually, you can cook a great steak straight from the freezer.

We cut a strip loin into eight steaks, cut each steak in half crosswise, put the pieces in vacuum-sealed bags, and froze them. We then thawed half of each steak in the refrigerator overnight and kept the other half frozen. We seared both sets of steaks in a hot skillet and then transferred them to a low oven until they reached medium-rare (125 degrees). Not surprisingly, the frozen steaks took longer to finish cooking through in the oven. What was surprising, though, was that the frozen steaks actually browned in the skillet just as well as, and in the same amount of time as, the thawed steaks. Furthermore, they had less moisture loss and thinner bands of gray, overcooked meat directly under the crust than the thawed steaks. Tasters unanimously preferred the cooked-from-frozen steaks.

A fully frozen steak is extremely cold, which prevents over-cooking while the surface reaches the very high temperatures necessary for browning reactions. As its slightly thicker gray band indicated, the steak that had been thawed had more overcooking around the edge, so it made sense that it also had greater moisture loss.

While we prefer to start with steak that's never been frozen for the best texture, if we do have frozen steaks on hand, from now on we'll cook them straight from the freezer. Freeze steaks, uncovered, overnight on a baking sheet (this dries them out to prevent excess splattering during cooking), then wrap them tightly in plastic wrap, place in a zipper-lock bag, and return to the freezer. To ensure that frozen steaks brown evenly, cook them in a large skillet with ⅛ inch of oil.

You can tell the doneness of a piece of meat by comparing its texture to the texture of your hand.

Sure, Fingerspitzengefühl *(literally, "feeling in the tips of the fingers") is one way to determine doneness, but you'll get better results with a thermometer.*

When meat is heated, the proteins inside the meat compress and contract, squeezing out some of the liquid trapped in the proteins, which then moves into the spaces created between the shrinking proteins. This process of muscle contraction explains why experienced chefs can determine the doneness of meat by pushing on it and judging the amount of resistance. The firmer the meat, the more shrinkage has occurred and thus the more cooked the meat is.

To help inexperienced grill cooks develop instinctive fingertip precision, chefs train them literally by hand: Different points on a relaxed, open palm replicate the texture of rare, medium-rare, and well-done meats. However, while professional cooks might rely on these "rules of thumb" to determine doneness, we find this method much too imprecise. An instant-read thermometer coupled with knowledge of how temperatures relate to desired doneness is a much more reliable path to success.

| **Rare** | **Medium-Rare** | **Well-Done** |

If ground meat turns brown in the package, it has gone bad.

∞

Fortunately, color changes of this nature are purely cosmetic—they have no bearing on the meat's flavor or wholesomeness.

Ever find that the ground meat you just brought home from the supermarket is red on the outside but dark purple or brown on the inside? If you feared that this is an indication that the meat is past its prime or that something bad has happened to it, worry no more. The color in meat comes from a muscle protein called myoglobin. When the meat is freshly cut, this protein is deep purple. As the meat sits in its packaging (or in the butcher's display case), the myoglobin converts to bright red oxymyoglobin on the meat's exterior, where it is exposed to more oxygen. Inside the meat, where less oxygen can penetrate, it will slowly convert to brown metmyoglobin, creating the color difference between the surface of the meat and the interior, but not affecting the freshness or flavor of the meat.

Pink poultry and pork are always unsafe to eat.

∞

Don't overcook these meats because you're afraid of a little pink.

In general, the red or pink color in meat comes from myoglobin in the muscle cells that store oxygen. Because the areas of the animal that tend to get the most exercise—the legs and thighs—require more oxygen, they contain more myoglobin, which makes them darker in color than the breasts. As turkey (or chicken) roasts in the oven, the oxygen attached to the myoglobin is released, and the meat becomes lighter and browner in color. However, trace amounts of other gases formed in a hot oven or grill may react with the myoglobin to produce a pink color, even if the poultry is fully cooked. Always rely on an instant-read thermometer to accurately ascertain doneness when roasting poultry.

As for pork, selective breeding has made today's pork much leaner than pork in the past, and if you cook it till all traces of pinkness are gone, the meat will be dry and tough. We think that the leanest cuts are best cooked to 145 degrees. At this point, the meat will still have a tinge of pink in the center.

However, pink pork isn't completely without risk. All meat may be subject to cross-contamination with pathogens such as salmonella. This can happen during processing, at the supermarket, or in your home. To reduce risk, food safety experts recommend cooking all meat to 160 degrees (well-done). But if you think it's worth taking a small risk to enjoy a rosy steak, you might as well do the same with pork.

Chicken is done when the juices run clear.

❧

It's true that the juices will change color during cooking, but this is an inaccurate way to gauge doneness.

One persistent cooking belief is that if you poke chicken with a fork and the juices that come out are clear rather than pink, the meat is done. But is this oft-cited "rule" actually true? A chicken breast is done when it reaches 160 degrees, while thighs are done at 175 degrees. But when we cooked whole chickens, in one case the juices ran clear when the breast registered 145 degrees and the thigh 155 degrees—long before the chicken was done. And when we pierced another chicken that we'd overcooked (the breast registered 170 degrees and the thigh 180 degrees), it still oozed pink juices.

Here's the scoop: The juices in a chicken are mostly water; they get their color from myoglobin. When myoglobin is heated, it loses its color. So there's some good reasoning behind this idea. The problem is that the exact temperature at which this color change occurs varies depending on a number of factors (primarily the conditions under which the chicken was raised and processed). The best way to check for doneness? Use a thermometer, and make sure that both the light meat and dark meat are at the proper temperature before removing the chicken from the heat. For more information on how to use a thermometer to check the doneness of poultry, see page 173.

Poultry should be rinsed before cooking.

*Rinsing poultry might actually cause
more problems than it solves.*

Both the U.S. Department of Agriculture and the Food and Drug Administration advise against washing poultry. According to their research, while rinsing may remove some bacteria, the only way to ensure that all bacteria are killed is through proper cooking. Moreover, splashing bacteria around in the sink can be dangerous, especially if contaminated water lands on other kitchen surfaces—or on food that is ready to be served.

Some people argue that chicken should be rinsed for reasons of flavor, not safety. After sitting in its own blood and juices for days, they say, chicken should be unwrapped and refreshed under running water. To find out if rinsing had any impact on flavor, we roasted four chickens—two rinsed, two unrinsed—and held a blind tasting. Tasters couldn't tell the difference. Our conclusion? Avoid rinsing raw meat and poultry. Rinsing is more likely to spread contaminants around the kitchen than to send them down the drain.

You should eat oysters only in months whose names contain the letter *R*.

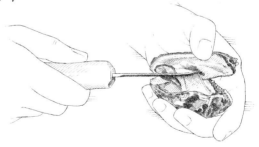

There was a good reason for this rule once upon a time, but it doesn't apply to modern oysters, so skip the superstition.

The "R" rule may have been true 30 or 40 years ago, but thanks to advances in aquaculture and refrigeration, it has fallen by the wayside. In days gone by, fishermen dug for oysters only in the colder "R" months (September through April) to avoid the spawning season. Warm waters (above 60 degrees) encourage spawning, rendering oysters milky, bland, soft-textured, and small. Once the spawning season is complete, oysters are generally plumper and better-tasting, thus commanding a higher price tag.

Today, oysters are more likely to be farmed than found, with farmers having more control over the conditions in which the bivalves are grown, harvested, and stored. This means that oyster cultivators can "plant" oysters in cold waters, thereby staggering spawning and keeping their product available year-round. So forget the "R" rule—any time is fine for eating oysters.

The best way to test a loaf of bread for doneness is by tapping on it to see if it sounds hollow.

✹

There are much more accurate ways to ensure that your bread is fully baked.

Long before cooks had handy tools such as instant-read thermometers to aid in determining doneness, tapping the bottom of a loaf of bread was one of the only ways to assess its readiness for the cutting board. Still, the technique requires a practiced ear, and not everybody embraces its utility. (*The Fannie Farmer Cookbook*, for instance, warns that bread "often" sounds hollow—even when it's not done.)

We baked our multigrain and American sandwich breads and then tapped the bottom crusts with our fingertips when they were below, at, and above their target temperatures. Some of our testers had no trouble recognizing the hollow sound of a fully cooked loaf, but to others, a tap on an underdone loaf sounded virtually the same. With practice, a baker might become adept at detecting when a tap sounds hollow, but we have found that it is much more effective to combine visual signs (the bread is properly browned) with the use of an instant-read thermometer. Rustic breads should be baked to an internal temperature of 200 to 210 degrees, while richer breads like brioche are done at 190 to 195 degrees. Make sure both the visual cues and the temperature match the doneness requirements for the specific recipe you're baking.

When you're making bread, use hot water to jump-start the yeast.

Do this only if you're feeling particularly murderous toward the yeast . . . and your chances of a good rise in your dough.

Since heat activates yeast, some bakers—and indeed, some yeast manufacturers—advise using 120- to 130-degree water for making bread doughs. According to the manufacturers, this will "guarantee yeast activity." However, those temperatures are dangerously close to the range at which yeast dies: 130 to 140 degrees. We suspect that the true intent is to guarantee yeast activity that is both rapid and visible. We know that yeast is perfectly active when combined with water at far colder temperatures (we use ice water when proofing doughs for several days to develop flavor)—the yeast just "wakes up" very slowly. Using hotter water would appeal to bakers for whom seeing dough bubble and rise (and seeing this happen quickly) is believing.

We advise patience, not only because hot water can kill the yeast, which means that your dough won't rise at all, but also because at the very least it can negatively affect the structure and flavor of the finished bread by encouraging overproofing or overheating during mixing. Both result in overactive yeast, which creates sour flavors and loss of dough structure (less rise) through overproduction of acids and carbon dioxide.

In other words, there are no real advantages to using water that's above 120 degrees in yeasted doughs—but there is a real risk of ruining them.

If you're baking only half a batch of cupcakes or muffins, you should fill the remaining cups with water.

Don't worry: Your baked goods (and your muffin tin) should be just fine without this messy extra step.

Proponents of this practice contend that filling any empty cups in a muffin tin with water serves two functions: preventing the tin from warping and also acting as a "heat sink" to ensure that muffins next to empty cups heat evenly (avoiding stunted growth or spotty browning).

We tested this theory by baking one batch of muffins in which all 12 of the muffin tin cups were completely filled with batter, one batch in which only six cups were filled with batter and the remaining six with water, and one batch in which six cups were filled with batter and the other six left empty. The results? All muffins had the same height, texture, and color, and none of the tins warped.

On reflection, the results make sense: In a full 12-cup muffin tin, all but the two center muffins are directly exposed to the oven's heat on at least one side to no ill effect. Furthermore, if your muffin tin warps, that's a sign that you need to find a better-quality tin.

Slamming the oven door (or walking too violently around the kitchen) will cause a cake to collapse.

⊗

As long as you don't have elephants wandering around your kitchen, you should be OK!

Cakes rise as tiny air bubbles in the batter expand in the heat of the oven. To find out if slamming the door would interrupt the process enough to spell disaster, we mixed batters for muffins, yellow cake, angel food cake, and cheese soufflé and loaded them into hot ovens. Just before each item reached its maximum height, we opened the oven door all the way and gave it a hard slam.

The sturdy muffins emerged unharmed, as did the yellow cake. Even the notoriously fragile angel food cake and the soufflé survived the vigorous slamming. Why? A properly developed foam—whether powered by baking soda, baking powder, or beaten egg whites—is pretty resilient. While very rough handling (dropping a half-baked cake, for example) can make it collapse, there's no need to worry about slamming doors or stomping around the kitchen.

In case you were wondering, the same is true for rotating cakes during baking. We made two each of the most delicate cakes we could think of: fluffy yellow layer cake and angel food cake, both containing whipped egg whites. One set of cakes we rotated at the halfway point, jostling them clumsily in order to drive the point home. The other we left alone. The result? Neither of the rotated cakes was worse for wear, and both were more evenly browned than the undisturbed cakes. It seems that even delicate cakes are fully set early on during baking, so there's little risk of collapse halfway through—and rotating your baked goods will only improve the results.

Room-temperature eggs are best for cakes.

∞

Sort of, but cold eggs are a problem only for specific recipes—and there's an easy way to warm them up.

Cake recipes often call for room-temperature eggs, which incorporate into the batter more readily than cold eggs. We wondered, though, if the difference between room-temperature and cold eggs was so great that it could actually ruin a cake recipe. To find out, we conducted a blind tasting of two yellow cakes: one made with room-temperature eggs, the other with eggs pulled straight from the refrigerator. The cake prepared with cold eggs produced a slightly thicker batter and took five minutes longer to bake. The cake made with room-temperature eggs had a slightly finer, more even crumb, but the cold-egg cake was entirely acceptable. Overall, tasters strained to detect differences between the two cakes, so we think it's fine to use cold eggs in most basic cake recipes.

However, cold eggs can cause problems in finicky cakes, such as angel food and chiffon, that rely on air incorporated into the beaten eggs as a primary means of leavening. In these cases, we found that cold eggs didn't whip nearly as well as room-temperature eggs and that the cakes didn't rise properly. As a result, these cakes were too dense when made with cold eggs. If you need to quickly warm whole eggs, place them in a bowl, cover them with hot—but not boiling—tap water, and let them sit for five minutes before using them.

Older eggs are better for baking than fresh eggs.

❀

Don't pass up farm-fresh eggs in hopes of baking a better cake—age doesn't matter.

Because egg whites thin with age, some bakers theorize that the weakened proteins of eggs even a few weeks old can stretch more than those from just-laid eggs, leading to cakes that rise higher and have a softer, more tender texture than cakes made with the freshest eggs. To test this theory, we made a yellow layer cake with 7-week-old supermarket eggs (we determined their age by the date on the carton) and Vermont farm eggs laid a few days before. Any differences we found were slight. The cake made with older eggs dissolved a little more quickly on the tongue, and the cake made with farm-fresh eggs was a little more attractive. But only a few tasters actually detected these variations in texture. And did one cake rise higher than the other? No. So grab fresh eggs if you can. But think about scrambling or frying any you don't use for baking, since those are dishes where freshness truly matters.

You can tell how fresh an egg is by putting it in a bowl of water—if it floats, it's bad.

❀

Older eggs do float, but that doesn't tell you anything about their quality.

You may have heard this common advice for testing the freshness of eggs without cracking them open: Put the egg in a bowl of cold tap water. If it lies flat on the bottom, it's fresh; if it stands up and bobs on the bottom, it's not as fresh, though still safe to eat; if it floats to the surface, it's bad. We decided to test this out with three cartons of eggs with sequential expiration dates exactly one month apart. Our results matched the description of the eggs' behavior based on their age: Most of the eggs from the freshest carton sank, most of those from the next-freshest carton bobbed, and all of those from the oldest carton floated.

Eggs take in air as they age, creating an air cell inside. An egg that floats has a good-size air cell, indicating that the egg is at least a month or two old. Based on other tests we've done on the shelf life of eggs, however, we know that an older egg is not necessarily a spoiled egg. We found minimal performance differences in fresh eggs and eggs that were up to three months old. If an egg smells odd or displays discoloration, however, then it's definitely time to pitch it.

If you start with hot water instead of cold water, your water will boil faster.

∞

Yes, it probably will, but there's a good reason you might want to use cold water and wait the extra couple of minutes.

Waiting for a pot of water to boil for pasta can feel like an eternity. It seems logical that starting with water that is hot from the tap might speed up the process. To test this, we filled two identical pots with 4 quarts of tap water, one hot and one cold, and brought them to a boil, uncovered. The hot tap water took 13½ minutes to reach a boil, while the cold water took 15 minutes. We then added 1 tablespoon of salt and 1 pound of pasta to each pot. When the pasta was done, we drained and tasted it plain (no oil, no sauce). None of our tasters could tell the difference between the two batches of pasta.

However, before you turn on the hot tap, you might want to consider what the U.S. Environmental Protection Agency (EPA) has to say about cooking with hot tap water. According to the EPA, water hot from the tap can contain much higher levels of lead than cold tap water. Even cold tap water should be run for a while to ensure that any lead deposits are flushed out of the system. All of a sudden that extra minute and a half doesn't seem quite so long.

Water will boil faster if you cover the pot.

⊗

True—and that's not the only reason you should use a cover.

When you heat water in an open pot, some of the energy that could be raising the temperature of the liquid escapes with the vapor. But as long as more energy is being added to the water than is being lost with the vapor, the temperature will continue to rise until the water boils. Covering the pot prevents water vapor from escaping, enabling the temperature to rise more quickly. How much more quickly? In our experience, not a lot. When we brought 4 quarts of water to a boil in identical covered and uncovered stainless-steel Dutch ovens, the covered pot boiled in just over 12 minutes and the uncovered pot boiled in about 13½ minutes. But why waste even a small amount of time when it's so easy not to?

If, however, you're heating water or another liquid for a recipe and you need an exact amount, you'll want to keep the lid on from the beginning. By the time 1 quart of liquid comes to a boil, it can lose more than 2 tablespoons in volume through steam if left uncovered. This might not seem like much, but it's enough to throw off a recipe for chocolate cake, make a pastry cream more like pasty cream, or turn the simplest boiled rice gummy. So the next time the recipe calls for boiling a precise amount of liquid, put a lid on it.

The best way to tell if pasta is fully cooked is to throw it against the wall to see if it sticks.

✄

This is certainly the best way to make a mess; there are better ways to tell if pasta is cooked.

We prefer pasta cooked al dente, which is an Italian term meaning "to the tooth," or fully cooked but still firm when bitten. The cooking directions on the pasta box are a good starting point to get an idea of how long the pasta will take to cook, but those times are usually too long and will result in mushy, overcooked pasta. Figuring out exactly when to stop cooking takes a little trial and error.

Throwing the cooked pasta at the wall won't tell you anything about how done it is. Instead, take a piece of pasta out of the pot and taste it. Testing the pasta a few minutes ahead of the cooking time prescribed on the box is the most accurate way we've found to determine the doneness. For further information on how to cook perfect al dente pasta, see pages 270-271.

You should add oil to your cooking water to keep the pasta from sticking together as it cooks.

✄

Don't waste your oil; this does nothing for the pasta.

Adding salt to your pasta cooking water is a must to season the pasta from the inside out, but you can definitely skip the oil. It will only coat the pasta when you drain it, and that prevents the sauce from adhering.

The best way to keep pasta from sticking is to use a large amount of water. We recommend 4 quarts of water to 1 pound of pasta. This means you should be cooking pasta in a 6- or 8-quart stockpot or Dutch oven. Stirring the pasta for a minute or two after you add it to the boiling water will also help keep it from sticking.

Adding salt to your cooking water dramatically increases the sodium level of the pasta.

✠

Salting the cooking water does add to the sodium content of the pasta, but probably not as much as you think.

Adding salt to pasta cooking water ensures that the pasta will be flavorful. Throughout the years we've zeroed in on a preferred ratio of 1 tablespoon of table salt to 4 quarts of cooking water per pound of pasta for the best-seasoned pasta of any shape or size.

We were curious to find out exactly how much sodium actually makes it into the pasta, so we sent samples of six different shapes—spaghetti, linguine, penne, rigatoni, campanelle, and orzo—all cooked al dente, to an independent lab for analysis.

The results? Give or take a few milligrams of sodium, all the shapes absorbed about the same amount of salt: 1/16 teaspoon per 4-ounce serving, or a total of 1/4 teaspoon per pound of pasta. The U.S. Department of Agriculture (USDA) Dietary Guidelines for Americans recommend less than 2,300 milligrams (1 teaspoon) daily for people under age 51 and less than 1,500 milligrams (3/4 teaspoon) for those age 51 and older, so even if you're watching your sodium intake, the amount that pasta absorbs is so small that it's probably not an issue.

Salt your cooking water only after it has come to a boil, since salt increases the time it takes for the water to boil and can cause pitting in your pan.

∞

These aren't major concerns, but it also won't hurt to add the salt later.

Culinary students are taught to add salt to a pan of heating water only after it has reached a boil. Two explanations are offered: (1) Salt increases the time it takes for the water to boil, and (2) salt can cause pitting (the formation of tiny white spots on the pan) unless added after the water has come to a boil.

Indeed, it's a scientific fact that salt will increase the boiling point of water. The generally accepted formula says that 1½ tablespoons of salt in 1 quart of water will raise the boiling point by about 1 degree. But those proportions yield a super-salty solution that is almost never used in cooking.

In the test kitchen, we used the same burner and the same pot to bring 4 quarts of water with and without 1 tablespoon of salt to a boil, uncovered. Both came to a boil in the same amount of time.

We also did not witness an occurrence of pitting when we conducted our tests. In any case, cookware manufacturers say that pitting does not affect the performance, only the appearance, of cookware. However, the quick dissolution of the salt (as occurs in boiling water) does help reduce the risk of pitting.

Our recipes almost always direct the cook to add salt to water after it has come to a boil. However, if you tend to be an absentminded cook for whom salting at the outset is the best way to ensure that it gets done, then go ahead and do it. If pitting is a concern, simply stir the water until the salt dissolves.

Salt is optional in most recipes— you can just leave it out.

Salt does much more than just flavor food.
Even if a recipe calls for only a pinch
of salt, resist the temptation to omit it.

Even the small amount of salt included in most baking recipes makes an enormous difference. We tested yellow layer cakes made with and without salt and found serious flavor differences. Tasters found the salt-free cake overly sweet but also bland—they called it "mild," "flat," and "dull," and could barely detect any vanilla flavor. The cake that included salt was also sweet, but the flavors of butter and vanilla were much more balanced and pronounced.

Salt doesn't just enhance flavors in foods; it also helps mask less agreeable tastes like bitterness. By suppressing bitterness, salt allows more desirable flavors—including sweetness and spices—to come through. In bread baking, salt controls the activity of yeast, strengthens gluten, and accents the bread's flavor; it should never be omitted. Adding even a small amount of salt to an egg dish keeps the proteins in the eggs from bonding to each other, thereby producing a weaker protein chain and more tender eggs.

Salt is also a crucial component of many recipes involving meat and vegetables. Salt helps improve the texture and flavor of nearly every kind of meat. When salt is applied to raw meat, juices inside the meat are drawn to the surface. The salt then dissolves in the exuded liquid, forming a brine that is eventually reabsorbed by the meat. This brine acts to change the structure of the muscle proteins, helping them hold on to more of their own natural juices. Vegetables like tomatoes, cucumbers, and eggplant can also benefit from being salted to draw out their moisture before they're used in a recipe.

Memorize This!

How to Use Your Refrigerator

A COMMON MISCONCEPTION IS THAT THE REFRIGERATOR IS simply a box of cold air, and you don't have to worry about how or where you store things inside it. We often think of our refrigerator as having a single temperature ("cold"), but every refrigerator actually has a whole set of microclimates, with warmer, cooler, and more humid zones. You can make this temperature variation work to your advantage by learning which types of food are best suited to each of the different zones.

A. Cold Zone *Back, Top to Bottom*
The area of the shelves at the back of the fridge (and the bottom of the door) are normally the coldest areas (around 33 degrees). Meat, dairy, and produce that is not prone to chilling injury should be stored here.

B. Moderate Zone *Front, Top to Bottom*
The areas at the front of the refrigerator, from the top to the bottom shelves, are generally moderate, with temperatures above 37 degrees. Put eggs, butter, and fruits and vegetables that are sensitive to chilling injury here.

C. Humid Zone *Crisper Drawer*
Crispers provide a humid environment that helps keep produce with a high water content from shriveling and rotting. However, if the humidity is too high, water can accumulate and hasten spoilage. You can regulate the humidity by adjusting the vents; the more cold air that is let in, the less humid the environment will be.

| **A.** Cold Zone | **B.** Moderate Zone | **C.** Humid Zone |

Thin asparagus spears are more tender than thick ones.

*Actually, thicker spears have better texture,
but certain sizes are better for different dishes.*

Asparagus spears are the plant shoots of an underground crown that can produce for up to 20 years. The thickness of a spear has nothing to do with its age—that is, a thin spear will not mature into a thick spear. Rather, diameter is determined by two factors: the age of the entire plant (younger crowns produce more slender stalks) and its variety.

So, which size is preferable? We snapped off the woody bottoms of fat and skinny spears, steamed them, and tasted them side by side, both plain and tossed with olive oil and salt. Both types tasted equally sweet, nutty, and grassy. To our surprise, the thicker spears had the better texture (if only by a hair). The reason? The vegetable's fiber is slightly more concentrated in thinner spears.

Since thick and thin spears are both good bets, choose the size that best suits your cooking method. Thicker stalks are better for broiling and roasting because they will stand up to the intense dry heat that would quickly shrivel skinnier spears. We also like thick spears for grilling since they are easier to manipulate. Quick-cooking thin spears are good candidates for steaming and stir-frying.

Adding a raw potato will help rescue a dish that's too salty.

*It won't, but there are other ways
you can correct an oversalted dish.*

Adding potatoes to oversalted foods simply doesn't help. Yes, the potatoes might absorb some of the salty liquid, but the remaining liquid will still be too salty. However, there is a way to help mitigate the effects if you went overboard on the salt: Add another ingredient from the opposite end of the flavor spectrum. Depending on the recipe, you can add an acid (such as vinegar, lemon or lime juice, or canned unsalted tomatoes) or a sweetener (such as sugar, honey, or maple syrup) to counteract the offending saltiness. Use your judgment to figure out which addition would best suit the dish in question.

This approach also works for food that is too sweet or too spicy/acidic. To balance sweetness, use an acid or seasonings like fresh herbs or cayenne pepper. For sweet dishes, try a bit of liqueur or espresso powder. If your dish is too spicy or acidic, counteract that with a fat (such as butter, cream, sour cream, cheese, or olive oil) or a sweetener. (For more information, see page 249.)

While these adjustments can help in mild cases, keep in mind that prevention is the best medicine: Whenever possible, season with a light hand during the cooking process, then adjust the seasoning just before serving.

Most of the heat in a chile pepper resides in the seeds.

∞

*While seeding a chile will lessen the fieriness a little bit,
most of the heat comes from other sources.*

Chiles get their heat—or "pungency," as the experts like to say—from a group of chemical compounds called capsaicinoids, the best known of which is capsaicin. To figure out where most of these compounds reside, we donned rubber gloves and separated the outer green-colored flesh, the inner whitish pith, and the seeds from 40 jalapeños. We then sent the lot to our food lab. As it turned out, there were just 5 milligrams of capsaicin per kilogram of green jalapeño flesh (not enough to really make much impact on the human tongue), 73 milligrams per kilogram of seeds, and an impressive 512 milligrams per kilogram of pith.

The reason why the seeds registered more heat than the flesh is simply that they are embedded in the pith; they are essentially guilty—or hot—by reason of association. So from now on, when we want to control the fire in a dish, we'll do it by means of the pith. The seeds will just be along for the ride.

On a related note, it's a common misconception that you can tell how hot a pepper is from the white lines on the outside, which are known as "corking." It turns out that corking is merely a genetic trait with no bearing whatsoever on chile heat.

You should never
wash fresh mushrooms.

∞

Washing mushrooms will not ruin them,
as long as you do it right.

You've probably heard that you should never, ever wash fresh mushrooms under running water. The thinking goes that their spongy nature will allow them to soak up water, making them soft and slimy in the final dish. But when preparing a mushroom-heavy dish, the painstaking task of gingerly wiping every mushroom with a damp cloth—the method recommended by most experts—had us questioning just how valid this "rule" really is.

After testing both methods (a damp cloth versus a quick rinse in a colander under running water), we found no difference in the texture of the finished dishes. Our rule of thumb? Wash mushrooms right before cooking; if you let rinsed mushrooms sit around for longer than 10 or 15 minutes, the texture will indeed begin to suffer.

White button mushrooms
taste better if they're older.

∞

Surprisingly, there might be some truth to
this one—but there's a fine line between aged
to perfection and just plain past their prime.

Freshly harvested white button mushrooms have firm caps, stems, and gills that are free of dark spots. That said, some chefs advocate the use of slightly older, blemished mushrooms, claiming that they are more flavorful than pristine, ultrafresh specimens. To test this claim for ourselves, we sautéed two batches of mushrooms, one fresh from the supermarket and one showing signs of age after a week in the refrigerator. In a side-by-side comparison, the results surprised us. Tasters found that the older mushrooms had a deeper, earthier flavor and were substantially more "mushroomy" than the unblemished samples. This is likely because some moisture had evaporated, allowing the flavors to concentrate.

The takeaway: There's no need to discard old mushrooms. In fact, their imperfections may even improve the flavor of your dish. Do not, however, use mushrooms that smell fermented or feel slimy.

It's impossible to overcook mushrooms.

⊗

While many foods we cook require precise attention to internal temperature and cooking time, mushrooms are remarkably forgiving.

Cooks often lump mushrooms into the category of vegetables, though they're actually a fungus. While mushrooms display characteristics of vegetables (high water content) as well as meat (savory flavor), they are unique in their ability to maintain a pleasant texture over a wide range of cooking times.

We cut ½-inch-thick planks of portobello mushroom, zucchini, and beef tenderloin and steamed them in a basket in a large Dutch oven for 40 minutes. At 5-minute intervals, we used a piece of equipment called a CT3 Texture Analyzer to determine how much force was required to "bite" into each piece of food.

After 5 minutes of steaming, the tenderloin, portobello, and zucchini required 186, 199, and 239 grams of force, respectively, to compress (or "bite") 3 millimeters into the food. Tasters noted that all the samples were tender. Over the course of the next 35 minutes, the tenderloin steadily toughened, eventually turning a whopping 293 percent tougher, while the zucchini decreased in firmness 83 percent and turned mushy and structureless. The portobello, meanwhile, increased in firmness just 57 percent over the same period of time; after a full 40 minutes of cooking, tasters found the mushroom to still be properly tender.

The key to mushrooms' resiliency lies in their cell walls, which are made of a polymer called chitin. Unlike the proteins in meat or the pectin in vegetables, chitin is very heat-stable. This unique structure allows us to sauté mushrooms for just a few minutes or roast them for the better part of an hour, all the while achieving well-browned, perfectly tender specimens.

You can speed-ripen green bananas by roasting them in their skins.

While this might make the skins of the bananas appear ripe, it doesn't actually affect the ripeness of the fruit.

S trategies for speeding the ripening of bananas abound, but as we worked our way through over eight cases of fruit while developing a banana bread recipe, we found most of them to be ineffective. One theory, for example, holds that freezing or roasting underripe bananas in their skins will quickly render them sweet and soft enough for baking. While these methods do turn the bananas black—giving them the appearance of their supersweet, overripe brethren—they do little to encourage the necessary conversion of starch to sugar.

The best way to ripen bananas is to enclose them in a paper bag for a few days. Fruit produces ethylene gas, which hastens ripening; the bag traps the gas while still allowing some moisture to escape. Since fully ripe fruit emits the most ethylene, placing a ripe banana or other ripe fruit in the bag with the unripe fruit will speed the process by a day or two. (For more information, see page 222.)

The best way to tell if an avocado is ripe is to squeeze it.

⊗

Yes, this is a good way to determine ripeness, but it's also a good way to mistake a bruised avocado for a ripe one.

Our favorite type of avocados is Hass—the variety with dark, pebbly skin that's probably the default at your grocery store. We find them to be creamier and more flavorful than the large, smooth-skinned varieties. Testing for ripeness can be a little tricky, though; while avocados do get softer as they ripen, squeezing to determine ripeness is not always the best gauge. Not only can you bruise the fruit by squeezing it, but a previously bruised fruit can also be mistaken for a ripe one this way.

Our preferred method for identifying a ripe avocado is to try to flick the small stem off the fruit. If it comes off easily and you can see green underneath it, the avocado is ripe. If it does not come off or you see brown underneath, the avocado is not yet ripe, or it's overripe and therefore unusable.

If you do end up with an unripe avocado, we recommend storing it in the fridge for a few days. It will ripen a little more slowly than on the counter, but the ripening will be more even—and once completely ripe, a refrigerated avocado will last longer (about five full days).

Blowing into a bag of salad greens will help them last longer.

Maybe—but that doesn't mean you should do it.

This notion seemed pretty wacky to us (not to mention unsanitary), but in the interest of science, we divided fresh salad greens into two batches, placing both samples in zipper-lock bags and lightly inflating one of them with a few exhales before sealing. The salad leaves stored in the regular bag started to wilt after five days, while—much to our surprise—those that had received a few puffs lasted almost twice as long.

Here's why: Fresh produce ripens and eventually decomposes by the process of respiration (the conversion of glucose into carbon dioxide and water). However, exposing produce to elevated levels of carbon dioxide can retard the process. Air contains only 0.03 percent carbon dioxide, human breath as much as 4 to 5 percent. A couple of breaths into a zipper-lock bag full of salad greens increased the concentration of carbon dioxide enough to decelerate the respiration process.

Despite its effectiveness, we don't recommend this practice, since human breath can contain airborne pathogens. However, if you have a seltzer maker, you can use that as a sanitary source of carbon dioxide; simply add a few puffs of gas before you seal the bag of greens.

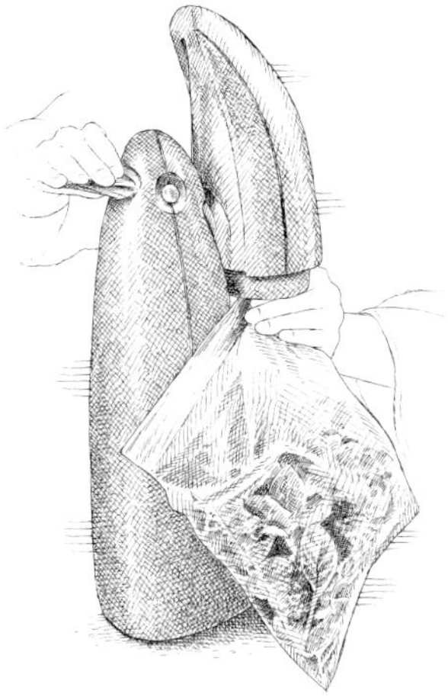

You can avoid crying while slicing onions by lighting a candle near your cutting board.

∞

It seems weird, but this does in fact work.

We can't tell you how many onions we've chopped over the years. Let's just say a lot. As a result, we've shed more than a few tears. What causes cut onions to be so pesky? When an onion is cut, the cells that are damaged in the process release sulfuric compounds as well as various enzymes, notably one called sulfoxide lyase. Those compounds and enzymes are separate when the onion's cell structure is intact; when the onion is cut, they activate and mix to form the real culprit behind crying, a volatile new compound called thiopropanal sulfoxide. When this evaporates in the air, it irritates the eyes, causing redness and tears.

Through the years we've collected dozens of ideas from readers, colleagues, magazines, and books, all aimed at reducing tears while cutting onions. We finally decided to put those ideas to the test. They ranged from the commonsensical (work underneath an exhaust fan) to the comical (whistle while you work or hold a toothpick in your teeth).

Overall, the methods that worked best were to introduce a flame near the cut onions or to protect our eyes by covering them with goggles or contact lenses. A flame, which can be produced by either a candle or a gas burner, changes the activity of the thiopropanal sulfoxide by completing its oxidization. Contact lenses and goggles form a physical barrier that the vapors cannot penetrate. So, if you really want to keep tears at bay when handling onions, light a candle—or put on some ski goggles, even if it does look a bit silly.

If you store cut scallions in a glass of water, they'll grow back.

∞

*This is a real, magical ingredient resurrection
that you can stage right in your kitchen.*

To test this tale of zombie alliums, we trimmed three bunches of scallions to about 3 inches above the white bulbs and set each bunch in a glass with 2 inches of tap water. We placed the glasses on a sunny windowsill, changed the water daily, and watched for developments.

We were happily surprised to find that the scallion tops grew back quickly—about an inch per day. After a week, we cut off the new green tops and tasted them. They were pleasantly pungent and even more crisp and fresh-tasting than many store-bought scallions. Encouraged, we repeated the process with the same scallions; this time the tops grew half as fast, came back skinnier, and tasted a bit milder.

The nutrients stored in the scallion's white bulb are sufficient to regrow the tops once or twice, but the plants eventually run out of fuel. If you use scallion greens more often than whites, though, this is a clever way to ensure that you'll always have a supply on hand. One shopping note: Select scallions with roots longer than ½ inch, as they'll grow faster.

Rinsing grapes before storing them makes them spoil more quickly.

∞

*It's true—washing and storage can make
a big difference in the freshness of this fruit.*

We took bunches of red and white grapes and removed any on-the-verge or obviously rotten ones. Then we rinsed and dried half of each bunch, leaving the other half unrinsed. We also wondered whether leaving the fruit on the stem hastens or delays spoilage, so we plucked some of the grapes from their stems and left the remaining clusters intact. Then we refrigerated all the samples in the perforated bags that we bought them in.

All the rinsed grapes spoiled within just a couple of days. Why? Even though we had dried them as much as possible, moisture exposure encouraged bacterial growth. The unrinsed loose grapes were the next to rot, as the now-exposed stem attachment point became an entryway for bacteria. Unrinsed stem-on grapes fared best, lasting nearly two weeks before starting to decay. In fact, as long as we periodically inspected the bunches and removed any decaying grapes, most of them— both red and white samples—kept for an entire month. So don't pull grapes from their stems before refrigeration. Simply discard any that show signs of rotting, and hold off on rinsing until just before you're going to eat the fruit.

Eating pine nuts can affect your sense of taste.

∞

If you've experienced this, you weren't going crazy—there really is something going on.

A mysterious phenomenon sometimes occurs when people eat pine nuts on their own or in a dish such as pesto: Their sense of taste is temporarily altered, causing most food and drink (including water) to taste bitter or metallic. The nuts themselves taste fine; the condition emerges hours or even days after ingestion and can linger for as long as two weeks. Doctors have labeled this condition "pine mouth," and while it is clearly linked to the consumption of pine nuts, its underlying explanation remains a mystery. One theory is that the reaction stems from rancid nuts. The most recent hypothesis suggests that new types of pine nuts introduced to the marketplace from China (now one of the largest—and cheapest—suppliers of the foodstuff) may be to blame. According to newspaper reports, Swiss researchers found at least two Chinese species for sale that had never previously been used for human consumption, which might explain the rising prevalence of pine mouth.

The good news? While the symptoms of pine mouth are downright unpleasant, the condition is temporary and does not seem to present any health concerns. But until the true source of pine mouth is understood, we recommend purchasing the more expensive Middle Eastern or European pine nuts and refrigerating or freezing them in a well-sealed container to stave off rancidity.

Cooking will completely evaporate any alcohol you add to a recipe.

∽∾

Though it is possible to cook off the majority of alcohol in a recipe, traces will always remain.

It's a commonly heard refrain: "Cooking removes all the alcohol." But the truth is much more complex. When alcohol and water mix, they form a solution called an azeotrope—a mixture of two different liquids that behaves as if it were a single compound. Even though alcohol evaporates at a lower temperature than water, the vapors coming off an alcohol-water azeotrope contain both alcohol and water. Because alcohol binds with water during cooking, trace amounts remain in food as long as there's still moisture.

We measured the alcohol content of the liquid in a beef Burgundy recipe before it went into the oven. Every hour, we sampled the liquid to measure the alcohol concentration, and every time, it had dropped—but not as much as might be expected. After three hours of stewing, the alcohol concentration of the stew liquid had decreased by just 60 percent. A major reason for the retention of alcohol in this dish is the use of a lid. If the surface of the liquid is not ventilated, alcohol vapor will accumulate, reducing further evaporation.

One way to quickly reduce the amount of alcohol in a liquid is to ignite the vapors that lie above the pan, a technique known as flambéing. But the degree to which a flambé will burn off alcohol depends on the temperature of the liquid underneath. In our tests, brandy ignited over high heat retained 29 percent of its original alcohol concentration, while brandy flamed in a cold pan held 57 percent. The diameter of the pan is also a factor; the wider the pan, the more total evaporation. (For more information about flambéing, see page 186.)

Beer in dark-colored glass bottles tastes better than beer in clear glass bottles.

✹

It's true—and there's a scientific reason why.

You may have heard the term "skunky brew." Turns out that's an accurate label for what happens to beer when it's exposed to light. Hops contain bitter molecules called isohumulones, and any type of light—natural or artificial—causes these molecules to produce free radicals. In turn, the free radicals react with a sulfur compound in beer to produce a compound known as MBT, which is a component of skunk spray. It takes very little MBT to produce a skunky off-flavor in beer: Some perceptive tasters have detected as little as one-billionth of a gram per 12 ounces of beer.

Hopefully, your favorite beer comes in cans or amber bottles. At the very least, avoid six-packs of clear glass bottles that have been sitting in the front of a store shelf or at the top of a commercial refrigerator near fluorescent lighting. For the best-tasting beer from start to finish, use a beer cozy to keep your brew cold and to block out as much light as possible from the bottle, be it colored or clear.

Wine needs to be allowed to "breathe" for several hours before you drink it.

✹

This is true only for some wines, and there are easy ways to speed up the process.

Red wines—especially young, undeveloped ones—often benefit from a "breathing" period after opening so that oxygen can break down the tannins and sulfur compounds, which helps soften any harsh flavors. But merely uncorking a bottle and letting it sit for a bit is insufficient. In order to truly aerate wine, you must expose as much of its surface area as possible to oxygen. Typically, this so-called hard decanting is accomplished by pouring the wine into a wide, shallow vessel and letting it rest for up to several hours.

While specialized wine-aerating gadgets can speed things along, immediate decanting can also be done with just two pitchers. We opened several recent-vintage bottles of Cabernet and Sangiovese (both known for their punchy, highly tannic flavors) and held a blind taste test of samples poured straight from the bottle and samples that had been poured back and forth from one pitcher to another 15 times. The results were remarkable: The undecanted wines were astringent and flat; the wines that had been decanted by pouring were bright and balanced, and their tannins were less prominent, with more complex aromas coming to the fore. Use this method the next time you need to let wine breathe in a hurry.

Cocktails that are shaken or stirred should be mixed quickly and not agitated for too long.

∞

As a matter of fact, depending on what kind of cocktail you like, you might want to keep mixing for a while.

Most recipes for a classic martini advise stirring with ice for about 30 seconds. To evaluate whether this was an ideal length of time, we made four martinis, combining 1¼ cups of ice, 3 ounces of gin, and 1 ounce of vermouth in each of four cocktail shakers. We then stirred the martinis for 15 seconds, 30 seconds, 1 minute, and 2 minutes, respectively.

Unsurprisingly, the longer a drink was stirred, the colder it got. What did startle us was just how different each martini tasted. Tasters found the martini that was stirred for 15 seconds to have not only a stronger alcohol flavor but also less noticeable aromatic herbal notes. The longer the drink was stirred, the more pronounced these other flavors became.

Why does a colder, more diluted cocktail exhibit a broader spectrum of flavors and aromas? First, chilling makes the harsh-tasting ethanol less volatile and assertive, allowing more pleasant, subtle flavors to come through. Second, the ethanol in gin (and other spirits like whiskey) dissolves some of the water-insoluble aroma compounds. Diluting with water (from the ice) drives these molecules—and their aromas—out of the solution and into the air.

If you're a fan of stiffer drinks that taste more of ethanol, by all means, stir for only 30 seconds. But if you'd like a martini that's more aromatic in flavor, be patient and keep stirring for a minute or two.

MSG will give you a headache.

✠

*Studies have found no connection between
MSG and "Chinese restaurant syndrome."*

In grade school we learned that we experience four primary taste sensations: salty, sweet, bitter, and sour. In recent years, scientists have determined that there is a fifth taste called umami, which is best described as "meaty" or "savory" and is produced by a common amino acid known as glutamate or glutamic acid. Glutamate is present in relatively high amounts in such foods as tomatoes, mushrooms, seaweed, and Parmesan cheese, as well as most proteins, including meat, dairy products, and soy.

MSG (monosodium glutamate) is simply the sodium salt form of naturally occurring glutamate. MSG is believed to enhance the response of our tastebuds, especially to meats and proteins. In our kitchen tests, we have found that MSG bumps up the flavor of food. When we added MSG, in the form of the supermarket product Accent, to our beef and vegetable soup, tasters raved about the "rich," "ultrabeefy" results. However, MSG has gotten somewhat of a bad rap in the press, in part because of "Chinese restaurant syndrome." The term was coined in the late 1960s, when people complained of headaches and digestive upset after eating Chinese food and suspected MSG was the cause. However, numerous studies failed to find a link between MSG and these symptoms. Some experts suggest that bacteria growing on room-temperature cooked rice was in fact the culprit. Given the prevalence of MSG in the American food supply today, there is no evidence that this additive causes medical problems.

Dark roast coffee has more caffeine than light roast coffee.

∞

*Nope—and if you're not careful in how you measure,
light roast will actually have quite a bit more caffeine.*

Roasting is the process that transforms green coffee beans into a far more complex-tasting product, and the degree to which the beans are roasted has as much of an impact on their final profile as their intrinsic flavors. We brewed two pots of coffee, one light roast and one dark roast, using the same volume of ground coffee per batch, and sent both to a lab for testing. When the results came back, we learned that the light roast had much more caffeine than the dark roast—60 percent more in this case. We made two more pots to send to the lab, this time measuring the coffee by weight instead of volume. As we added ground coffee to the scale, we noticed that it took more dark roast than light roast to reach 1½ ounces. Nevertheless, when the results came back, both pots had virtually the same amount of caffeine.

It turns out that as the beans roast, they lose water and also puff up slightly—and the longer the roast time, the more pronounced these effects. Dark roast beans will thus weigh less (and be slightly larger) than light roast beans. When the ground beans are measured by volume, the light roast particles will be denser, weigh more, and contain more caffeine than the dark grinds, producing a more caffeinated brew. The only way to ensure that you're getting the same amount of caffeine with different roasts (all other variables being equal) is to weigh the coffee. If you measure by volume, you'll end up with more of a buzz from a light roast than a dark roast.

Oil and vinegar don't mix.

⌘

Left to their own devices, these two liquids won't naturally combine . . . but you can make them.

I t's true, oil and vinegar do not ordinarily mix. The only way to combine them is to whisk them together so strenuously that the vinegar breaks down into tiny droplets—eventually so tiny that they remain separated by the oil, evenly suspended throughout it. The two fluids are then effectively one homogeneous mixture, called an emulsion (in this case, a vinaigrette).

Unfortunately, as soon as you stop mixing the oil and vinegar, those tiny dispersed droplets of vinegar will start to find each other and coalesce. When enough vinegar droplets find each other, the emulsion "breaks," and the vinegar and oil separate again. Then, when you pour the vinaigrette over your greens, you'll get some oily leaves and some sour leaves, and no delicious salad.

To help an emulsion stay stable for longer, you can include an ingredient that acts as an emulsifier, such as egg yolk or mustard. Emulsifiers work by forming a shield around the dispersed droplets in an emulsion, keeping them from recombining and separating out. This is why we often include a little mustard in our vinaigrette recipes—it might not be enough to noticeably affect the flavor of the dressing, but it can have a serious impact on the chemistry of the mixture.

Never use canned goods that are past their "best by" date.

There's a lot more leeway in "best by" dates than you might think.

The "best by" date printed on canned foods is not a hard-and-fast "expiration" date: It refers strictly to the manufacturer's recommendation for peak quality, not safety concerns. In theory, as long as cans are in good shape and have been stored under the right conditions (in a dry place between 40 and 70 degrees), their contents should remain safe to use indefinitely.

That said, natural chemicals in foods continually react with the metal in cans, and over time, canned food's taste, texture, and nutritional value will gradually deteriorate. The question is when. Manufacturers have an incentive to cite a "best by" date that is a conservative estimate of when the food may lose quality. But it's possible that some canned foods will last for decades without any dip in taste or nutrition. In a study conducted by the National Food Processors Association and cited in *FDA Consumer* magazine, even 100-year-old canned food was found to be remarkably well preserved, with a drop in some nutrients but not others.

Dates aside, cans with a compromised seal (punctured, rusted through, or deeply dented along any seam) should never be used. And discard immediately any cans that are bulging or that spurt liquid when opened: These are warning signs of the presence of the rare but dangerous botulism bacteria, *Clostridium botulinum*.

Baking soda can remove unpleasant odors from your refrigerator or freezer.

⊗

Unfortunately, a box of baking soda is not the magic bullet you might hope it would be.

Baking soda is sodium bicarbonate, an alkali used as a leavening agent in baking. To test whether it can also absorb or neutralize odors from the refrigerator or freezer, we placed equal amounts of sour milk, stinky cheese, and spoiled fish in two airtight containers, then added an open box of baking soda to one container and left the second alone. We sealed the samples and let them sit at room temperature. Finally, we asked a panel of "sniffers" to smell each container after 24 hours and again after 48 hours. The results were inconclusive, with some sniffers claiming they couldn't detect much difference and others swearing they could.

As it turns out, food scientists dismiss the notion that baking soda has deodorizing power in the fridge. While it does neutralize acids, the likelihood of gaseous molecules from acidic sour milk migrating through the refrigerator and interacting with the baking soda is slight. No single chemical has the ability to deactivate all the complex gaseous chemicals that make things smell bad.

But don't rule out baking soda altogether. When this alkaline powder comes into direct contact with smells, it can in fact make a difference. We recently tested different approaches to removing garlic and onion smells from a cutting board and found that scrubbing with a paste of 1 tablespoon baking soda and 1 teaspoon water was the most effective option.

You should never use soap on a cast-iron pan.

∞

A little dish soap will not ruin a
well-seasoned cast-iron pan.

When fat is heated at a certain temperature for a particular length of time, it forms a coating of polymerized triglyceride molecules on the surface of the pan. To keep food from sticking to or reacting with the metal of a cast-iron pan, you need to develop and maintain that coating, known as seasoning. By applying oil to the pan and heating that oil, you can cause the fat molecules in the oil to break down and reorganize into a layer of new molecules that adhere to the pan, creating a fairly durable surface that acts much like an all-natural Teflon coating. But many sources caution that using dish soap on a seasoned cast-iron pan will degrade the seasoning and ruin the pan.

In the process of developing recipes in the test kitchen, we have generated hundreds of dirty cast-iron skillets and thus had plenty of opportunities to test different cleaning methods. We experimented with a variety of cleansers, including dish soap and scouring powders. We found that a small amount of dish soap is not enough to interfere with the polymerized bonds that make up the protective layer on the surface of a well-seasoned cast-iron skillet. Don't scrub the pan with abrasives like steel wool or use harsh cleansers like Comet, and don't soak the pan, but it's OK to use a few drops of regular dish soap if you need to clean up a particularly greasy pan, or even if that just makes you feel more comfortable. Just rinse the pan clean and wipe it dry when you're finished.

You should never cook acidic ingredients in cast-iron cookware.

∞

You certainly can—as long as you follow some simple rules.

When acidic ingredients are cooked in cast iron for an extended period of time, trace amounts of molecules from the metal can loosen and leach into the food. Although these minute amounts are not harmful to consume, they may impart unwanted metallic flavors, and the pan's seasoning can be damaged as well. To test how fast this happens and how noticeable it is, we made a highly acidic tomato sauce and simmered it in a well-seasoned cast-iron skillet, testing it every 15 minutes to check for off-flavors and damage to the pan. Our tasters could detect metallic flavors in the tomato sauce only after it had simmered for a full 30 minutes.

So, while an acidic sauce can enjoy a brief stay in a cast-iron pan with no dire consequences, you have to be careful. First, make sure your pan is well seasoned, as seasoning keeps the acid from interacting with the iron—to a point. You should also remove acidic dishes from the warm skillet soon after they finish cooking. (These rules do not apply to enameled cast-iron skillets; the enamel coating makes it safe to cook acidic ingredients for any length of time.) If you do accidentally oversimmer an acidic ingredient, you may have to throw out the food, but you can simply reseason your skillet and get back to cooking in it again; it won't cause any permanent damage.

Plastic cutting boards are more sanitary than wooden ones.

∞

Maintenance, not material, provides the greatest margin of safety when it comes to cutting boards.

We asked four staff members to donate their used boards, two wooden and two plastic, to our testing efforts. We found very little bacteria growing on these boards when we sampled them, so we took the boards to a local lab to have them artificially inoculated with bacteria. A drop of a medium containing millions of bacteria was placed on each board, the boards were left to sit for 40 minutes to allow for absorption of the bacteria, and an attempt was then made to recover the bacteria. In repeated tests, between 6.0 and 8.1 percent of the bacteria were recovered from the plastic and between 1.3 and 6.2 percent from the wood. Given that the number of bacteria recovered from each type of board was well into the hundreds of thousands, there was little to assure us that one was any safer than the other.

Scrubbing the boards with hot, soapy water changed the story drastically. Once the contaminated boards had been cleaned, we recovered an average of only 0.00015 percent from the plastic and 0.00037 percent from the wood—or fewer than 100 bacteria from each board. So, while both plastic and wooden boards can hold on to bacteria for long periods of time and can thus allow for transference of bacteria to foods, we found that scrubbing with hot, soapy water was an effective (though not perfect) way of cleaning both kinds of boards. The USDA also recommends the regular application of a solution of 1 teaspoon of bleach per quart of water to all types of cutting boards.

Simply put, use whichever type of board you want, but make sure to keep it clean and well maintained.

Pyrex dishes can shatter when you cook in them.

There is a small chance of this happening, but you can minimize the risk.

S hattering is relatively rare, but it can happen when tempered glassware such as Pyrex is exposed to sudden temperature changes (known as thermal shock), extremely high heat (over 425 degrees), or direct heat. In fact, we have experienced three such incidents in the test kitchen.

Precautions you can take to avoid shattering include fully preheating the oven before placing glassware inside (to avoid exposure to the very high temperatures that some ovens initially use to jump-start preheating); covering the bottom of the dish with a little liquid prior to cooking foods that may release juices (to keep the temperature of the dish even); placing hot glassware on a dry cloth or trivet (to avoid contact with a cool or wet surface); never placing glassware on a burner or under the broiler; never adding liquid to hot glassware; and never moving a glass dish directly from the freezer to the oven or vice versa. Both of the leading glassware brands in this country, Anchor Hocking and World Kitchen (the U.S. manufacturer of Pyrex) offer more detailed instructions on all packaging and on their websites.

Clear glass cookware has many advantages: It's inexpensive, provides even browning, and makes it easy to monitor progress. But if you want to avoid glassware altogether when baking, we recommend broiler-safe ceramic baking dishes.

Some people are good cooks and others are bad cooks—that's just the way it is!

※

Anyone can become a good cook,
but it does take some effort!

What separates success from failure in the kitchen? It's the ability to think on your feet and make adjustments as you cook. And, despite what you might think, years of experience and a natural predilection for cooking aren't prerequisites for being a good cook (although they do help). Cooking is a skill that can take a lifetime to master, and even the best cooks occasionally produce disappointing results. Cooking isn't complicated, but it is complex. Small variables can have a significant effect on the quality of the finished dish.

We think everyone should start by learning the basics, such as how to read a recipe, how to sharpen a knife, and how to measure properly. Good cooking requires a solid foundation in all these essentials, from key techniques to knowing your ingredients to understanding how seasoning works. You also have to get to know your own particular tastes; each person's palate is unique.

To some extent, good cooking is about familiarity and predictability. There are definite calculable, scientific aspects to the culinary arts, and once you understand the whys and hows of cooking, you're much more likely to use the proper techniques. But you also have to know the rules before you can efficiently and effectively break them. Once you have a handle on the basics, that's when creativity begins. And that's why we have one final word of advice: Be inquisitive in the kitchen. That may be the most important lesson we can teach anyone who wants to become a better cook.

Cheat Sheet

Equivalents and Conversions

CHEFS KNOW HOW TO CALCULATE INGREDIENT AMOUNTS AND measurements almost instinctively, but for the home cook those kinds of calculations are not always so easy. This is worrisome, because a misstep in measuring can be costly—and potentially ruin a dish. Whether your tablespoon measure has gone missing for the moment or you want to halve or double a recipe, this chart will help. Ounce measurements are for liquids only.

Equivalent Measures

3 teaspoons	= 1 tablespoon	
4 tablespoons	= ¼ cup	
5 tablespoons + 1 teaspoon	= ⅓ cup	
8 tablespoons	= ½ cup	
10 tablespoons + 2 teaspoons	= ⅔ cup	
12 tablespoons	= ¾ cup	
16 tablespoons	= 1 cup	= 8 fluid ounces
2 cups	= 1 pint	= 16 fluid ounces
2 pints	= 1 quart	= 32 fluid ounces
2 quarts	= ½ gallon	= 64 fluid ounces
4 quarts	= 1 gallon	= 128 fluid ounces

Conversions for Common Baking Ingredients

BAKING IS AN EXACTING SCIENCE. BECAUSE MEASURING BY WEIGHT is far more accurate than measuring by volume, and thus more likely to yield reliable results, in our recipes we provide ounce measures in addition to cup measures for many ingredients. Refer to the chart below to convert these measures into grams.

Ingredient	Ounces	Grams
1 cup all-purpose flour*	5	142
1 cup cake flour	4	113
1 cup whole-wheat flour	5½	156
1 cup granulated (white) sugar	7	198
1 cup packed brown sugar (light or dark)	7	198
1 cup confectioners' sugar	4	113
1 cup cocoa powder	3	85
Butter**		
4 tablespoons (½ stick, or ¼ cup)	2	57
8 tablespoons (1 stick, or ½ cup)	4	113
16 tablespoons (2 sticks, or 1 cup)	8	227

* U.S. all-purpose flour does not contain leaveners, as some European flours do. These leavened flours are called self-rising or self-raising. If you are using self-rising flour, take this into consideration before adding leavening to a recipe.

** In the United States, butter is sold both salted and unsalted. We generally recommend unsalted butter. If you are using salted butter, take this into consideration before adding salt to a recipe.

Kitchen Substitutions

How Much Can I Get Away With?

Substituting ingredients and equipment in the kitchen is a delicate art, and you can't always count on common sense to lead you to success. For instance, yogurt can often be substituted for buttermilk and sour cream for yogurt—but does that mean sour cream can be substituted for buttermilk? You should probably double-check before you ruin that batch of pancakes.* Still, no one wants to run out to the supermarket in the middle of a recipe for just one missing ingredient, so we've put together a guide to the substitution questions we've fielded over the years, both common and . . . creative, in the hopes that we can save you a trip to the store, or at least keep you safe from the possible disappointment of Thai curry made with coconut water instead of coconut milk.

* *Actually, sour cream makes a great substitution for buttermilk in pancakes—you should try it. Just thin it with a little milk to get it closer to buttermilk texture.*

Test Your Cooking IQ

Smart Swap or Terrible Trade?

PLAYING AROUND WITH SWAPPING REPLACEMENT INGREDIENTS or tools in place of those listed in a recipe can be a dangerous game. Pick the substitutions that you think would actually work in a pinch.

1
Baking Powder
for
Baking Soda
SWAP *or* SKIP?

2
Club Soda
for
Seltzer
SWAP *or* SKIP?

3
Coconut Water
for
Coconut Milk
SWAP *or* SKIP?

4
Regular Limes
for
Key Limes
SWAP *or* SKIP?

5
Almond Butter
for
Peanut Butter
SWAP *or* SKIP?

6
Salted Butter
for
Unsalted Butter
SWAP *or* SKIP?

7
Dried Herbs
for
Fresh Herbs
SWAP *or* SKIP?

8
Whole-Wheat Flour
for
All-Purpose Flour
SWAP *or* SKIP?

9
Paper Towels
for
Cheesecloth
SWAP *or* SKIP?

10
Fresh Pumpkin
for
Canned Pumpkin
SWAP *or* SKIP?

Answers

1 SKIP (page 71)
2 SWAP (page 127)
3 SKIP (page 96)
4 SWAP (page 105)
5 SKIP (page 81)
6 SKIP (page 90)
7 Sometimes SWAP but mostly SKIP (page 107)
8 SWAP—but not 100% (page 64)
9 SWAP (page 128)
10 SWAP—with some extra work (page 97)

I often keep bacon on hand, but rarely have pancetta in my refrigerator. Can bacon be substituted for pancetta?

It's an imperfect substitution, but this can work if you make a few adjustments.

Bacon and pancetta are both cut from the belly of the pig, but the products are not identical. Bacon is cured with salt and then smoked. Pancetta (sometimes called Italian bacon) is cured with salt, black pepper, and spices and rolled into a cylinder. It is never smoked.

Replacing pancetta with bacon won't ruin a dish, but because bacon is overtly smoky, many sources recommend blanching it before swapping it for pancetta. We tried this in a few recipes, first blanching the bacon in boiling water for two minutes and then proceeding with the recipe. As we prepared the recipes, we noticed that blanching had removed a considerable amount of the fat from the bacon. In fact, for a stew recipe, we had to supplement the bacon with a small amount of oil to properly sauté the aromatics. And when we tasted the finished dishes, we noticed that despite the blanching, subtle hints of smokiness remained. Even so, tasters deemed the substitution acceptable in each case.

I love cooking with bacon fat, but my girlfriend is a vegetarian. Is there a good meatless substitute?

Sorry, but nothing tastes like bacon fat except bacon fat.

In an attempt to build a vegetarian substitute that would mimic bacon fat's savory, smoky, sweet, and fatty qualities, we tested a variety of fats (coconut oil, vegetable oil, olive oil, Crisco, and butter) flavored with a range of ingredients, including soy sauce, smoked paprika, chipotle chiles in adobo, miso paste, dried porcini mushrooms, liquid smoke, maple syrup, apple cider vinegar, and more. The closest substitute was a combination of ¼ cup of refined coconut oil, 2 teaspoons of miso paste, 1 teaspoon of maple syrup, and ¼ teaspoon of liquid smoke. The concoction was satisfactory as a cooking medium, but it lacked the unmistakable porky qualities of bacon, and was annoyingly complicated to make.

Because bacon fat's smoke point is close to those of olive oil and canola oil, either will work as a substitute for cooking; they just won't yield the same flavor results. Nothing else captures the complex combination of flavors of bacon fat.

Can I use "ground turkey breast" in a recipe that calls for "ground turkey"?

You might not even realize there is a difference between these two products, but there definitely is, and it's an important one.

Ground turkey is typically 93 percent lean and is made by grinding both light and dark meat, including the skin and fat. Ground turkey breast (which often costs twice as much) is 99 percent lean and is made from only breast meat. To see whether we could use the two products interchangeably, we made batches of turkey burgers, turkey meatballs, and turkey chili using each. Our tasters preferred the fattier, richer ground turkey in every dish. The samples using the ultralean ground turkey breast were deemed "dry," "chalky," and "like cardboard."

I don't keep anchovies on hand. Is there anything I can substitute so I don't have to buy a whole tin of anchovies just to make one recipe?

We've come up with a few simple, fishy pantry substitutions if you don't want to keep anchovies around.

In the test kitchen, we often use anchovies in pasta sauces, stews, and even salad dressings to add a savory, indefinable flavor that isn't identifiably fishy. To see whether other pantry ingredients could substitute for anchovies in a pinch, we gathered soy sauce, dried porcini mushrooms, fish sauce, and canned tuna (selected for their similar umami depth) and used them in place of the anchovies in pasta sauce and Caesar salad dressing.

The salty soy and intensely mushroomy porcini missed in both the sauce and dressing. The fish sauce (which is made from fermented anchovies anyway) was acceptable in the cooked sauce, but it made the dressing too thin. So in recipes where anchovies are used to add background flavor, feel free to substitute ½ teaspoon of fish sauce per anchovy fillet. To our surprise, finely chopped canned tuna was nearly indistinguishable from the anchovy in both the sauce and dressing. For a more all-purpose anchovy replacement, use 1 tablespoon of minced water-packed tuna per teaspoon of minced anchovy (about 2 fillets).

Is there a homemade vegetarian substitute for fish sauce?

We came up with a simple one that relies on the same compounds that give fish sauce its savory depth.

Fish sauce is rich in glutamates, tastebud stimulators that give food the meaty, savory flavor known as umami. Glutamates are often found in animal proteins, and in the case of fish sauce, they come from fermented fish.

Knowing that seaweed is a potent (and vegetarian) source of glutamates, we optimistically tried subbing a strong salted kelp broth for fish sauce in a Thai dipping sauce. When it failed to contribute sufficient depth, we turned to another source of savory flavor: nucleotides.

When flavor-boosting nucleotides are paired with glutamates, the perception of umami is significantly increased. Sure enough, a salty broth made with dried shiitake mushrooms (rich in nucleotides) and soy sauce (glutamates) provided just the right meaty punch as a one-to-one substitute for fish sauce. Here's how to make it: In a saucepan, simmer 3 cups of water, ¼ ounce of dried sliced shiitake mushrooms, 3 tablespoons of salt, and 2 tablespoons of soy sauce over medium heat until reduced by half. Strain, cool, and store in the fridge for up to three weeks.

I have a recipe that calls for prawns, but my grocery store sells only shrimp. Is there really any difference?

There is definitely a biological difference, but when it comes to taste, it's not very noticeable.

Biologically speaking, there is a difference between shrimp and prawns, and it's mainly about gill structure—a distinguishing feature that is hard for the consumer to spot. This simple fact may be why the terms are often used interchangeably or can vary depending on factors as random as custom and geography. "Prawn" is a term often used in the southern United States, for example, while northerners might refer to the same specimen as "shrimp." In the United Kingdom and in many Asian countries, it's all about size: Small crustaceans are called shrimp; larger ones, prawns. Size is actually not a good indication of a true shrimp or a true prawn, as each comes in a wide range of sizes, depending on the species. Taste won't provide a clue either: Each type can sometimes taste more or less sweet, again depending on the species.

In our tests, we found no problem substituting one for the other in any recipe. The most important thing is to make sure that the count per pound (which indicates the size) is correct so that the same cooking times will apply.

I often see wild salmon for sale at the market. How does it differ from farmed salmon?

Several variables affect how different types of salmon behave in a recipe. We prefer wild salmon in every application.

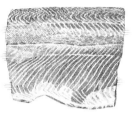

Setting aside environmental and sustainability issues, we tasted fresh wild Alaskan king salmon alongside fresh farmed salmon from Norway in a basic pan-fried application as well as in a salmon cake recipe, noting variations in fattiness, flavor, aroma, and color. Sometimes labeled "Atlantic salmon," farmed salmon is also widely bred in Canada, Chile, and the United Kingdom.

The wild salmon exuded more oil in the pan than the farmed salmon but tasted leaner overall, with a buttery texture and sweet, fresh flavor. The farmed salmon, which get less exercise and consume more fat than wild salmon, tasted fishy, with slimy, soft flesh and a musty, fatty aftertaste. In the salmon cakes, the same flavor and texture differences were noted. The leanest wild salmon also contains less fat, about half as much as farmed salmon, so there is less fat to provide lubrication and the perception of juiciness when cooked. Because of these differences, we prefer wild salmon cooked to just 120 degrees, while farmed salmon should be cooked to 125 degrees.

The flavor and texture of wild and farmed salmon will vary depending on a host of factors, including the species, season, and place of origin. In all our tests, however, we preferred the wild Alaskan salmon to the Norwegian farmed salmon.

If I have all-purpose flour, do I need to buy cake flour and bread flour? Can I just use all-purpose for everything (as the name implies)?

There are real chemical differences between various types of white flour—and they can make a big difference in your recipe.

The main difference between types of white flour is protein content. The amount of protein in flour affects how it will behave in a recipe: The higher the protein content, the more structure and chew in the end product; the lower the protein content, the more tender the end product. Besides texture, protein level also affects moisture retention, since proteins absorb moisture.

All-purpose flour is 10 to 12 percent protein. Bread flour has the highest protein, 12 to 14 percent. Then there is pastry flour, at 8 to 10 percent, and cake flour, at 6 to 8 percent. The names suggest the types of recipes each protein content is most useful for—lower protein means less structure and a softer crumb, which is ideal for a cake, while higher protein content generates height and chew, just what you need in a loaf of bread.

For best results, you should use the flour called for in the recipe whenever possible. However, if all you keep on hand is all-purpose flour, it can make an acceptable one-to-one substitute for bread flour and pastry flour. You can also make an approximation of cake flour: Simply use ⅞ cup of all-purpose flour plus 2 tablespoons of cornstarch for every cup of cake flour called for in a recipe. We don't recommend using bread, pastry, or cake flour in a recipe that doesn't specifically call for that type of flour.

Can I use whole-wheat flour in place of all-purpose flour to make my baked goods healthier?

Don't do this if you want your baked goods to still turn out edible.

Whole-wheat flour is ground from the entire wheat berry—the outer bran layer, the germ, and the endosperm (the heart of the berry)—whereas all-purpose flour is ground from just the endosperm. While the germ layer gives whole-wheat flour more protein than all-purpose flour, it also inhibits the formation of gluten. Gluten provides lift and structure to baked goods, so less of it results in a denser crumb. Additionally, the germ and bran particles in whole-wheat flour contribute to greater chewiness. Thus, if you simply replace all the all-purpose flour in a recipe with whole-wheat flour without making other modifications, you'll end up with dense, tough, chewy baked goods.

That doesn't mean you can't use any whole-wheat flour at all. We found that you can replace about 25 percent of the all-purpose flour called for in a recipe with whole-wheat flour without any adverse effects. If you want to bake with more whole-wheat flour than that, we recommend you seek out recipes specifically designed for that ingredient.

What is the difference between bleached and unbleached flour, and should I buy one over the other?

We prefer unbleached, especially for baking.

When flour is first milled, it has a yellowish cast that some consumers find unappealing. Within a few months after milling, however, the pigments naturally whiten. Because it is expensive to naturally "age" flour, some producers expedite the process chemically. In flours labeled "bleached," benzoyl peroxide has likely been used to fade the yellow color. In baking tests, bleached flour was criticized for tasting flat or having "off" flavors, but we didn't find any issues with the flavor of a savory sauce made with bleached flour. So it's fine to use small amounts of bleached flour to thicken sauces, but avoid it for baking.

I hate to sift flour. Is it really necessary?

Sifting does more than just get rid of lumps, and skipping this step can cause major problems down the line.

Sifting not only removes lumps but also aerates flour so it can be incorporated more easily into batters. Additionally, sifted flour weighs 20 to 25 percent less per cup than unsifted flour. We've found that just one additional ounce of flour can cause a normally moist and level cake to bake up drier and with a domed top, so if you use unsifted flour, you might be dooming your cake to failure before it even goes into the oven.

If you really hate sifting, you can try whisking the flour instead. When we tested equal weights of sifted versus whisked flour in recipes, we found that both methods delivered similar results. Cakes made with sifted flour were a tad taller (sifting does aerate the flour more than whisking), but the differences were minimal.

Can I use white and yellow cornmeal interchangeably in recipes? Do they taste the same?

Feel free to swap white and yellow cornmeal, but pay close attention to the grind.

The color of cornmeal comes from the variety of corn from which it is milled. Besides the common white and yellow, some companies also mill red and blue varieties. To determine whether there was a noticeable flavor difference, we made corn muffins, hush puppies, and polenta with yellow cornmeal and then with white cornmeal. With the muffins, a few tasters detected sweeter notes, stronger corn flavor, and a more delicate crumb in the yellow cornmeal batch. However, in the hush puppies and polenta, we did not find strong flavor or textural differences (though many preferred the look of yellow cornmeal).

Our testing did confirm a more important distinction: Coarseness is key. When a recipe calls for a specific grind of cornmeal, be sure to use what's called for. If the recipe does not specify, use finely ground.

I've seen recipes calling for masa, masa harina, and *masarepa*. Can I just use whichever is easiest to find?

While all three come from corn, they are actually three quite different products.

Masa and masa harina are made from hominy, which is dried corn that has been soaked or cooked in a solution of water and calcium hydroxide to remove the germ and hull. This process, called nixtamalization, imparts a distinctive flavor that differentiates masa-based products from other forms of dried corn like cornmeal.

Masa is a moist dough made from finely ground hominy. It can be flattened into rounds to make corn tortillas or enriched with other ingredients to make tamales and pupusas. Fresh masa is hard to find outside Mexico and the American

Southwest. More commonly available, masa harina is made by drying fresh masa and processing it into a flour. It can be cooked with water and used in place of fresh masa to make tortillas, tamales, or pupusas, but it has a less intense corn flavor.

Unlike masa and masa harina, masarepa, a form of instant precooked corn flour, has not been treated with calcium hydroxide. In the test kitchen, we found that it had the weakest flavor of the three products. Masarepa is typically mixed with cold water to make arepas, corn cakes that are split and filled like a sandwich, and then grilled, fried, or baked.

What are the differences between old-fashioned and quick-cooking oats? Which should I use for baking? Which is best for homemade oatmeal?

Choose old-fashioned rolled oats for all your baking needs, as well as your morning oatmeal.

Both old-fashioned and quick-cooking oats are flattened between rollers to speed cooking. For even faster cooking, quick oats are steamed, toasted, and cut into smaller pieces before packaging.

After making and tasting two batches of oatmeal cookies, one with quick oats and the other with old-fashioned rolled oats, we found that the cookies made with old-fashioned oats were more attractive and had a fuller oat flavor and a pleasing chew. The cookies made with quick oats were acceptable, though, even if we did have to peer long and hard to spot the oats. They were lighter and cakier while still retaining their chew. So if the only oats you have in the cupboard are quick oats, go ahead and use them.

We also prepared quick oats and old-fashioned rolled oats as simple oatmeal and found that they both tasted fine, but the quick oats turned out a bit mushy. In the microwave, the quick oats take 90 seconds to cook, while the old-fashioned oats take about a minute longer. Given all this, we recommend that you buy old-fashioned oats. They have the best texture and take only a minute longer to cook.

Are there differences between long-, medium-, and short-grain rice aside from the length of the grains?

When picking rice, keep in mind that there is a correlation between length of grain and stickiness.

Generally speaking, the shorter the grain, the stickier the rice. In long-grain rice, the grains are more than three times as long as they are wide. Well-known varieties include basmati, jasmine, and Carolina Gold. Both medium- and short-grain rice are often marketed and sold as short-grain to set them apart from long-grain, since both have a fatter, more rounded look. But medium grains are up to three times longer than they are wide, and short grains are less than twice as long as they are wide. Most varieties of Japanese rice are medium- to short-grain, as are Italian Arborio (used for risotto) and Spanish Valencia (used for paella).

The stickiness of rice, referred to as "waxiness" in the rice industry, is related to its relative amount of amylose, a starch that does not gelatinize during cooking. The less amylose, the stickier the rice. Short-grain rice consists of 15 to 20 percent amylose, making it the waxiest of all rice types. Medium-grain rice has an average amylose content of 18 to 26 percent, putting it right in the middle of the waxiness spectrum. Finally, long-grain rice is 23 to 26 percent amylose, causing it to cook up light and fluffy.

Short-grain   **Medium-grain**

Long-grain

My grocery store recently started carrying Carolina Gold and Charleston Gold heirloom rice—will they work in recipes that call for regular long-grain rice?

These heirloom varieties cook in about the same time as long-grain white rice, but you might notice some flavor differences.

Any produce billed as heirloom is simply an older variety that is not associated with large-scale commercial production. The smaller yields often mean that more care is taken in growing, harvesting, and packaging—and you pay more for that. We tested the two varieties of heirloom rice you spotted, Carolina Gold and Charleston Gold, next to our favorite long-grain white rice in a simple boiled preparation, rice pilaf, and rice pudding.

In all three applications, both heirloom varieties cooked at similar rates to the long-grain rice. They did, however, have different flavors and textures. Tasters noted that the Carolina Gold rice tasted "nutty" and "sweet," with notes of barley and popcorn; it also had more of an al dente chew than our favorite long-grain rice. The Charleston Gold rice had smaller kernels, and some tasters commented that it was "stickier," with a "perfumed" flavor similar to that of basmati rice, making ordinary white rice taste "plain" in comparison. Each of these heirloom varieties has a unique flavor and texture that make them worth trying.

Do different colors of quinoa taste different? Do they need to be used differently?

White and red quinoa are interchangeable,
but black quinoa should be used more carefully.

White quinoa is the most commonly found variety of these tiny seeds native to South America, but red and black varieties are increasingly available. To see whether color made a difference, we prepared quinoa pilaf using all three types. White quinoa, which has the largest seeds of the three, had a slightly nutty, vegetal flavor with a hint of bitterness; it also had the softest texture. The medium-size red seeds offered a heartier, nutty crunch. Black quinoa seeds, the smallest of the three, have the thickest seed coat. They were notably crunchy in our recipe and retained their shape the most during cooking, but many tasters disliked their slightly sandy texture. Based on these results, you should feel free to use white and red quinoa interchangeably, but you're better off reserving black quinoa for recipes specifically tailored to its distinctive texture and flavor.

Can I use active dry yeast and instant yeast interchangeably?

Active dry yeast and instant yeast may be similar
in appearance and origin, but substituting one
for the other will yield vastly different results.

When we baked a variety of bread recipes using equal amounts of active dry yeast and instant (also known as rapid-rise) yeast, the active dry batches consistently took longer to rise and baked up denser than the instant batches. These two forms of yeast have different degrees of potency owing to differences in processing: Active dry yeast is dried at higher temperatures, which kills more of the exterior yeast cells (so this yeast requires an initial activation in warm water), whereas instant yeast is dried at more gentle temperatures (so it can be added directly to the dry ingredients in a recipe).

If you have only active dry yeast on hand and a recipe calls for instant, there's an easy fix: To compensate for the greater quantity of inactive yeast cells in the active dry yeast, simply use 25 percent more of it. (Conversely, use about 25 percent less instant yeast in a recipe that calls for active dry.) Also, don't forget to dissolve active dry yeast in a portion of the water from the recipe, heated to 105 degrees, and let it stand for five minutes before adding it to the remaining wet ingredients. If you're using instant yeast in recipes that call for active dry, simply add it to the dry ingredients.

What's the difference between baking soda and baking powder? Can I substitute one for the other?

The chemical makeup of your recipe determines which of these leaveners you can successfully use.

Both baking soda and baking powder are chemical leaveners. Baking soda causes baked goods to brown more and contributes deeper flavor, thanks to the Maillard reaction. However, to do its work, baking soda, which is alkaline, relies on acid in a recipe, provided by ingredients such as buttermilk, yogurt, or molasses. Baking powder, on the other hand, is baking soda mixed with a dry acid, such as cream of tartar, and double-dried cornstarch. The cornstarch keeps the baking soda and dry acid apart during storage, preventing premature production of carbon dioxide. When baking powder becomes wet, the dry acid comes into contact with the baking soda, producing the gas. Cooks use baking powder rather than baking soda when there is no natural acidity in the batter or to provide more sustained leavening (since it's activated by higher temperatures later in the baking process).

You cannot substitute baking powder for baking soda. If you want to substitute baking soda for baking powder, however, just add cream of tartar: For every 1 teaspoon of baking powder called for, use ¼ teaspoon baking soda plus ½ teaspoon cream of tartar. Use this mixture right away (that is, do not prepare it and then store it for future use).

In many recipes, we call for both baking soda and baking powder because the combination gives us better control over how fast (and when) leavening occurs in a recipe, as well as the alkalinity of the dough or batter.

Is it possible to substitute granulated sugar for other types of sugar?

Yes, you can doctor granulated sugar to approximate other types.

I t's happened to all of us: A recipe calls for confectioners' sugar, or brown sugar, but the only thing on hand is plain old white sugar. However, given that all three of these sweeteners are nothing more than commercially processed granulated sugar, we wondered whether we could "process" the white stuff ourselves to serve as a stand-in. Though it's certainly more convenient to buy a particular sugar when you need it, each of our substitutes worked just fine.

Superfine Sugar
Process 1 cup plus 2 teaspoons granulated sugar in a food processor for 30 seconds.
Yield 1 cup superfine sugar

Confectioners' Sugar
Pulverize 1 cup granulated sugar with 1 teaspoon cornstarch in a spice grinder or blender (a food processor cannot crush the sugar fine enough) for at least 1 minute, until fully powdered. Strain through a fine-mesh strainer to remove any large particles that remain.
Yield 1 cup confectioners' sugar

Brown Sugar
Pulse 1 cup granulated sugar with 1 tablespoon dark molasses (for light brown sugar) or 2 tablespoons dark molasses (for dark brown sugar) in a food processor until fully combined.
Yield 1 cup brown sugar

I don't use corn syrup very often and usually have only one type on hand at any given time. Can I substitute light corn syrup for dark (and vice versa)?

If you can't make it to the grocery store, go ahead and use whatever corn syrup you've got in the pantry.

Light corn syrup is made by adding enzymes to a mixture of cornstarch and water to break the long starch strands into glucose molecules. It is then clarified to remove all color and impurities, giving it a sweet, mild flavor. (Vanilla is also added.) Dark corn syrup is a mixture of corn syrup and refiners' syrup (a type of molasses), to which caramel color and flavor are added to give it a deep brown color and stronger flavor.

We tried each type in three different recipes (oatmeal lace cookies, hot fudge sauce, and pecan pie) to determine whether the two varieties could be used interchangeably. Tasters detected few flavor differences in the samples. The cookies made with light corn syrup were lighter and chewier than the darker, crispier cookies made with dark corn syrup, but tasters found both acceptable. Colorwise, both samples of the hot fudge sauce and the pecan pie looked the same. In the hot fudge sauce, the dark corn syrup yielded a richer chocolate flavor and a slightly looser texture. In the pecan pie, several tasters found that the dark corn syrup made for a runnier texture and a richer caramel flavor that masked some of the pecan flavor.

Our conclusion? Yes, there are some subtle flavor and textural differences between light and dark corn syrups, but they are far from earth-shattering, so you can use either type in most recipes.

I've recently seen a sweetener called agave nectar at my supermarket. Is it a good substitute for sugar?

Agave nectar is too different from granulated sugar to make a reliable substitute—unless you're sweetening drinks.

Agave nectar comes from the sap of the thorny, thick-leaved agave plant native to Mexico. The nectar ranges in color from pale gold to amber, depending on the amount of filtration during processing. Lighter nectar has a relatively neutral flavor, while darker nectar has a caramel-like taste. Agave contains 2.9 calories per gram compared to sugar's 4 calories per gram. Agave is also sweeter than sugar, so less of it is needed, further reducing the caloric intake.

We tested agave as a replacement for sugar in oatmeal cookies, yellow cake, sweet iced tea, and margaritas, using a proportion of ⅔ cup of agave nectar for every cup of sugar. We found that the cookies were marred by a soft, bready texture, while the cake had a layer of tough, chewy agave that settled on the bottom of the pan. On the bright side, there were no off-flavors.

When we used agave in beverages, the results were more to our liking. In the sweet tea, tasters found the agave a perfectly acceptable substitute, despite the slightly bitter after-taste some of the more discerning tasters detected. The agave margaritas were hugely popular, which makes sense given that tequila is also derived from the agave plant. Another bonus: Because it is a liquid, the nectar dissolves better in drinks than granulated sugar.

Is it OK to substitute blackstrap molasses in recipes that call for mild molasses?

Yes, but you have to doctor the intense blackstrap molasses first.

Molasses is produced by boiling down sugarcane juice. Light molasses comes from the first boiling, dark from the second, and blackstrap from the third. As the molasses is boiled, the sugar caramelizes and the minerals in the sugarcane juice become more concentrated. While both light and blackstrap molasses have about the same amount of total sugar (55 to 70 percent), their mineral content differs: Light molasses contains 2 percent minerals, while blackstrap contains a whopping 10 percent.

To find out how different types of molasses affect recipes, we made batches of Boston baked beans and molasses cookies with both light and blackstrap molasses. The vast majority of tasters found the flavors of the blackstrap molasses too potent in both recipes. We went back into the kitchen to see whether we could mix blackstrap molasses with another ingredient to approximate light molasses. We replaced half of the blackstrap molasses with light corn syrup and then with honey in two more batches of cookies and beans. Tasters said the batches made with honey lacked distinct molasses flavor, but declared the corn syrup–blackstrap cookies just as good as the light-molasses cookies. The corn syrup–blackstrap baked beans were tender and flavorful.

So, if you want to use blackstrap in a recipe that calls for light molasses, temper its brashness by replacing half of it with light corn syrup for an approximation of mild molasses. (We have also found that mild, dark, robust, and full molasses all taste similar and can be used interchangeably.)

What's the difference between semisweet, bittersweet, and dark chocolates?

It turns out these labels don't mean as much as you might think they do.

All chocolate begins as cacao beans. The inner meat (or nib) of the bean is removed from the shell and ground into a paste, called chocolate liquor (although it contains no alcohol). Chocolate liquor consists of cocoa solids and cocoa butter. It is then further processed and mixed with sugar and flavorings to create various types of chocolate.

Semisweet and bittersweet chocolates, which are both considered "dark chocolate," must contain at least 35 percent chocolate liquor, although most contain more than 55 percent and some go as high as 99 percent. Typically, manufacturers use the label "bittersweet" for chocolates that are higher in cacao (and therefore less sweet) than their "semisweet" offerings. Thus, "bittersweet" and "semisweet" can be useful terms for comparing products within one brand but are imprecise across different brands. Cacao content matters more than name, and we have found that the flavor and texture of 60 percent cacao (whether called semisweet, bittersweet, or just "dark") is ideal for most cooking applications.

Is there any way to use dark chocolate and unsweetened chocolate interchangeably?

There are some useful substitutions, but they don't work in all types of recipes.

Unsweetened chocolate is not the same as dark (bittersweet or semisweet) chocolate. It is limited by the amount of cocoa butter it can contain, which must be between 50 and 60 percent. Lower fat means more cocoa solids, and therefore richer chocolate flavor.

You can replace 1 ounce of dark chocolate with ⅔ ounce of unsweetened chocolate and 2 teaspoons of granulated sugar, but the unsweetened chocolate will not provide the same smooth, creamy texture. That means that while this substitution will work well with fudgy brownies, it could wreak havoc on a delicate custard or an airy cake.

To replace 1 ounce of unsweetened chocolate, you can either use 3 tablespoons of unsweetened cocoa powder plus 1 tablespoon of vegetable oil or use 1½ ounces of dark chocolate and then remove 1 tablespoon of sugar from the recipe, but we recommend these substitutions only in recipes that call for small quantities of chocolate.

Is it OK to melt chocolate chips instead of chopping my own chocolate?

Good news—this shortcut works for many recipes!

When a recipe calls for melted chocolate, we usually reach for quality bar chocolate, but the idea of using chocolate chips instead is appealing. Chips require no prep, whereas chopping up a block of bar chocolate makes a mess. We baked four batches of brownies—one with bittersweet bar chocolate, one with semisweet bar chocolate (the recipe calls for either), a third with commonly available semisweet chips, and a fourth with bittersweet chips.

Surprisingly, the texture and appearance of all four pans of brownies were the same. There were some slight differences in flavor, but if all you have is chocolate chips, this swap can work. Just try to use the same sweetness level as called for in the recipe.

Chocolate chips do tend to contain less cocoa butter than bar chocolate, however, and this lower fat content means that they might take a bit longer to melt than chopped bar chocolate; they may also contain stabilizers designed to help them hold their shape when baked into cookies. As a result, we don't recommend using them in chocolate sauces or puddings where a perfectly smooth texture is necessary.

Why is some cocoa powder labeled "natural" and some labeled "Dutched"? What's the difference and which one should I use?

In most applications, you can use either—there will be some texture and flavor differences, but you won't ruin a recipe.

In the world of cocoa powder, there are two main categories: natural and Dutched. The natural product is made mainly of unsweetened cocoa solids that have had much of their fat removed and are then dried and ground to a powder. Dutching refers to the step of adding an alkali to neutralize the powder's acidity and to mellow its astringent notes; it also darkens the color.

We tested a half-dozen recipes side by side, using both types of cocoa in each recipe. The biggest finding was that none of the recipes failed, even those with a high proportion of cocoa powder, and thus the potential to be most strongly affected. But that didn't mean there weren't differences in appearance, texture, and flavor. Not surprisingly, Dutch-processed cocoa produced cakes, cookies, and hot cocoa with a darker color than the versions made with natural cocoa. In terms of texture, natural cocoa produced slightly drier baked goods, as well as cookies with less spread than did Dutch-processed. Finally, we found that baked goods and hot chocolate made with Dutched cocoa displayed more of the fruity, bitter notes of dark chocolate, while natural cocoa delivered a more straightforward chocolate flavor.

Both natural and Dutched cocoa will work in most recipes; unless a recipe specifically calls for one or the other, use whichever fits your preferences in terms of flavor, appearance, and texture.

Many chocolate desserts call for a small amount of instant espresso powder, which I don't usually have on hand. Is there an easy substitute?

Instant coffee can be used as a substitute, but the proportion depends on the type of recipe you're making.

Instant espresso powder is often used to boost the intensity of chocolate flavor. Because instant espresso isn't always available, we wanted to determine how much instant coffee should be used in place of instant espresso. We prepared three recipes—*pots de crème*, triple-chocolate espresso brownies, and devil's food cake—each with the amount of instant espresso called for in the recipe, an equal amount of instant coffee, and twice the amount of instant coffee.

The pots de crème made with instant espresso had a rich, dark chocolate flavor. When the espresso was replaced with an equal amount of a popular brand of instant coffee, the chocolate flavor was weak and lacked depth. Doubling the amount of instant coffee, however, made the flavor comparable to the original recipe. The opposite was true with the espresso brownies, which exhibited a bitter, overwhelming coffee flavor when twice the amount of instant coffee was used. Tasters preferred the brownies made with a one-to-one conversion, which had a strong, but not undesirable, coffee flavor. As for the cake, tasters couldn't detect much of a difference among the three batches.

If you can't find instant espresso powder, we recommend replacing it with the same amount of instant coffee in baked goods and with double the amount in creamy applications like puddings, frostings, and mousses, which contain proportionally more chocolate as a percentage of the total ingredients. You can also just grind your own espresso beans at home, but avoid this substitute in recipes that require a supersmooth texture; freshly ground espresso tends to be gritty and doesn't dissolve the same way instant espresso powder does.

I've recently seen powdered peanut butter in the grocery store. What is it and can I use it in place of regular peanut butter?

Not if you follow the directions on the jar, but there is another way to make it work.

Marketed as a lower-fat alternative to regular peanut butter, powdered peanut butter is a byproduct of peanut oil production: Roasted peanuts are pressed to extract the peanut oil, and the leftover, defatted peanut bits are dried and ground into a powder, which can be reconstituted if desired.

We purchased four brands of powdered peanut butter and followed the package directions to reconstitute them with water. We matched these against our favorite creamy peanut butter in peanut butter cookies, milkshakes, and peanut butter sandwiches.

Tasters were easily able to pick out the applications made with the powdered varieties. The cookies were noticeably leaner. In the milkshakes, the peanut flavor was less pronounced, and the texture was decidedly chalky. The sandwiches, according to tasters, seemed as if they were made with reduced-fat peanut butter.

These comments made sense when we compared nutrition labels. While 2 tablespoons of Skippy has 190 calories and 16 grams of fat, 2 tablespoons of reconstituted powdered peanut butter has about 45 calories and 1.5 grams of fat.

Knowing that peanut oil is removed from powdered peanut butter, we also tried reconstituting the powder using peanut oil instead of water. It made the product much more similar to regular creamy peanut butter and yielded superior results to the water-constituted version. Of course, this does add back some of the fat removed from powdered peanut butter, so if you're looking for a diet product, you may not like this solution.

Peanut allergies have become so commonplace. Can I substitute other nut butters for peanut butter in cookie recipes?

Unless the recipe is specifically designed for alternative nut butters, you probably won't get great results with a direct swap.

To find the answer to this question, we substituted almond butter and cashew butter, the two most commonly available "alternative" nut butters, for peanut butter in chewy peanut butter cookies. The cashew butter cookies were very similar in texture and appearance to those made with peanut butter, but the cashew flavor was so subtle that it was easy to miss, making this nut a poor stand-in for peanuts. The almond butter cookies fared worse: The almond skins made the cookies taste noticeably bitter, and the cookies also spread more than their peanut and cashew counterparts, ending up comparatively flat and unattractive.

It turns out that almonds contain not only slightly more fat than peanuts and cashews (which share a similar fat percentage) but also a much higher proportion of unsaturated fat. Because unsaturated fat has a lower melting point, cookies made with almond butter are more fluid, allowing the batter to spread before their structure is set.

In a nutshell: If you're concerned about peanuts, look for cookie recipes specifically designed for other nut butters. However, if you'd consider a non-nut replacement, we did have good results with sunflower seed butter. Spread on bread, subbed for peanut butter in cookies, and mixed into dipping sauces for crudités, it was surprisingly good. It has the pleasantly vegetal, slightly nutty flavor characteristic of the seeds, and though runny, its texture was still perfectly acceptable. We think it makes an interesting alternative to peanut butter, even if you aren't avoiding nuts. Like peanut butter, sunflower seed butter comes in both smooth and crunchy varieties.

Memorize This!

Baking 911

THE SCIENCE INVOLVED IN BAKING MAKES IT VERY HARD TO FIND substitutions that won't mess with the chemistry that creates the delicate crumb of a cake, the dense fudginess of a brownie, or the crisp crust of a loaf of bread. Luckily, we have tested scores of possible ingredient substitutions to figure out which ones do the trick under which circumstances and which ones simply don't work.

Dairy

To Replace	Amount	Substitute
Whole Milk	1 cup	⅝ cup skim milk + ⅜ cup half-and-half
		⅞ cup skim milk + ⅛ cup heavy cream
		⅔ cup 1 percent milk + ⅓ cup half-and-half
		¾ cup 2 percent milk + ¼ cup half-and-half
Half-and-Half	1 cup	¾ cup whole milk + ¼ cup heavy cream
		⅔ cup skim or low-fat milk + ⅓ cup heavy cream
Buttermilk	1 cup	¾ cup plain whole-milk or low-fat yogurt + ¼ cup whole milk
		1 cup whole milk + 1 tablespoon lemon juice or distilled white vinegar
Sour Cream	1 cup	1 cup plain whole-milk yogurt (Nonfat and low-fat yogurts are too lean.)
Plain Yogurt	1 cup	1 cup sour cream

Flour, Sugar, and Chocolate

To Replace	Amount	Substitute
Cake Flour	1 cup	⅞ cup all-purpose flour + 2 tablespoons cornstarch
Bread Flour	1 cup	1 cup all-purpose flour (Recipes may bake up with slightly less chew.)
Baking Powder	1 teaspoon	¼ teaspoon baking soda + ½ teaspoon cream of tartar (Use right away.)
Brown Sugar	1 cup	1 cup granulated sugar + 1 tablespoon molasses (for light brown sugar) or 2 tablespoons molasses (for dark brown sugar) (Pulse molasses in food processor along with sugar or simply add it along with other wet ingredients.)
Confectioners' Sugar	1 cup	1 cup granulated sugar + 1 teaspoon cornstarch (Grind together in blender. Works well for dusting, less so in frostings and glazes.)
Unsweetened Chocolate	1 ounce	3 tablespoons unsweetened cocoa powder + 1 tablespoon vegetable oil 1½ ounces bittersweet or semisweet chocolate (Remove 1 tablespoon sugar from the recipe.)
Bittersweet or Semisweet Chocolate	1 ounce	⅔ ounce unsweetened chocolate + 2 teaspoons sugar (Works well for fudgy brownies. Do not use in a custard or cake.)

When should I use pasteurized eggs versus unpasteurized eggs? Does pasteurization change the flavor or cooking properties of the eggs?

Most of the time you can use either, but it might take a little extra work to whip pasteurized eggs properly.

Pasteurization of eggs has become popular as a way to combat potential salmonella bacteria. The pasteurization process involves passing the eggs through a series of warm water baths. The combination of time and temperature heats the eggs enough to kill potentially harmful bacteria but not enough to cook the eggs. The eggs are then chilled and coated with an all-natural wax sealant to prevent recontamination and to maintain freshness.

To see how pasteurized eggs stacked up against the unpasteurized variety, we made Caesar salad dressing with both pasteurized and unpasteurized raw yolks, and meringues from the whites of each. We didn't detect any differences in the two dressings, but that was not the case with the meringues. We immediately noticed that the pasteurized whites were much looser and more watery than their unpasteurized counterparts. What's more, the pasteurized whites took more than twice as long to whip into a stiff and glossy meringue.

On the whole, we still prefer and continue to use ordinary eggs for most recipes, especially those for baked goods. But if you are wary of making mayonnaise, eggnog, or Caesar salad dressing using raw eggs, pasteurized eggs are a safe and acceptable option.

If a recipe calls for whole milk, can I use low-fat or skim milk?

While skim milk probably won't ruin a recipe, whole milk or even 1 percent milk will make it that much better.

We've all seen those recipes that specify what kind of milk to use: whole, low-fat, nonfat. But in the end, does it really matter? Can the average palate detect a difference, or are they pretty much interchangeable? We tested whole milk (which is 3½ percent fat), 1 percent milk, and skim milk (which must contain less than ½ percent fat) in three recipes: pancakes, yellow layer cake, and chocolate pudding. Each recipe originally called for whole milk.

While a couple of very particular tasters could pick out the pancake made with skim milk, the majority could not discern much difference between any of the pancakes. That's good news: You can use whatever you have in your fridge.

Not so with the yellow cake, though. Tasters found the cake made with skim milk to be dry and tough and the cake made with whole milk to be moist and tender. Surprisingly, the cake made with 1 percent milk was very similar in tenderness to the whole milk cake. Clearly, this cake needs milk with some fat.

The pudding made with skim milk was by no means a disaster, but it was nowhere near as rich and creamy as the pudding made with either the 1 percent or whole milk. Moreover, the puddings made with the higher-fat milks were thought to taste more chocolatey and decadent, with the whole-milk pudding having a distinctly velvety mouthfeel. Fat is a flavor carrier, which would explain the discrepancy.

What is the difference between whipping cream and heavy cream? Are they interchangeable?

Despite its name, whipping cream is not your best bet for homemade whipped cream.

By law, heavy cream (also called heavy whipping cream) must consist of at least 36 percent milk fat, and whipping cream (also called light whipping cream) must have at least 30 percent but no more than 36 percent. This may not sound like much of a difference, but after whipping up more than a few bowls of cream, we learned that it can be. Other factors that can make a difference include whether it's ultrapasteurized or simply pasteurized (the difference is the temperature to which the cream is heated during processing), and whether it contains any additives.

In our testing, we found that while whipping cream reached stiff peaks faster than heavy cream, it lost those peaks and became watery after just a few hours, while the whipped heavy cream maintained its texture for up to a day. The higher-fat heavy cream also made the thickest and best-tasting whipped cream; we especially liked the pasteurized version we tried, which also had no additives. Additives, as well as the process of ultrapasteurization, compromise the sweet, delicate flavor of cream. All told, pasteurized heavy cream, with a fat content of 40 percent (or 6 grams per tablespoon), is the best all-purpose cream to use for whipping. The next best choice is ultrapasteurized heavy cream. We don't recommend light whipping cream.

What exactly is buttermilk, and can I use some combination of butter and milk if I don't have any on hand?

There are several easy buttermilk substitutes you can make with common dairy products—but none of them involve butter.

Buttermilk is a misleading word. Many assume the product is infused with butter and thus high in fat, when the truth is quite the opposite. The name refers to the watery end product of butter making—the "milk" left behind after the solid fat has been removed through the process of churning cream into butter. Today, buttermilk is made more after the fashion of yogurt, in which harmless bacteria are added to milk to break down the milk sugar (lactose) and in the process create lactic acid, which thickens the milk and helps produce a tangy flavor.

The easiest substitute for buttermilk is "clabbered" or thickened milk. This is made by adding an acid to regular milk. Our go-to is lemon juice—1 tablespoon stirred into each cup of milk. You can also use the same amount of distilled white vinegar. Another option is cream of tartar, which has a less noticeable flavor than lemon juice or vinegar. Since cream of tartar can clump when you stir it into milk, it should be whisked into the dry ingredients instead (1½ teaspoons of cream of tartar for each cup of milk). We also like powdered buttermilk, which is easy to use (simply follow the instructions on the package), has a longer shelf life than liquid buttermilk, and is also cheaper.

In baking applications, you can also substitute low-fat yogurt for buttermilk. A one-to-one swap will work for thicker batters like cakes or biscuits; for thinner batters like pancakes, you should first thin the yogurt with low-fat milk or water. We do not recommend substituting yogurt for buttermilk in savory recipes like buttermilk mashed potatoes.

Are regular yogurt and Greek yogurt interchangeable in recipes?

It's not a one-for-one swap, but you can make it work.

Greek yogurt is thicker and creamier than typical full-fat American-style yogurt—and has more than twice the fat. Most brands of full-fat plain yogurt contain between 7 and 9 grams of fat per 1-cup serving, while Greek yogurt usually contains upwards of 20 grams of fat. Nearly all the whey (the watery liquid that separates from the solids) is strained out of Greek yogurt, giving it a rich, smooth texture that is slightly thicker than that of sour cream. In terms of flavor, Greek yogurt is fairly mild, with a slight tang.

You can make your own version of Greek yogurt by straining the whey out of full-fat plain yogurt. Put the yogurt in a fine-mesh strainer lined with several layers of cheesecloth (paper towels or coffee filters will also work) and set it over a bowl to catch the whey. Cover the bowl with plastic wrap and place it in the refrigerator. After 24 hours, the yogurt will have reduced in volume by about half and achieved a thick, rich consistency closely resembling that of Greek yogurt.

If, on the other hand, all you have is Greek yogurt and your recipe calls for regular yogurt, you can add moisture back in: Use only two-thirds of the amount of yogurt called for in the recipe and make up the difference with water.

Can I substitute Greek yogurt for sour cream in recipes?

In a pinch, it'll work. Just be wary of using it in recipes that require high heat.

Greek yogurt and sour cream are both thick, sour-tasting dairy products, so it's not crazy to think they could be interchangeable. To test this, we tried Greek yogurt in our drop biscuits, in a sour cream–based horseradish sauce, and in beef stroganoff.

In the biscuits and the cream sauce, our testers thought that the Greek yogurt was a fine substitute; it felt slightly leaner than the sour cream in both applications, but overall it was acceptable. However, the Greek yogurt broke when it was added to the hot sauce in the beef stroganoff. While tasters said it tasted fine—albeit less rich—it was visually unappealing.

Why did the yogurt break in the stroganoff? While 1 cup of sour cream has 40 grams of fat, the same amount of whole-fat Greek yogurt has less than half that amount, making it much less stable when exposed to high heat.

What's the best substitute for crème fraîche if I can't find the real thing?

Crème fraîche is not quite like any other dairy product, but you can make an approximation with more common ingredients—as long as you've got time to wait.

Authentic crème fraîche has a silky-smooth, almost cream-cheesey texture and a rich, faintly sour yet slightly sweet, nutty flavor. The traditional way of making it in France is simply to leave heavy cream out at room temperature to let the inherent lactic bacteria do their job of thickening it and blooming its flavor.

If you can't find crème fraîche and have at least 24 hours before you need to use it, the best approximation of the real thing is to whisk 1 tablespoon of buttermilk into 1 cup of heavy cream and let the mixture sit at room temperature for 24 hours to thicken. This version of crème fraîche can then be covered and stored in the refrigerator, where it will thicken still further. We also found that leaving the mixture, covered, at room temperature for another two days further developed the flavor. The finished product can be stored in the refrigerator for about two weeks.

What if you can't wait a day and want to serve something milder and sweeter than sour cream but more tangy than whipped cream? Try mixing 1 part sour cream and 1 part heavy cream; letting it sit out for even an hour or two helps thicken the mixture and meld the flavors. If you're adding this mixture to a soup, be aware that it will separate if boiled.

Is it OK to replace unsalted butter with salted butter if I reduce the total amount of salt in the recipe?

This may seem like it makes sense, but we don't recommend it.

We advise against cooking with salted butter for three reasons. First, the amount of salt in salted butter varies from brand to brand—it can range from 1.25 percent to 1.75 percent of the total weight, making it impossible to offer conversion amounts that will work with all brands. Second, because salt masks some of the flavor nuances found in butter, salted butter tastes different from unsalted butter. Finally, salted butter almost always contains more water than unsalted butter. The water in butter ranges from 13 to 19 percent. In baking, butter with a low water content is preferred, since excess water can interfere with the development of gluten. In fact, when we used the same brand of both salted and unsalted butter to make brownies and drop biscuits, tasters noticed that samples made with salted butter were a little mushy and pasty; they preferred the texture of baked goods made with unsalted butter.

Can whipped butter be substituted for stick butter in recipes?

It depends on what you're going to use it for.

Whipped butter is made by incorporating air into butter; manufacturers do this to increase the butter's spreadability. Adding air increases the volume of the butter, but not the weight. In other words, a 4-ounce stick of butter measures ½ cup in volume, while 4 ounces of whipped butter measures 1 cup.

We compared butter cookies, pound cake, and buttercream frosting made with unsalted whipped butter and unsalted stick butter. Tasters found the cookies to be nearly identical and even slightly preferred the whipped-butter version for its crispier, flakier texture. The same held true for the pound cake: Although the butter for each cake was creamed for exactly the same time—5 minutes—some tasters deemed the cake made with whipped butter to be lighter, fluffier, and more tender. The buttercream was a different story. While the stick butter produced a fluffy, off-white frosting, the whipped-butter frosting was foamy, with an intense yellow color and a plasticlike texture.

So, unsalted whipped butter makes a fine substitute for unsalted stick butter in baked goods, but do not make the swap in uncooked applications, such as frosting. And remember to make the substitution based on weight, not volume. A standard tub of whipped butter weighs 8 ounces, equal to two sticks of butter.

Can I use shortening and butter interchangeably in cookie recipes?

Sure, but it's going to change the texture of your cookies.

The type of fat used has a big impact on the flavor and texture of cookies. We prepared several different kinds of cookies with butter and with shortening. In general, tasters preferred the flavor of the cookies made with butter. For instance, shortening made especially bland chocolate chip cookies. This flavor deficit was less noticeable in snickerdoodles; these cookies are so heavily coated with cinnamon sugar that the differences between the batches made with butter and shortening were harder (although not impossible) to detect.

In addition to flavor differences, cookies made with shortening were crispier, largely because shortening adds no water to dough. Unlike butter, which is at least 80 percent fat and 13 to 19 percent water, shortening is 100 percent fat. Cookies made with butter were thus softer and cakier.

Our advice? You can use butter in cookie recipes that call for shortening; the cookies may be more flavorful, but they are also likely to be less crisp.

I love using lard to make flaky pie crust. Can I substitute it in place of butter when I make biscuits?

This will work, but you have to use the right kind of lard.

Many home cooks swear by lard, which is rendered pork fat (and not vegetable shortening, such as Crisco, as many people think), for pie crusts and biscuits. However, most chefs find supermarket lard to be of subpar quality.

We made two batches of biscuits: one with butter and one with lard from the supermarket. The butter biscuits were a clear winner, as our tasters found the biscuits made with supermarket lard dense and gummy, with a slightly sour aftertaste. Why were the lard biscuits so bad?

Butter's capacity to create flakiness comes from its relatively high water content (13 to 19 percent). This water converts to steam in the oven, producing pockets of air that yield flaky biscuits. Lard contains no water.

But not all lard is created equal. Higher-quality leaf lard, which is rarely found on supermarket shelves but can be ordered from a butcher, is made from the fat around the pig's kidneys. Leaf lard has a higher melting point, thereby providing a more effective coating of fat around the other biscuit ingredients. This keeps the dough from gumming up in the oven, instead allowing it to bake and set into tender biscuits.

Our tests confirmed: Leaf lard made incredibly tender biscuits with a notably rich flavor, though perhaps not as flaky as those made with butter.

Can liquid oil be used as a substitute for shortening or butter in pie crust recipes?

Nope—liquid oil just doesn't behave the same way that solid shortening does.

We prepared a pie crust recipe that called for both butter and vegetable shortening, using liquid canola oil in place of the solid shortening. Though the crust made with butter and oil got slightly darker than the crust made according to the recipe, it looked fine. When we broke into the crust, however, all was not fine. Whereas the butter and shortening crust was tender and flaky, the butter and oil crust was crisp and crumbly, not something we look for in a pie crust.

Why the discrepancy? Shortening is a solid fat, so it can be worked into small bits that leave behind tiny spaces when they melt in the oven, creating flaky layers. The oil, of course, is already a liquid and thus leaves no spaces behind as it heats up. The result is a crisp texture, more like that of a cookie.

What should I use when a recipe calls for vegetable oil? Can I use olive oil? Olives are vegetables, right?

Although "vegetable oil" may sound vague, it does refer to something fairly specific.

Loosely speaking, vegetable oil is an edible oil made from any number of plant sources, including nuts, grains, beans, seeds, and olives. In the more narrow confines of recipe writing, it refers to one of the more popular brands of supermarket cooking oil whose label reads "Vegetable Oil." These are typically made from soybeans.

"Vegetable oil" is often the ingredient of choice in recipes that call for an oil with a completely neutral flavor. Corn and canola oil make good substitutes, although corn oil can impart unwanted flavors to recipes like vinaigrette. Some other plant-based oils, such as peanut and olive, have much more distinct flavors and might not be appropriate substitutes in a recipe that calls for vegetable oil. Olive oil also has a lower smoke point, making it an inferior choice for high-heat applications like deep-frying.

If a dressing recipe calls for red wine vinegar and I have only white wine vinegar, is that a safe substitution to make?

Absolutely; just use what you have.

Though we like to keep a well-stocked pantry, there are definitely occasions when we have red wine vinegar or white wine vinegar, but not both. To find out whether we could distinguish between the two in a salad dressing once it was tossed with greens, we made batches of vinaigrette using red wine vinegar and white wine vinegar. We used each to dress mild Bibb lettuce and asked tasters whether they could pick out which was which.

Some could tell the two dressings apart, but most could not. Those who did notice a difference found the dressing made with white wine vinegar to be brighter in flavor, but none considered either one to be unacceptable, despite the difference.

What's the difference between Parmesan and Pecorino Romano cheeses? Some recipes call for either, and I'm never sure which one to buy.

The choice matters more when you're using lots of cheese.

Made from cow's milk, Parmesan is a hard, dry, aged cheese with a sharp, nutty flavor and a granular texture that lends itself to grating. Pecorino Romano, on the other hand, is an aged sheep's-milk cheese with a firm-to-hard, slightly grainy, oily texture and a salty, piquant flavor that borders on lemony. Because Parmesan and Pecorino Romano cheeses have similar textures and flavors, they can generally be used interchangeably, especially when the amount called for is moderate. In larger quantities, however, Pecorino Romano can be fairly pungent and may require the addition of a small amount of Parmesan to balance its bold flavor.

If you must choose one cheese over the other, Parmesan is the more flexible option for the broadest range of recipes.

I keep seeing coconut water in the grocery store. Is it similar to the canned stuff I cook with?

Nope, they are totally different products, and you can't cook with coconut water.

Coconut water, also referred to as coconut juice, is the thin liquid found in the center of a coconut. It has become increasingly trendy lately, in part because of its purported hydrating qualities.

Coconut water is very different from canned coconut milk. While coconut water is naturally occurring, canned coconut milk is made by steeping coconut flesh in water and then straining out the solids. Coconut water has a much lower fat content than canned coconut milk (less than 1 gram per cup as opposed to about 50 grams per cup). It therefore tastes thinner and less rich. It also tastes sweeter, which makes sense given that it typically contains more than three times the sugar of canned coconut milk. Because it is so vastly different, coconut water is not a suitable substitute for coconut milk. Furthermore, do not confuse canned coconut milk with canned coconut cream (the ratio of coconut meat to liquid is higher) or cream of coconut (which is sweetened and containers thickeners and emulsifiers).

You may also see a type of refrigerated coconut milk sold in a carton near the soy and almond milk and labeled "coconut milk beverage." This product is made by blending canned coconut milk with water and additives, which make it creamy, despite the water it contains. It can be used as a replacement for dairy milk, but since coconut milk beverage has about an eighth of the fat content of canned coconut milk and does not taste strongly of coconut, it's not a good substitute for canned coconut milk.

Can I use canned tomatoes in place of fresh tomatoes when fresh ones are out of season?

Definitely; canned tomatoes can be a much safer bet than out-of-season specimens.

Nothing tastes better than juicy, fresh tomatoes—on the rare occasion that they're in season, that is. The pale, mealy options available during the rest of the year would ruin dishes like a fresh tomato sauce. We found that canned tomatoes make a much better stand-in than those flavorless, off-season fresh options. For every pound of fresh tomatoes needed, simply substitute one 14.5-ounce can of drained diced tomatoes, plus 1 tablespoon of the drained liquid. And since canned diced tomatoes are firmer than fresh tomatoes, they should be pressed against the side of the pan with a wooden spoon to help them break down more naturally as they cook.

Baking recipes usually call for canned pumpkin—can I substitute fresh pumpkin?

This substitution works, as long as you're willing to do the work, but you can't use just any pumpkin for a pie.

For starters, make sure you're using a sugar pumpkin, which is 8 to 10 inches in diameter and usually has a darker orange exterior compared with jack-o'-lantern pumpkins. And be aware that fresh pumpkin puree does not taste exactly like canned pumpkin; it tends to taste a bit more vegetal and less sweet, though definitely acceptable. This is less of an issue in strongly flavored recipes like pumpkin pie, which tastes predominantly of the spices added to the pie.

To make homemade pumpkin puree, halve a sugar pumpkin from top to bottom and then scoop out the seeds and pulp. Place the halves cut side down on a parchment-lined rimmed baking sheet and roast in a 375-degree oven until the flesh can be easily pierced with a skewer, 45 minutes to 1 hour.

Turn the halves over and continue to roast 30 minutes longer. Scoop the flesh from the skins and puree it in a food processor until smooth. Drain the puree in a fine-mesh strainer set over a bowl for at least 1 hour. To test the consistency, pack the puree into a small drinking glass and unmold it onto a plate. It should slump gently toward the base but otherwise hold its shape. Loosen as necessary with drained liquid, or return the puree to the strainer and continue to drain it if it is still too loose. The puree can be refrigerated for up to four days or frozen in an airtight container with parchment pressed on its surface for up to two months. You can substitute this puree for an equal amount of the canned product.

I often see cornichons listed in recipes but have a hard time finding them in the supermarket. Is there something else I can use instead?

There is no substitute for the real thing,
but in a pinch, a dill pickle makes a good stand-in.

Cornichon is the French word for a pickled gherkin cucumber. They are most often served as a condiment with rich foods such as pâtés and cured meats. Although they look like the sweet gherkins found in the supermarket, the similarities end there. Cornichons are pickled in vinegar and flavored with onions, mustard, and aromatics. Sweet gherkins, on the other hand, contain a fair amount of sugar or corn syrup along with spices such as cloves and allspice.

To find an acceptable substitute, we tasted plain cornichons, sweet gherkins, and chopped dill pickles straight up and in French potato salad and homemade tartar sauce. In the end, tasters felt that chopped dill pickles came the closest to the tart, briny flavors of cornichons. Sweet gherkins tasted too "candy-like," and their spices upset the balance of flavors.

Can I buy pitted olives to save the work of pitting them myself?

Sorry—sometimes the easiest option is not the best option.

To evaluate differences between pitted and unpitted olives, we gathered green and black brine-cured olives from the deli section at the supermarket, as well as olives packed in jars and plastic containers. After tasting many samples, it became clear that the pitted olives suffered on two counts: They tasted saltier and their flesh was mushier. They also lacked the complex, fruity flavors of the unpitted kind. Here's why: Before being packed for sale, fresh-picked olives are soaked in brine for up to a year to remove bitterness and develop flavor. The olives are then pitted and prepared for packing, which means returning them to the brine, which can penetrate the inside of the olive and turn it mushy and pasty, as well as increase the absorption of salt. That saltiness can mask subtler flavors. So, if you have the time, it's better to buy unpitted olives and pit them yourself, especially if they are a major part of a dish.

Is there any flavor difference between red and green cabbage? Can I use them interchangeably?

Go ahead! There are slight flavor differences, but nothing major.

Although both are part of the Brassicaceae family, red and green cabbage are two different varieties. We made batches of coleslaw and braised cabbage with both types and tasted them side by side. Tasters didn't notice any textural differences. In terms of flavor, however, the green cabbage tasted notably milder in both applications, with tasters commenting on its vegetal flavor in the coleslaw. The red cabbage tasted sweeter and "fruitier" in both recipes, though this was more pronounced in the braised sample. If you have a preference based on those qualities, choose your cabbage accordingly. Otherwise, use whatever is convenient.

The eggplant varieties that I see most frequently in my supermarket are large globe, small Italian, slender Chinese, and apple-shaped Thai. Does it matter which kind I use in a particular dish?

They're all eggplants, but that's pretty much where the similarities end.

To find out whether the four most common varieties of eggplants can be used interchangeably in recipes, we prepared each type of eggplant in five dishes calling for different cooking methods: roasted and pureed in baba ghanoush, sautéed in *pasta alla norma*, baked in eggplant Parmesan, stewed in Thai curry, and stir-fried with sweet chili-garlic sauce.

Only the globe eggplant was a true multitasker, suitable for all dishes and responding well to all cooking methods. The smaller varieties were prevented by their size from being good choices in eggplant Parmesan, and their excessive amount of seeds made for overly coarse baba ghanoush. Italian eggplant, which has a spicy flavor, and Chinese eggplant, which has an intense, slightly sweet profile, are both good when sautéed, stewed, or stir-fried. Thai eggplant, with its crisp, applelike texture, is also a good choice for those cooking techniques and is notable for tasting bright, grassy, and appealing even when simply eaten raw.

Can green beans and wax beans be used interchangeably?

They definitely can—and depending on your dish, yellow wax beans might actually be the better choice.

Green beans get their color from chlorophyll, and yellow wax beans are simply green beans that have been bred to have none of this pigment. We wondered whether chlorophyll contributes to the flavor of green beans—and whether we'd miss it if it wasn't there.

We tasted green and wax beans steamed until crisp-tender and also braised. In both applications, tasters found very little difference in the flavors of the two, calling both sweet and "grassy." But wax beans did have one advantage over green: Because they have little color to lose during prolonged braising, their appearance changes less than the appearance of green beans, which tend to turn a drab olive. So if you're making a long-cooked bean dish and are picky about aesthetics, go for the gold.

What's the difference between broccoli rabe, broccolini, and broccoli?

These three vegetables are in fact quite different: Broccoli rabe is more bitter than broccoli and a bit spicy; broccolini is sweeter.

Most Americans are familiar with broccoli, but not the other two. Broccoli, broccolini, and broccoli rabe are all cruciferous vegetables, but broccoli rabe is more closely related to turnips, another member of the Brassicaceae family. Broccolini looks like broccoli stretched into a long, skinny form.

Broccoli rabe has a bitter bite that can be polarizing: People who love dark leafy greens are typically fans, while others can be turned off by its pungent flavor. In a recent tasting, our tasters lauded its "sharp," "minerally" flavor and spicy finish. Broccolini is a bit sweeter than broccoli, with a flavor some tasters likened to a cross between spinach and asparagus.

What is white asparagus, and how does its taste compare to green asparagus?

Less color means less flavor for most of the white asparagus you can get at the supermarket.

White asparagus is simply green asparagus that has never seen the light of day. The plant is grown under soil or some other covering to block out the sun's rays, preventing photosynthesis and the development of chlorophyll, which is what normally turns the spears green. Most of the white asparagus available in American supermarkets is imported from Peru. When we pan-roasted Peruvian white asparagus and green asparagus and sampled them side by side, tasters dubbed the green spears "vegetal," "sweet," and "grassy," with a "slightly mineral" aftertaste. The white spears had a less pronounced flavor, reminding tasters of a cross between peas and turnips. Overall, the white spears didn't wow us, presumably because their delicate flavor had faded during shipping and storage.

If you have the opportunity to try freshly picked white asparagus, give it a try. As for the usual supermarket offerings, given the hefty price difference (we paid $3.99 per pound for green and $5.99 per pound for white), we say stick with the green stuff.

How different are white and brown mushrooms? Can I just use whatever I have when a recipe calls for mushrooms?

Technically, they're not very different, but there are definite variations in flavor.

Despite their differing appearance, white button and cremini mushrooms (also known as baby portobellos) belong to the same mushroom species, *Agaricus bisporus*. Creminis are a brown-hued variety, and portobellos are simply creminis that have been allowed to grow large. We think of creminis as a recent introduction to the marketplace, but all button mushrooms were actually brown until 1926, when a mushroom farmer in Pennsylvania found a cluster of white buttons growing in his beds, which he cloned and began selling as a new variety. But does the loss of color mean a loss of flavor? To find out, we sautéed white button and cremini mushrooms and tasted them side by side in risotto and atop pizza. The flavor of the creminis was noticeably deeper and more complex. This difference was also apparent, though less obvious, when we compared both types of mushrooms sprinkled raw over salads. If bolder mushroom flavor is what you're after, it's worth shelling out a little extra for creminis, but otherwise the two are largely interchangeable.

I recently saw purple and white sweet potatoes at the market. Can I substitute these for the orange kind in sweet potato pie?

These varieties are definitely worth trying on their own merits, but they don't make a great substitute for orange sweet potatoes, especially in baking recipes.

While you may see just one or two kinds of sweet potatoes at the grocery store, there are actually hundreds of varieties, with varying flesh and skin colors. To determine what the differences were in flavor and texture, we tasted common varieties of white and purple sweet potatoes boiled, mashed, and in sweet potato pie next to their more common orange-fleshed cousins.

Overall, the white sweet potatoes we tried tasted citrusy and floral, while the purple sweet potatoes tasted more neutral. Both, however, shared some of the sweet, pumpkinlike flavors we're used to with orange sweet potatoes. But the differences in texture were more noticeable.

Both white and purple sweet potatoes have lower moisture contents and are generally starchier—more akin to regular white or yellow potatoes. For this reason, they cooked differently: The mashed sweet potatoes made with white or purple sweet potatoes were thicker and needed to be thinned significantly with stock or cream to reach the texture of the mashed orange sweet potatoes.

In the pie, both white and purple sweet potatoes resulted in a denser filling than the orange control batch. And while the purple sweet potato pie was visually very interesting, tasters commented that it seemed "starchy" or even "gluey" or "mealy," so it's probably not a worthwhile swap.

What's so special about Key limes? Will using regular limes in a Key lime recipe ruin it?

Conventional lime juice won't ruin a Key lime recipe—and it's a much easier ingredient to use.

Key lime aficionados herald the fruit's "distinctive" flavor and fragrance compared with conventional Persian limes, but we wondered whether our tasters could tell the difference in a blind taste test.

Sampled plain, the Key lime juice tasted slightly less tart and bracing than its Persian counterpart, and a quick lab test confirmed that impression: The juice from the conventional limes had a lower pH than the Key lime juice, indicating higher acidity. When we made Key lime bars with both varieties, once again the Persian-lime version tasted a bit more tart, though tasters were split over which variety made the better bar. The deciding factor may be the amount of work involved: To get the ½ cup of lime juice called for in our bar recipe, we had to squeeze three Persian limes. With the tiny Key limes, it took almost 20!

Both Key lime juice and regular lime juice are sold in shelf-stable bottles, and we wondered whether these would do in a pinch. The short answer? No way. The four brands we tried were at best "bracingly bitter" and, in some cases, "just plain rancid." What's more, many baking recipes (including ours) call for the addition of zest—a tough proposition with a glass bottle.

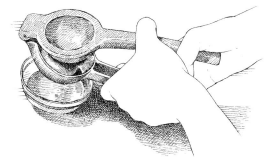

What makes jelly, jam, preserves, and marmalade different? Does it matter which one I use in a particular recipe?

There is a method to the processed-fruit madness, and which product you use in a recipe can definitely make a difference.

Commercial jellies, jams, preserves, and marmalades are all made in the same basic manner: by cooking fruit down with sugar and an acid. What differentiates the types, according to the standards of identity regulated by the U.S. Food and Drug Administration, are the size and structure of the fruit products used. Jelly is made from fruit juice and cooks up into a thick, clear, homogeneous mixture. Jam contains fruit pieces (crushed, chopped, sliced, or pureed) and has a slightly chunky, slightly firm texture. Preserves are made with large chunks or even whole fruits and are usually described as fruit suspended in thick syrup. Preserves tend to be less sweet than jams and jellies. Marmalade is almost always made from citrus fruits and contains pieces of rind, which gives it a unique texture and also a faint bitterness.

We reserve each type of product for specific uses according to its characteristics. Jelly can be melted and used as a glaze; other products won't function in this capacity because they contain seeds or chunks of fruit. We use jam as a filling for pastries and other desserts because of its texture, which is firm but relatively uniform. Preserves and marmalade are reserved for spreading on toast, muffins, or other baked goods because the larger pieces of fruit and rind in these products make them harder to reliably incorporate into recipes.

Can I use the dried form of an herb if I don't have the fresh version on hand?

*In some cases this substitution can work,
but be careful about when you use it.*

It can be tempting to use dried herbs when a recipe calls for fresh—after all, they are more convenient and a lot cheaper than buying bunches of fresh herbs from the supermarket. We purchased fresh and dried versions of basil, chives, dill, oregano, parsley, rosemary, sage (in coarsely crumbled and rubbed forms for the dried version), tarragon, and thyme. Then we cooked our way through 24 recipes (including marinades, sauces, and braises), making each with fresh and dried herbs and comparing differences in flavor.

In all but one application, tasters preferred fresh herbs to dry. Chili was the exception; in this dish, dried oregano was the favorite. Still, there were a few instances in which dried herbs, though not preferred, were a passable substitute. In addition to oregano, dried rosemary, sage, and thyme fared reasonably well in recipes involving fairly long cooking times (more than 20 minutes) and a good amount of liquid.

So, when a recipe calls for delicate herbs, it's best to stick with fresh (as well as in all recipes that use herbs raw or to finish a dish). However, if a recipe calls for fresh hardier herbs such as oregano, rosemary, sage, or thyme, dried can be an acceptable substitute. Just keep in mind that ounce for ounce, dried herbs are more potent than fresh. You need to use only about one-third as much dried herbs as you would fresh.

Have you tried the herbs in a tube sold in the produce section of the supermarket? Can I use these as a substitute for fresh herbs?

Fresh herb taste without the hassle of washing, drying, and chopping, with no waste and an extra-long shelf life? If it sounds too good to be true, it probably is.

We gave basil, lemon grass, and cilantro versions of these herbs-in-a-tube products a try. To taste the products, we used them in common recipe applications, comparing them side by side with fresh herbs. As per the package instructions, we used teaspoon-for-teaspoon substitutions. For the basil, the difference was obvious to tasters in both appearance and taste in a tomato-basil vinaigrette. The vinaigrette made with the tubed product was noticeably more emulsified than the fresh herb version, perhaps because of the oil and stabilizers that have been added to all these products. Interestingly enough, most tasters preferred the tubed herb version for its sweeter, more balanced flavors.

The results for the other two herbs were not as favorable. We used the lemon grass to infuse plain chicken broth. While the flavor was much more pronounced using the tubed lemon grass, one taster complained that it tasted "like candy" and smelled "like Pledge." We also blended a small amount of cilantro with sour cream to make a simple dip. Comments for the tubed cilantro version ranged from "so fake, tastes like soap" to "disgusting and tastes stale." Used again in a salsa, the tubed cilantro tasted dull and looked "ugly as hell." Not exactly a ringing endorsement.

My local grocery store carries frozen basil, parsley, cilantro, and dill in small blister packs. How do they stand up to fresh herbs?

Skip this "convenience" product—but think about making your own!

We also found these frozen herbs—stabilized with water, soybean oil, starch, dextrose, and salt—at the supermarket, packaged in small ice cube tray–like containers. According to the label, one cube is equivalent to 1 teaspoon of chopped fresh herbs. We tried them in six applications. Other than marinara sauce, tasters overwhelmingly preferred fresh herbs to their frozen counterparts.

It is possible, however, to make decent homemade frozen herb cubes from parsley, sage, rosemary, or thyme. Place the chopped fresh herbs in an ice cube tray, cover them with water, and freeze. Then simply add the cubes to sauces, soups, or stews.

What's the difference between various types of parsley?

We have strong feelings about this issue, but it really depends on the situation.

Restaurants often favor curly parsley for chopping because its upright carriage and drier nature make the going easier, but this ignores its inferior taste. Flat-leaf, or Italian, parsley, on the other hand, with its big green flavor, is an indispensable culinary herb. We prefer flat-leaf parsley for its fresh, grassy presence and tender texture and find curly-leaf parsley to be bitter or tough. However, these differences are not as noticeable in heavily flavored dishes where you're using only a little bit of parsley.

The moral of the story? If you're making a dish in which parsley gets star billing, go for flat-leaf. However, if you're sprinkling a little parsley into a stew or onto pasta, don't worry if you have only the curly stuff on hand.

When a recipe calls for "mint," do they mean peppermint or spearmint? Can I use these two interchangeably?

When you see "mint" in an ingredient list,
it usually means spearmint, and if you buy "mint"
at the supermarket, you'll probably be fine.

I t may sound rather simplistic, but when we call for mint as an ingredient, we are thinking of the fresh herb that is available in the grocery store, which is often labeled simply as "mint." After doing a little research, we learned that super-market mint is in almost all cases spearmint *(Mentha spicata)* rather than peppermint *(Mentha piperita)*. While peppermint certainly can be (and sometimes is) used in cooking, it is more commonly used as a flavoring or scent in commercial products—everything from medicine to toothpaste to cigarettes. And there is a world of difference between the two types of mint.

Visually, the differences are easy to spot: Peppermint leaves are a deeper green than spearmint leaves, and peppermint's stalks are a darker brown. The flavor of peppermint can also be described as deeper and darker than that of spearmint. We made teas from a handful of each to better taste the differ-ence. The peppermint, true to its name, has a spicier, peppery character (tasters called it medicinal), while spearmint has a lighter, sweeter flavor. On the whole, the spearmint sold in grocery stores is your best bet for cooking.

Can I substitute dried lemon grass for fresh?

If you can't find fresh lemon grass or don't want to deal with preparing it, you can substitute dried—but not in every type of dish.

Woody stalks of lemon grass, a grassy herb native to India and tropical Asia, are used in many South Asian dishes, imparting citrusy and floral flavors to soups, curries, and stir-fries. Lemon grass is also sometimes dried and sold in jars.

To test the difference between fresh and dried, we used some of each to make a curry paste (which we then stirred into vegetable broth), a Thai chicken soup, and a snow pea stir-fry. (Because dried herbs are more concentrated in flavor than fresh herbs, we followed our general rule of using one-third as much dried lemon grass as fresh in each recipe.)

In all three cases, tasters found that the fresh lemon grass imparted a bright mix of citrus, floral, and minty notes, while the dried lemon grass contributed a less complex, woodsy flavor. That said, we still found the dried lemon grass to be an acceptable substitute for fresh in the paste and the soup, both of which also had a lot of other flavors in the mix. But we don't recommend the dried herb at all in stir-fries. With this dry-heat cooking method, the parched pieces of lemon grass could not hydrate, and thus retained the texture of hay.

So, if you're going to substitute dried lemon grass for fresh, make sure to use it only in recipes in which there is enough liquid for the herb to hydrate and soften.

When a recipe calls for onions,
I usually reach for the yellow kind,
as it's the variety I normally
keep on hand. Can Spanish
or white onions also be used?

*We recommend different types of onions for different
applications, but yellow onions are your best all-around pick.*

Different onion varieties have subtle flavor differences, mostly due to the sulfur content of the soil in which each is grown. The sulfur level of the soil yields varying levels of sulfur compounds within each onion type, resulting in greater or lesser pungency. White onions tend to have the least amount of sulfur compounds and the sweetest flavor; Spanish tend to have the most, for a far more pungent taste.

We tasted all three onions raw in salsa, sautéed in oil, and simmered in French onion soup. In salsa, tasters found low-sulfur white onions to be mild and well-balanced, high-sulfur yellow onions notably stronger but still balanced, and Spanish onions decidedly strong, with a lingering harshness. When briefly sautéed, the sweetness of white onions intensified to a caramel flavor, Spanish onions retained their pungency, and yellow onions turned earthy and sweet. In French onion soup (a recipe that calls for deeply caramelized onions), white onions became too sweet for many tasters and Spanish onions left a slight astringent aftertaste, while yellow onions offered just the right balance of sweet and savory.

While such flavor differences may not ruin a recipe, we recommend mild white onions for raw applications and Spanish onions for cooked applications in which a heartier onion flavor is desired. If you want to stock just one type of onion in your pantry, make it yellow onions, which fall somewhere between these two on the pungency scale.

Is there a reason for using shallots instead of onions? My grocery store sells shallots for $2.99 a pound and onions for $1.29 a pound. Why pay twice as much for shallots?

There are definitely recipes in which shallots are worth the added expense.

Shallots have a unique flavor that is milder and more delicate than that of onions. When shallots and onions are cooked, these differences show up even more. In a quick-cooking pan sauce for steak, for example, a shallot's mild flavor will meld much more smoothly with that of the other ingredients. A finely minced shallot will also melt into the sauce until it's all but indiscernible. No matter how finely you mince an onion, it's not going to disappear into an otherwise silky sauce. An onion also needs much more cooking time before its flavor will mellow. When used raw, a shallot will add gentle heat to a vinaigrette or salsa, with a minimum of crunch. Use a raw onion in the same recipe and the pungent onion crunch may seem out of place.

What is the difference between spring onions, green onions, and scallions? Can they be used interchangeably?

Scallions and green onions are different names for the same vegetable and can be used interchangeably with spring onions.

In the United States, green onions and scallions are the same thing. We refer to them as scallions, as this is a slightly more widely used term.

Spring onions and scallions are both species of the genus *Allium*, along with garlic, shallots, chives, ramps, and leeks. Scallions never form a bulb, so their white bases do not bulge.

Spring onions look like scallions with small white bulbs; they are typically harvested in spring and are not available year-round. We tried them both raw, roasted with oil and salt, in a compound butter (which we tossed with potatoes), and in a barbecue sauce recipe. They tasted very similar. Tasters called both of them "strong and oniony," with the scallions being slightly more pungent and reminiscent of raw onion than the spring onions. The spring onions, however, fared the best in our roasting tests because of their sweetness and slightly larger size.

You can use spring onions and scallions interchangeably in raw applications where they are chopped. But be careful about using them in cooked applications, as the larger spring onions may require longer cooking times.

What is the difference between dehydrated garlic and garlic powder? Is either an acceptable replacement for fresh garlic?

Most of the time we prefer fresh garlic, but there are a few specific situations where you might want to use garlic powder.

Dehydrated garlic is simply minced fresh garlic that is dehydrated before packaging. Garlic powder is made from dehydrated garlic that's been pulverized and, unless you buy a high-quality brand, often includes a slew of artificial ingredients and flavorings meant to improve flavor and extend shelf life.

We compared garlic powder and dehydrated minced garlic to the real thing in our recipes for Caesar salad dressing, pasta with garlic and oil, and garlic bread. In the dressing, flavor differences were minimal; the assertive flavors of lemon, anchovies, and Worcestershire sauce masked any processed garlic taste. In the pasta and garlic bread, however, tasters preferred the unmistakable bite of real garlic.

Our opinion? In most instances, nothing compares to fresh cloves, especially when garlic is the predominant flavor in the recipe. We don't recommend dehydrated garlic, which takes a while to rehydrate and is quite mild. However, there are a few cases in which garlic powder makes sense. We like its mild roasted flavor in spice rubs for meat and in dishes such as oven-roasted potatoes (unlike minced fresh garlic, garlic powder will not burn in the oven). Substitute ¼ teaspoon of garlic powder for each clove of fresh garlic called for.

Is prepeeled garlic a good shortcut product to eliminate the prep associated with fresh garlic?

It's probably not worth the time it saves
unless you use a whole lot of garlic.

We tasted both prepeeled garlic and freshly peeled garlic raw in aïoli, sautéed in spaghetti with garlic and olive oil, and lightly cooked in stuffed rolled flank steak. In all cases, results were mixed, with neither freshly peeled nor prepeeled garlic claiming victory. However, we did notice a difference in shelf life: A whole head of garlic stored in a cool, dry place will last for at least a few weeks, while prepeeled garlic in a jar (which must be kept refrigerated) lasts for only about two weeks before turning yellowish and developing an overly pungent aroma, even if kept unopened in its original packaging. (In fact, in several instances we found jars of garlic that had already started to develop this odor and color on the supermarket shelf.)

But if you go through a lot of garlic, prepeeled cloves can be an acceptable alternative. Just make sure they look firm and white with a matte finish when you purchase them.

I've seen packages of black garlic displayed in the produce section of my grocery store. What is it? Can I use it in place of regular garlic?

Black garlic isn't a go-to substitute for regular garlic, but you might still want to try it.

Aged, fermented "black" garlic was introduced to the Korean market in 2007. The version we've recently found in American supermarkets is fermented in a temperature- and humidity-controlled machine for 30 days, followed by 10 days of air-drying. The resulting bulbs have loose-fitting, grayish-purple skin and opaque black cloves. Straight from the bag, the cloves have a sticky, chewy texture and a concentrated, notably sweet flavor reminiscent of molasses or reduced balsamic vinegar, with a mild aftertaste.

To evaluate the product in everyday cooking applications, we finely minced two black garlic cloves and added them to a simple vinaigrette. We also sliced and roughly chopped two cloves and used them to garnish pasta, risotto, and pizza. In the acidic vinaigrette, the black garlic's flavor was hard to detect, save for subtly sweet undertones. If the garlic was left in larger pieces, its flavor was more pronounced, adding complexity to pasta, risotto, and pizza. Still, while black garlic might be worth trying, it's no substitute for the potent taste of ordinary garlic.

I've started seeing enormous bulbs of "elephant garlic" at my supermarket. Can I use it just like regular garlic?

Don't use elephant garlic in place of regular garlic. Or at all, for that matter.

D espite the name, elephant garlic is not actually garlic. Though both aromatics are members of the *Allium* genus, they are different species. And while at first glance elephant garlic might look like garlic on steroids (it's two to three times larger), closer examination reveals some differences.

Conventional garlic heads can boast as many as 20 cloves, but elephant garlic never has more than about six, and its cloves have a yellowish cast. To see how their flavors compared, we made aïoli and garlic-potato soup, using regular garlic in one batch and the same amount of elephant garlic in another.

Raw in aïoli, the elephant garlic had a mild, garlicky onion flavor. This weak flavor virtually disappeared when it was simmered in soup. Tasters much preferred the sharper, more pungent taste of regular garlic in both recipes. It turns out that elephant garlic produces the same flavor compounds as regular garlic when it's crushed—as well as those produced by onions and leeks—just less of each type. The upshot is that elephant garlic doesn't taste as potent other alliums.

Is there a difference between chili powder and chile powder? I've seen both spellings used.

Chili and chile are not synonyms.

Chili powder (or chile powder) is a tricky term; it is often applied to both the blend of ground ingredients that goes into the seasoning mix many Americans use to make a pot of chili and any powder made from a single type of chile pepper, be it ancho, pasilla, or otherwise. In general, recipes calling for a powder made from a single type of chile will specify the type—as in ancho chile powder. If you see only "chili powder" in an ingredient list, you can be pretty sure it's referring to the blend, which usually contains one or two ground red chiles as well as cumin and oregano and sometimes salt, paprika, and other seasonings.

Can I use white pepper and black pepper interchangeably? Are there times when I really need one or the other?

It depends how much pepper is called for and whether aesthetics are a concern for your dish.

Some recipes call for white pepper when uniformly light-colored results are desired. But if looks aren't a consideration, does it matter if you substitute black pepper when a recipe specifies white? If the recipe calls for a large enough amount—yes. We made two pots of hot-and-sour soup (which traditionally calls for white pepper), using 1 teaspoon of black pepper in one batch and 1 teaspoon of white pepper in the other. Tasters noted that the soup with black pepper was more aromatic and had more heat but preferred the soup with white pepper for its floral, earthy flavor and greater complexity. However, when we tried the swap in a stir-fry that called for a lesser amount of white pepper, tasters had a hard time distinguishing them.

Black and white pepper come from the same plant. The difference in flavor and color relates to how they are processed. To make black pepper, unripe berries from pepper plants are gathered and dried until the skins are blackened, which gives black peppercorns their characteristic aroma and sharp bite. White peppercorns are fully ripened berries that have been soaked in water to ferment, and their outer skin is removed before drying. Although stripping the skin removes much of the volatile oils and aroma compounds, allowing the berries to ripen longer lets them develop more complex flavor, while fermenting adds another layer of flavor.

How can I substitute sweet paprika in recipes that call for hot paprika?

Sweet paprika + cayenne pepper = hot paprika

Both sweet and hot paprika come from the dried pods of *Capsicum annuum L.*, which includes a large swath of pepper varieties ranging from sweet red bell peppers to hot chile peppers. The type of pepper used will influence the flavor, spiciness, and intensity of the paprika. Sweet paprika is made from only the middle layer of the pepper's outer wall (the mesocarp), while hot paprika also contains some of the white veins (the placenta) and seeds, where most of the heat resides. Most paprika labeled "paprika" or "mild paprika" is of the sweet variety.

Heat aside, we wanted to find out whether there were any other flavor differences between the two varieties and whether one was better suited for a particular type of recipe than another. We used each in three applications: chicken paprikash, barbecue sauce, and a dry rub for baked chicken breasts. Most tasters found the sweet paprika to be a better choice in the chicken paprikash; the hot paprika was less flavorful, aside from its pronounced heat. The differences were even more apparent in the spice-rubbed chicken breasts, where the hot paprika took on an unpleasant bitter edge. In the barbecue sauce, however, tasters found both varieties perfectly acceptable, and some preferred the sauce made with the hot paprika.

If yours is going to be a one-paprika household, we recommend stocking the more versatile sweet; add a pinch or two of cayenne pepper to replicate the flavor of the hot stuff. Paprika also comes in a smoked variety, which is produced by drying the peppers (either sweet or hot) over smoldering oak embers. Since smoked paprika has a deep, musky flavor all its own, we do not recommend using it for regular paprika applications; it is best used to season grilled meats or to add a smoky aroma to boldly flavored dishes. If a recipe ever calls for smoked paprika, make sure that's what you're using.

On a recent visit to a spice shop, I was surprised to see three different kinds of cardamom pods for sale: white, green, and black. How do they differ, and which one should I use if my recipe simply calls for "cardamom"?

Green is your best all-purpose bet, but it depends on how much cardamom flavor you want in your dish.

The delicate complexity of cardamom makes it a popular spice in several cuisines, most notably Middle Eastern, Indian, and Scandinavian. Green cardamom is the most commonly found variety in the United States, and white cardamom is simply green cardamom that has been bleached so as not to discolor light-colored baked goods and other foods. Black cardamom (also called large cardamom) is not true cardamom but a relative.

To test for flavor differences, we removed the seeds from the inedible green, white, and black cardamom pods, ground the seeds in a coffee grinder, and used the spice to flavor sugar cookies. We also crushed all three kinds of pods and steeped them in the rice cooking water for separate batches of chicken biryani.

All three forms of cardamom boasted similar flavors—piney, sweet, and floral, with a peppery, warm finish—but intensity levels varied. In both applications, the green cardamom was the most vibrant and balanced. Not surprisingly, the flavor of the bleached pods paled in comparison to the green; since they cost almost twice as much, we won't purchase them again. Black cardamom offered hints of eucalyptus, and as it is generally dried over fire, it boasted smoky nuances that we appreciated in savory biryani but not in cookies. For an all-purpose choice, we'll be going green when it comes to cardamom.

What should I look for when picking saffron? Are threads better than powder?

Powdered saffron is a great choice if you want to save time and effort.

S affron is available in two forms—threads and powder. Conventional wisdom says that deep, dark red threads are better than yellow or orange threads. We held a small tasting of broths infused with different saffron samples, and the threads with considerable spots of yellow and orange did in fact yield the weakest-colored and flattest-tasting broths. The reddest threads yielded intensely flavorful, heady, perfumed broths—so much so that less ardent saffron fans would have been happier with a little less saffron.

Conventional wisdom also cautions against the use of powdered saffron. Some sources say that inferior threads are used to produce the powder and that coloring agents may be added. While this may be true, we found powdered saffron purchased from a reputable source to be just as flavorful and fragrant as even the highest-quality threads. What's more, powdered saffron offers a few advantages over threads. First, a smaller amount can be used (about one-third to one-half the volume measurement of threads); second, the powder is easier to measure and does not need to be crumbled before use; finally, it releases its flavor much more rapidly (a boon for quick recipes but not so important for simmered dishes such as paella and bouillabaisse).

Can I use whatever kind of salt I have on hand when a recipe calls for just "salt"?

In a purely scientific sense, salt is salt—but that doesn't mean you can simply substitute different types one for one.

While there is technically the same amount of sodium chloride in a pound of table salt as in a pound of kosher salt, you can dramatically change how salty your dish tastes by using the wrong kind of salt.

The three types of salt we use most often are table salt, kosher salt, and sea salt. Table salt consists of tiny, uniformly shaped crystals that dissolve easily, making it our go-to for most applications. Kosher salt has larger, coarser grains than table salt and is our top choice for seasoning meat. The large grains distribute easily and cling well to the meat's surfaces. The two major brands of kosher salt—Morton and Diamond Crystal—work equally well; however, their crystal sizes differ considerably, and this makes a difference when measuring by volume. (In the test kitchen, we use Diamond Crystal kosher salt.) Sea salt is the product of seawater evaporation, a time-consuming, expensive process that yields irregularly shaped, mineral-rich flakes. Don't bother cooking with pricey sea salt; mixed into food, it doesn't taste any different from table salt. Instead, use it as a "finishing salt" where its delicate crunch can stand out. Look for brands boasting large, flaky crystals.

You can substitute kosher or sea salt for table salt, but you'll need more of them, since the small size of table salt crystals makes it "saltier" (because more grains fit in a measuring spoon). Use the ratios below. Kosher salt and coarse sea salt do not dissolve as readily as table salt; for this reason we do not recommend using them in baking.

1 teaspoon table salt	=	1½ teaspoons Morton Coarse Kosher Salt
1 teaspoon table salt	=	2 teaspoons Diamond Crystal Kosher Salt
1 teaspoon table salt	=	2 teaspoons Maldon Sea Salt

Can I use pastis in place of Pernod? What about schnapps, sambuca, or ouzo?

Beware: Not all anise-flavored liqueurs are created equal when it comes to cooking.

Pernod and pastis are often sipped in cafés in the south of France, as well as used interchangeably in many classic recipes for Provençal soups and stews that call for a hint of anise flavor. But unless you do a lot of southern French cooking, a whole bottle of either one could spend years in your liquor cabinet. Would other, slightly more common anise-flavored liqueurs such as schnapps, sambuca, and ouzo (which you might already have on hand) work just as well?

In our side-by-side test, tasters consistently condemned the schnapps and sambuca for being far too sweet, but the ouzo proved itself an admirable stand-in. It can be used interchangeably with Pernod and pastis.

What is the difference between wine and vermouth? Can I use vermouth in place of wine when cooking?

In small amounts, vermouth can be a great substitute for wine.

Vermouth starts out as a basic table wine. Traditionally, the wine was flavored with flowers, herbs, spices, and roots and then fortified with alcohol, bringing the total alcohol content up from the 12 to 13 percent typical of wine to about 18 percent. Today the process is much the same, although some large commercial producers use liquid concentrates rather than the botanicals themselves to achieve the characteristic flavor of vermouth.

Our tests showed that dry vermouth is a viable substitute for white wine, especially when the quantity called for isn't all that much (½ cup or less) and when the dish has other flavors that balance and dilute the flavor of the vermouth. Red vermouth is sweeter than white vermouth (and considerably sweeter than red wine), but it still makes an acceptable substitute for red wine when used in recipes that call for a relatively small amount. If the extra sweetness bothers you, try toning it down with a few drops of lemon juice or red wine vinegar.

Considerations of flavor aside, vermouth has a couple of things going for it. First, at $5 or $6 for a 750-ml bottle, it is cheaper than most wines. Second, an open bottle can keep in the refrigerator for three to nine months, versus just a few days for wine. When you don't want to open a bottle of wine just to pour off a small amount for a recipe, vermouth can be used as a substitute.

I often see recipes that call for dry sherry. Is it OK to substitute cream sherry?

With a few adjustments, sweet and dry sherry can be effectively interchanged.

Sherry is a fortified wine that originated in the Andalusia region of southern Spain. Dry sherry is made from Palomino grapes, and cream (also called sweet) sherry comes from Pedro Ximénez grapes. In our tests, we found that only a few tasters objected to the sweetness of the cream sherry when it was substituted for dry sherry, and this can be fixed with a squeeze of lemon juice to help balance out the flavors.

We've also found that it's possible to create a reasonable facsimile of cream sherry by stirring 2 teaspoons of dark brown sugar into ½ cup of dry sherry. (But don't try serving a glass of the sweetened dry sherry to your great-aunt Sadie as a sub for her favorite tipple; it's suitable only for recipes.)

No matter what, avoid "cooking sherry" from the supermarket shelf. Loaded with salt and artificial caramel flavoring, it will ruin the flavor of most dishes. (We feel similarly about any alcohol sold specifically for cooking.)

If I don't have sherry or port on hand, can I substitute ordinary white or red wine?

This can definitely work—just make sure you sweeten the deal a little.

Sherry, which tasters describe as "nutty" and "musky," is traditionally made with white wine, while port, with heavy notes of dried fruit, is developed with red. We tried adapting recipes for sherry-cream sauce with leftover Chardonnay and a port-cherry reduction with leftover Merlot. In each application, the regular wine's sharper alcohol flavor stood out immediately, but adding a sweetener fixed that. Brown sugar's caramel-molasses flavor best resembled that of the aged fortified wines.

Our suggestion is to substitute white wine for sherry and red wine for port, adding light brown sugar in increments of ¼ teaspoon until the boozy aftertaste is masked by the sweetness of the added sugar.

Can I substitute tawny port for the ruby variety in a recipe?

These two are pretty different for drinking, but you can mix them up for cooking.

The difference between tawny and ruby port lies in the aging process. Before it is bottled, tawny port spends at least two years (and as many as 40 years) in wooden barrels, where it picks up a caramel color and toasty, nutty flavors. Ruby port, on the other hand, is typically aged for only two years and spends little or no time in wood, so it retains a vibrant red color and a more straightforward, fruity character. Ruby port is generally used in cooking because it tends to be less expensive than tawny, and its brilliant red hue adds visual appeal. However, if you don't mind sacrificing some of your expensive tipple, go ahead and use tawny port instead; the nuances of flavor are pretty much lost in cooking.

What are the best nonalcoholic substitutions for beer and wine in cooking?

Our favorites are just nonalcoholic versions of beer and wine.

Our first impulse was to replace wine with an equal amount of broth, but during our testing we found that sauces prepared this way lacked acidity and balance. To make that up, you can add a small amount of wine vinegar (red or white, depending on the recipe) or lemon juice, about 1 teaspoon per ½ cup of broth. We also tried dealcoholized wine in a pan sauce and a stew. While all tasters could easily detect the sweet and less acidic notes of the dealcoholized wine in both dishes, most thought it was still acceptable. When we added some lemon juice or wine vinegar to cut the sweetness, both dishes got near-universal compliments.

We tried using nonalcoholic beer in two of our recipes (carbonnade and beer-braised short ribs) and had great success. Because both of these dishes are simmered over a long period of time, much of the alcohol is cooked off anyway. In the end, what's left is the beer's hoppy, malty flavor profile. Therefore, using a nonalcoholic beer makes sense.

What is the difference between apple cider and apple juice? Can I use them interchangeably?

These two products may seem like essentially the same thing, but you shouldn't treat them as such.

To make apple cider, apples are simply cored, chopped, mashed, and then pressed to extract their liquid. Most cider is pasteurized before sale, though unpasteurized cider is also available. To make apple juice, manufacturers follow the same steps used to make cider, but they also filter the extracted liquid to remove pulp and sediment. Apple juice is then pasteurized, and potassium sorbate (a preservative) is often mixed in to prevent fermentation. Finally, apple juice is sometimes sweetened with sugar or corn syrup.

We tried using unsweetened apple juice in recipes for pork chops and glazed ham that call for cider. Tasters were turned off by excessive sweetness in the dishes made with apple juice, unanimously preferring those made with cider. This makes sense: The filtration process used in making juice removes some of the complex, tart, and bitter flavors that are still present in cider. (When we tested the pH level of both liquids, the cider had a lower pH than the apple juice, confirming its higher level of acidity.)

However, while a direct swap of apple juice for cider may not work, we did find one that did: For each cup of cider, you can substitute a mixture of ¾ cup of apple juice plus ¼ cup of unsweetened applesauce.

Are there any differences between club soda, seltzer, and sparkling mineral water? Can they be used interchangeably?

Yes, there are some important differences, and you should be careful which product you use for certain applications.

Club soda and seltzer are both made from water charged with carbon dioxide to give them bubbles. Club soda often contains sodium bicarbonate. In contrast, mineral water gets its more delicate effervescence from naturally occurring springs and, as the name suggests, contains more minerals than the other water types.

To find out whether these three effervescent waters could be used interchangeably, we tasted seltzer, club soda, and mineral water straight up and in shrimp tempura, a dish where the fizz of seltzer plays an important role in the development of an ethereally light batter.

Sipped from the bottle, the seltzer had a neutral taste, the club soda had a slightly acrid bite, and the mineral water had a subtle salty earthiness that tasters preferred for drinking.

In the tempura, club soda and seltzer both made a crisp, perfectly light crust that evenly coated the shrimp. Mineral water, however, produced a thin, weakly adhering batter that fried up soggy. We attributed this to the fact that mineral water contains less gas than club soda and seltzer. So, while club soda and seltzer can be used interchangeably in recipes, sparkling mineral water is best for drinking.

I've had a hard time finding cheesecloth at my grocery store—is there anything else I can use in place of it?

If cheesecloth eludes you, a very common household item can be used as a stand-in.

Cheesecloth is useful to have around for straining out those last bits of herbs and veggies from your broth or stock. Luckily, cheesecloth is a multiuse item, so if you can't find it at your local grocer, you may be able to track it down in hardware, paint, fabric, and craft stores.

Still can't locate cheesecloth? If you were planning to use it to strain a recipe like a broth, don't worry: Simply line a mesh strainer with at least three layers of plain, white paper towels (no prints, please) and slowly pour the broth through. You can also use several layers of paper coffee filters.

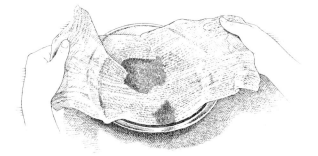

What's so special about kitchen twine? Can't I just use any old twine or string?

You probably shouldn't use industrial twine to tie your pork roast.

A recipe calls for kitchen twine, but the only twine you have is a skein from the hardware store. Should you use it? Probably not. Because it's not intended for cooking, it's probably not food-safe. Still, we thought we'd give it a try with some nylon twine from the hardware store. Although it didn't melt or burn, the day-glo yellow colorant leached onto the pork roast we had tied with it.

A common recommended alternative to kitchen twine is unwaxed dental floss, but it is so thin that it often cuts through a piece of meat while being tied. After cooking, this whitish, almost translucent filament is all but invisible and thus can be difficult to remove. We also found that dental floss is particularly ill suited to grilling because it easily singes and then breaks.

As for bona fide kitchen twine, you can buy cotton or linen. We found linen twine easier to tie, and it holds a tight overhand knot well. In addition, it pulls away from the cooked meat easily, taking a minimum amount of seared crust with it. That said, cotton twine worked nearly as well as linen and is a more economical choice. Look for a midweight cotton twine; of the four weights we tested, we liked 16-ply best.

These days almost all recipes for bread seem to call for a stand mixer. If I don't have one, can I just knead by hand? What kind of adjustments do I have to make?

No major adjustments are required—you can get great results from hand-kneading, as long as you're willing to put in the elbow grease.

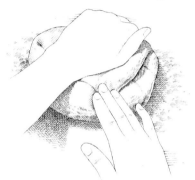

A stand mixer or food processor is our tool of choice for mixing and kneading bread doughs. But some cooks don't own either, and a handheld mixer is simply too lightweight. Using your hands, of course, is certainly an option.

Over the years, we've found that the following method works with most bread doughs: Start by mixing the wet ingredients in a large bowl. Add about half of the flour and mix with a wooden spoon until combined. Stir in the remaining flour, leaving aside ¼ to ½ cup. At this point, the mixture should form a shaggy dough. Turn out the dough onto a lightly floured work surface and knead, adding the reserved flour as necessary, until the dough is smooth and elastic.

Most doughs will require 10 to 15 minutes of kneading by hand. Expect to get a good upper-body workout, but your efforts will pay off. As long as you resist the temptation to add too much flour, hand-kneaded breads compare favorably with those made from machine-kneaded doughs.

I don't have a stand mixer. Is there an easy way to cream butter and sugar by hand? Or could I use a different tool instead?

You can definitely do it by hand, but we also came up with a shortcut using an unexpected ingredient that might save you time and effort.

Creaming does more than just combine two ingredients. As sugar is rapidly mixed into fat, it creates millions of tiny air pockets that expand in the heat of the oven, giving baked goods lift. Skip the creaming step and your cakes and cookies may turn out squat and dense. Creaming softened butter and sugar by hand using just a bowl and a wooden spoon is hard labor: It'll take you 20 minutes compared with a mere 3-minute hands-off stint in the mixer. Our search for an easier way led us to an unlikely product: whipped butter.

We made a cookie recipe and a cake recipe, first using two sticks of unsalted butter and mixing in a stand mixer, and then using an 8-ounce tub of whipped unsalted butter and mixing by hand. To our surprise, the cookies were indistinguishable, and the cake made with whipped butter was every bit as fluffy as the one made according to the recipe. Just make sure you use pure unsalted whipped butter, at room temperature, and substitute by weight, not volume.

If you're looking for an alternative tool, a hand mixer will work, although we found it took twice as long to achieve a light, fluffy mixture as it did in a stand mixer.

Can I bake any cake batter in a Bundt pan, or does it need to be specially formulated for that pan?

Most cake batters will work in a Bundt pan with a few adjustments in cooking time—and in your expectations about what the cake will look like.

A Bundt pan is a great shortcut to a picture-perfect cake. To see how a regular layer-cake batter (formulated for two 9-inch cakes) would fare in a Bundt pan, we tried making yellow, chocolate, and carrot cakes in a 15-cup Bundt pan and compared each to its original layer-cake version.

All three worked well, though none were identical to their original counterparts. Because the batter wasn't divided into multiple thinner layers, the leavener had more work to do in the deeper Bundt pan and wasn't as effective. All three came out denser than their light, fluffy layer-cake counterparts, though the crumbs were still lighter than a classic Bundt cake's. Also, because they all required a longer baking time in the deeper Bundt pan (twice as long for the yellow and chocolate and three times as long for the carrot), they were all slightly drier toward the edges, though still acceptable. The cakes baked in Bundt pans also developed a thicker crust— just as you'd expect to find on a classic Bundt cake.

Is there any way to make a dark-colored pan work like a light-colored pan?

The color of a pan can have a dramatic effect on how your recipe turns out, but there are ways to work around this.

D ark-colored pans absorb heat more efficiently than light-colored pans, so the sides and bottoms of items baked in dark pans will cook more quickly. This is an asset when baking cinnamon rolls and deep-dish pizza, where a brown crust is desired, but it can be a problem with other recipes. Because the batter near the edges in a dark pan will reach its maximum temperature sooner than the batter near the edges in a light pan, a cake baked in a dark pan will have sides that are overly brown and set early, leading to stunted height while the center continues to rise.

If you own only dark pans, you can wrap them in aluminum foil to mimic a light-colored pan. A cake baked in a dark pan wrapped in foil will look identical to a cake baked in a light-colored pan: level, with lightly browned sides and bottom. Make sure to wrap the exterior of the pan with foil as snugly as you can. At the top of the pan, fold the edges of the foil back onto itself; do not fold the foil over onto the interior.

Why do some recipes call for a tube pan? Can I make those cakes in any other kind of pan?

There's a good reason angel food and chiffon cakes are always baked in tube pans, and it's not just aesthetics.

These specialty vessels help delicate cakes rise. Because egg foam–based cakes like angel food and chiffon contain very little flour—and therefore very little of the structure-building network called gluten—the batter needs something to cling to as it bakes or it will collapse. Enter the tube pan's tall sides: As the egg foam heats up, it will climb the sides (and conical center) of the pan. But its lofty structure isn't sturdy until the cake cools, which is why angel food and chiffon cakes are often cooled upside down on the pan's tripod feet. For this reason, we don't recommend you try baking traditional angel food or chiffon cakes in any other kind of pan; they will fall.

Is there a rule of thumb for converting a quick bread into muffins? What about for converting a layer cake into cupcakes?

For most recipes, you can just dump the batter into a muffin tin and adjust the baking time, but there are a few important exceptions.

To answer this question, we chose a handful of quick bread and cake recipes with different mixing techniques and varying ratios of ingredients: banana bread, cornbread, carrot cake, angel food cake, chiffon cake, devil's food cake, and yellow layer cake. After preparing the batters as directed in each recipe, we simply portioned them into greased 12-cup muffin tins and baked them on the middle rack at the oven temperature specified for about half the time called for.

All the quick breads turned out very nicely as muffins. However, the cake results were a mixed bag. The cupcakes made from angel food and chiffon cakes, batters that receive lift from whipped egg whites, failed miserably. They came out of the oven looking perfect but quickly collapsed as they cooled. The devil's food and yellow cakes fared better. They baked up with flat tops (ideal for a layer cake but not so much for a cupcake), and several stuck to the pan because of their high sugar content, but overall they were acceptable.

So, with the exception of angel food and chiffon cakes, the next time you want to transform your favorite batter into muffins or cupcakes, go ahead. Divide your batter into a greased 12-cup muffin tin (use paper liners for tender layer cake batters) and bake until a toothpick inserted in the center comes out with just a few crumbs attached, about (or a little less than) half the time called for in the original recipe. Rotate the muffin tin halfway through baking.

Is there an easy way to convert a muffin recipe into a loaf recipe?

Yes, there are some pretty simple
rules to follow to make this switch.

Because muffins are small, they are generally baked at relatively high temperatures so they develop browning before their interiors overcook. In general, muffins bake for 15 to 20 minutes. Loaves, on the other hand, have a greater volume-to-surface-area ratio and thus require longer baking at a lower temperature. We tested several fruit and nut muffin recipes, as well as a plain one, baking each in 8½ by 4½-inch pans at a range of oven temperatures and times.

Our findings? To convert a muffin recipe to make a loaf, set the oven rack in the middle position, decrease the oven temperature by 50 degrees, and bake until a toothpick inserted in the center of the loaf matches the visual cue given for the muffins (either "with a few moist crumbs attached" or "clean"), 1 hour to 1 hour 10 minutes. Recipes with sugary toppings like streusel should be tented with foil during the last 20 to 25 minutes to prevent them from getting too dark.

Is there a rule of thumb to follow for converting layer cakes into sheet cakes? I find it much easier to frost a cake baked in a 13 by 9-inch baking dish than a multiple-layer cake.

Good news for cooks who hate the fuss of
frosting layer cakes: This is an easy swap!

When we tried this substitution with a few of our layer cake recipes, we found that each sheet cake version required about 5 extra minutes of baking, but after that they came out perfect. So the next time you want to prepare a recipe for two 9-inch layer cakes in a 13 by 9-inch baking dish, bake the cake as usual and add about 5 minutes of baking time to the original recipe (checking for doneness a few minutes early to prevent overbaking). Let the cake cool completely before frosting it in the pan or turning it out to be frosted.

Is there any way to successfully cook delicate foods in a traditional skillet if I don't have a nonstick skillet on hand?

In lieu of a nonstick skillet, a stainless-steel skillet coated with vegetable oil spray can work nearly as well.

To find out if we could make a regular stainless-steel skillet more nonstick with the help of a vegetable oil spray, we sprayed the entire surface of a 10-inch skillet and heated it over medium heat (any hotter and the spray discolored) until shimmering before adding an egg, which we also sprayed on top. For comparison, we heated 1 tablespoon of vegetable oil (a generous amount for a 10-inch pan) in an identical stainless-steel skillet over medium heat until shimmering before adding an egg, which we drizzled with oil before flipping.

The spray easily trumped the oil. Why? As oil heats up, it tends to form an uneven layer because the surface of the pan heats unevenly, causing the oil to pool in cooler areas and disappear in other areas. Vegetable oil sprays prevent sticking better because they contain more than just oil—they also include lecithin, an emulsifier that bonds the oil to the pan so it forms a thin, complete layer of oil between the pan and the food.

Be sure to spray the entire surface of the pan, including the flared sides. Note that foods like scrambled eggs won't work with this method; because the food is moved around the pan during cooking, the layer of nonstick spray is lifted from the bottom of the pan.

What makes an omelet pan special? Do I really need one in order to make a great omelet? What about a crêpe pan? Are these just a scam?

We have found that a few good, basic, multitasking pans are a better investment than a set of specialized tools.

Although pricey, specialized skillets often do little to enhance the products they produce, omelets and crêpes do benefit from different pan surfaces. Because omelets require constant, gentle movement and only a glancing acquaintance with the bottom of the pan, a 10-inch nonstick skillet works best for cooking them. In recent tests, the omelets we made in our favorite nonstick were fine-pored, delicately pale, and—unlike those cooked in the skillet's specialized counterpart—incapable of sticking.

A crêpe, on the other hand, tastes better when a sticking point or two yields a few brown spots; we found pale crêpes to be uninteresting in flavor and texture—rather omelet-like, in fact. This makes traditional pans (without a nonstick surface) a must for crêpes. A heavy traditional skillet performed as capably as a French crêpe pan—and in some regards even better, as the heat was more even.

Of course, these two pans—a nonstick skillet and a traditional skillet—are great tools for a wide variety of other cooking tasks as well, unlike the more specialized pans.

Can I reuse a disposable baking pan?

While they're not our favorite vessels, you can reuse disposable baking pans a few times, as long as you wash them by hand between uses.

W e don't typically use disposable pans for baking because they don't hold heat well and aren't as stable as metal, ceramic, or glass options, so baked goods don't brown well in them. That said, we've found that you can somewhat overcome these issues by placing your filled disposable pan directly on a preheated rimmed baking sheet in the oven.

Using this hack, we tried baking three batches each of brownies, sticky buns, and pie in succession in the same disposable baking pans (hand-washing them after each use). We tested with our winning disposable pan, Glad OvenWare, which is made of sturdy plastic, and with a generic disposable aluminum pan. After three rounds in the oven, both the plastic and aluminum pans showed some wear and tear but didn't exhibit any significant issues. A Glad company representative confirmed that the OvenWare pans should last for "at least three uses" on average.

Many recipes call for placing the oven rack in "the middle position," but my oven has six rack positions, so there is no true middle. Should I use the upper-middle or the lower-middle rack?

We say err on the side of the cooler, and therefore lower, rack position.

In the test kitchen, we have ovens with both an even and an odd number of rack positions. If you have an odd number of racks, finding the middle position is easy. If you have an even number, you can place the rack in either the upper-middle or the lower-middle position. To find out which position is preferable, we baked batches of cookies and cake in both positions and compared the results.

After an afternoon of baking, we found it was better to use the lower-middle rack, which put the food a little closer to the exact middle of the oven (since the food itself sits higher than the rack).

Recipes often call for cooling baked goods on a wire rack. Is a rack really necessary, or is it OK to cool foods on a flat surface?

That cooling rack is actually doing a lot for your baked goods—skip it at your own risk.

The chief concern when cooling baked goods is preventing sogginess. When an item is cooled on a wire rack, air can circulate beneath it, allowing steam to escape, rather than condensing and causing the food to turn mushy. To prove this theory, we baked up two identical batches of cookies and two pies. We cooled one batch of each recipe on a wire rack and compared it to batches cooled directly on a heatproof counter. The cookies cooled on a rack were crisp and evenly textured from the edge to the center. The counter-cooled cookies were less crisp overall and chewier in the center. The pie test was equally convincing: The bottom crust of the pie cooled on the wire rack maintained its crispness despite the moist apple filling. The pie cooled on the counter, on the other hand, developed a gummy, wet bottom crust.

If I don't have a carving board, I can just use a regular cutting board, right?

You can, but you need another piece of equipment to make it work.

Good carving boards come with a handy well in the center and a moat around the edges to capture juices from the meat that would otherwise drip onto the countertop and floor. Your regular, completely flat cutting board doesn't have that well, so if you use it to carve a juicy roast or whole turkey, you'll end up with juices all over the counter. As a makeshift solution, we recommend putting the flat cutting board inside a rimmed baking sheet before carving; the raised lip will keep the juices from leaking out as you carve.

If I don't have a garlic press, can I simply mince the garlic really small with a knife for the same results?

If you're an expert garlic mincer, this should be just fine, but if you doubt your skills, we recommend a garlic press.

Ever since we first tested garlic presses, we've started recommending pressed garlic in our recipes. We compared minced and pressed garlic in a variety of recipes, and our tasters couldn't tell the difference between properly minced garlic and pressed garlic. Professional chefs may well be able to produce piles of perfectly minced garlic in no time flat, but we've found that home cooks often don't mince garlic as finely as many recipes require, which can lead to uneven cooking. A garlic press produces not only a very fine mince (almost a puree) but an evenly fine mince, which ensures even cooking and even distribution of flavor throughout the dish. If you don't want to invest in a garlic press, just make sure you practice your knife skills.

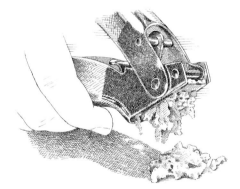

What is the difference between a food mill and a ricer? Why would I need to own one or the other?

One of these tools is definitely more useful than the other.

Ricers are most often used to make smooth, creamy mashed potatoes. The peeled, cooked potato is put in the basket of the ricer's lower half and forced through small holes when the upper handle is closed, thereby mashing—actually, pureeing—the potato.

A food mill purees food and strains it at the same time. Food is placed in the hopper, and a hand-crank mechanism turns a conical blade in the hopper against a perforated disk, forcing the food through the disk. Most food mills have three interchangeable disks with various-size holes. A food mill can thus not only make mashed potatoes but can make them from unpeeled potatoes, forcing the flesh through the holes in the disk while holding back the skins. Food mills can also puree apples to make flawlessly smooth applesauce with no need to peel and core the apples first, and can puree cooked tomatoes, removing the skin and bitter seeds for you.

Some cooks swear by the ricer for making superior-quality mashed potatoes, arguing that there's less likelihood that the potatoes' starch cells will be ruptured, which can make for gluey potatoes. But if you're looking for one kitchen tool that will mash potatoes and make all sorts of other purees, the food mill is the way to go.

Wide, shallow goblets (or coupes) were once the stemware of choice for champagne, but these days you're more likely to get a glass of bubbly in a tall, narrow flute. Is one better than the other, or is it just a matter of aesthetics?

There's actually a scientific reason for using a flute over a coupe glass.

In addition to the fact that the compact shape of a flute can keep champagne from warming too fast, a flute limits the exposed surface area of the champagne, which slows the release of carbon dioxide. The bubbles deliver much of champagne's flavor (by way of smell): As the bubbles rise through the liquid, they carry aromatic compounds to the surface and deliver them to your nose. So, slowing down the production of bubbles ensures good flavor from first sip to last. The larger exposed surface area of champagne in a coupe would logically translate into the faster release of bubbles and thus a more quickly dissipated flavor.

Naturally, we had to see (and taste) for ourselves, so we compared the same bubbly served in flutes and in wider goblets. Most tasters found the champagne in wider glasses to be fizzier yet flatter in taste; they described the champagne as "sweet" and "acidic," with little complexity. The flutes delivered champagne with "citrusy," "floral," and "fruity" aromas. So while your grandmother's goblets may look retrochic, we suggest that you serve your champagne in flutes.

Cheat Sheet

Finding Substitutes for Less-Common Ingredients

SUPERMARKETS ARE GETTING BETTER ABOUT STOCKING ALL THE ingredients necessary for cooking dishes from around the world, but some ingredients can still be hard to find. Here are a few of the items that we stock in our pantry, along with suggestions for approximating their flavors if unavailable.

If you don't have

Coconut Milk

Try Do not use canned cream of coconut, which is sweetened. Bring equal parts whole milk and unsweetened shredded coconut to a simmer and let steep, covered, for 15 minutes. Grind the mixture in a blender or food processor and let steep for another 15 minutes. Strain the mixture, pressing down on the coconut in the strainer to extract the most flavor. This will make an acceptable substitute for curries and stir-fry sauces, but it's less reliable in baked goods.

Fish Sauce

Try A mixture of 1 tablespoon of soy sauce plus 1 finely minced anchovy fillet will make a crude stand-in for 1 tablespoon of this salty, pungent Thai sauce.

Mace

Try Mace and nutmeg are both harvested from the fruit of the Indonesian nutmeg tree; whole nutmeg is the fruit's pitlike seed, and mace is found in the waxy red layer that separates the seed from the fruit's flesh. The flavors of the two spices are similar, but mace is much stronger than nutmeg. If a recipe calls for mace and you have only nutmeg, use it, but double the amount.

Mirin

Try To replace 2 tablespoons of this sweet Japanese rice wine, substitute an equal amount of white wine or sake plus 1 teaspoon of sugar.

Queso Fresco

Try Popular in Mexico, *queso fresco* (also called *queso blanco*) is a fresh, crumbly-soft mild cheese made from either cow's or goat's milk. If you can't find queso fresco, fresh farmer's cheese or a mild feta is a suitable substitute.

Savory

Try This aromatic Mediterranean herb is found in two varieties: winter and summer savory. The types are quite similar, though the flavor of the latter is slightly more delicate, and the former has a coarser texture. Summer savory is more widely available, but if you can't find either type, you can substitute a combination of 2 parts fresh thyme to 1 part fresh sage.

Tahini

Try To make a replacement for this sesame paste, grind up an equal amount of sesame seeds in a blender with just enough peanut or vegetable oil to make a fairly smooth mixture. Add 1 teaspoon of toasted sesame oil (or to taste) and use the mixture as a one-for-one substitute for tahini. Another option is to blend 3 parts peanut butter with 1 part toasted sesame oil and use half the quantity of tahini called for in the recipe.

Tamarind

Try Sweet-tart, brownish-red tamarind is a necessary ingredient for authentic pad thai, but you can still make a good pad thai using lime juice and water. To replace 2 tablespoons of tamarind paste soaked in ¾ cup of hot water and strained, mix ⅓ cup lime juice and ⅓ cup water.

Thai Basil

Try If you can't find Thai basil, do not substitute regular basil; its flavor is too gentle. An equal amount of mint makes a better substitute.

3

Kitchen Confidence

How Would a Test Cook Do That?

For most of us, once we learn to do something a particular way, that's the way we'll do it for the rest of our lives. This rule applies both in the world at large and in the kitchen in particular; if your aunt who makes the best cherry pie taught you to pit cherries using a knitting needle and a glass soda bottle, then that's probably the way you'll always do it. But here in the test kitchen, our test cooks try many different approaches before deciding on the best way to execute a particular task. The average recipe in our kitchen is tested more than 30 times before being published, and in the process of all that testing, we've also come up with some best practices for all kinds of kitchen work. Those tips and tricks are outlined here to help you learn new skills, level up your existing abilities, unlearn some bad habits, and tackle all your kitchen challenges with the confidence of a test cook.

Test Your Cooking IQ

Bench Test

A BENCH TEST IS A HANDS-ON EXAM DESIGNED TO MAKE SURE that a cook has the basic culinary talents required to do a job, from measuring to knife skills to following a recipe from start to finish. This multiple-choice quiz gets at just some of the foundational knowledge you need to be a successful cook.

1 If a recipe calls for searing a piece of meat, which of the following should you do?
A. Use moderate heat.
B. Move the meat around in the pan a lot.
C. None of the above.

2 Which of these techniques can make raw kale softer and easier to chew?
A. Massaging the leaves with your hands.
B. Soaking the leaves in hot water.
C. Either A or B.

3 If your silicone spatula gets really stained, you can clean it using
A. A bucket of salt.
B. Toothpaste.
C. Hydrogen peroxide.

4 If you accidentally oversoften butter, you can fix it by
A. Letting it sit until it congeals again and then resoftening.
B. Cooling it quickly with ice cubes.
C. Mixing in some additional cold butter.

5 When a recipe calls for "one-second pulses" in a food processor, which of the following actions you should you take?

A. Press and hold the button for a full second.

B. Press the button, release it, and repeat after 1 second.

C. It depends on how your food processor works.

6 It's easiest to separate eggs when they are

A. Cold from the refrigerator.

B. At room temperature.

C. Cold or room temperature; it doesn't matter.

7 Professional chefs season food from way above the counter

A. Because it changes the taste of the seasoning.

B. Because it helps distribute the seasoning more evenly.

C. For no good reason—it just looks cool.

8 If a recipe calls for tenting meat with foil after cooking, you should

A. Ignore it and leave the foil off.

B. Wrap the meat tightly in foil.

C. Loosely cover the meat with foil.

9 If you're beating cream by hand, the most efficient way to use the whisk is to

A. Beat in loops that take the whisk up and out of the bowl.

B. Stir in circles like a spoon.

C. Use side-to-side strokes back and forth in the bowl.

10 The best way to keep meat from getting stuck to the pan while searing is to

A. Let it cook without touching it.

B. Press down on the meat while it cooks.

C. Move the meat around a lot while it's cooking.

Answers

1 C (page 188)   2 C (page 155)
3 C (page 168)   4 B (page 202)
5 C (page 195)   6 A (page 203)
7 B (page 150)   8 C (page 158)
9 A (page 182)   10 A (page 189)

Why do TV chefs sprinkle salt from way up in the air? Is this just kitchen theatrics, or is there a reason behind this practice?

This showy technique actually seasons food more effectively.

We've seen chefs season food by sprinkling salt from a good 10 or 12 inches above the counter. To see whether there's any advantage to this trick, we sprinkled chicken breasts with ground black pepper from different heights—4 inches, 8 inches, and 12 inches—and found that the higher the starting point, the more evenly the seasoning was distributed. And the more evenly the seasoning is distributed, the better food tastes. So go ahead and add a little cheffy flourish the next time you season.

Is it better to season food early in the cooking process or just at the end?

Salt takes time to do its work, so season early in the process. If you're salting at the end, use a very light touch.

Most recipes (and culinary schools) advise seasoning food with salt early in the cooking process, not just at the end. We know that salt penetrates food slowly when the food is cold. (We have found that it takes a full 24 hours for salt to diffuse into the center of a refrigerated raw turkey.) While the process is faster during cooking (the rate of diffusion of salt into meat will double with every 10-degree increase up to the boiling point), it's still not instantaneous. And salt penetrates vegetables even more slowly than it does meat, because the salt must cross two rigid walls surrounding every plant cell, while the cells in meat contain only one thin wall. Adding salt at the beginning of cooking gives it time to migrate into the pieces of food, seasoning them throughout; if you add salt only at the end, it provides a more concentrated, superficial coating that immediately hits your tongue.

For the most even seasoning and well-rounded flavor, we strongly encourage seasoning food early in the cooking process as we direct in our recipes. However, if you forget, do not try to make up for it by simply stirring in all the salt at the end. Instead, start with a very small amount of salt and then taste and season further as desired. On the flip side, if you are watching your salt intake, you could wait until the end of cooking to season your food, knowing that you'll be able to get away with a lesser amount.

What's the best way to remove the seeds from a pomegranate?

Our favorite method involves using a bowl of water to your advantage.

While many sources recommend removing the seeds from a pomegranate by placing half of the fruit cut side down on a work surface and hitting the end with a rolling pin or wooden spoon, we've found an even better way that removes every seed without any mess.

1 Cut off the bump on the blossom end and score the outside of the fruit from pole to pole into six sections.

2 Insert your thumbs into the blossom end and pull the fruit apart in sections.

3 Submerge the sections in a bowl of cold water and then bend the rind backward to release the seeds. Pull out any stragglers and let the seeds sink to the bottom of the bowl. Discard the rind and any bits of membrane that float to the surface, and then drain the seeds in a colander. The seeds can be refrigerated in an airtight container for up to 5 days.

What kind of citrus peel garnish should I use for my fancy cocktails?

It depends on what you're going for. Bartenders aren't just showing off when they make those fancy twists—there's a good reason for them.

There are three common citrus peel garnishes for cocktails: The first is a twist, a simple strip of citrus peel that is twisted over the drink to release essential oils and then rubbed around the rim of the glass and discarded. The second is a flamed twist, in which a flame is held between the drink and the peel so that when the peel is twisted, its oils ignite briefly. The third type is a swath, a band of zest with a little pith attached that is twirled and placed in the drink. We made all three types of garnishes with orange peel and tasted each in a simple Negroni cocktail. We found that the twist contributed bright orange notes that enlivened the drink. The flamed twist offered sulfurous undertones and had a somewhat subdued orange fragrance. The swath added citrus notes along with mild bitterness from the pith. In sum, fancy citrus peel garnishes are more than just ornamental: Your choice should hinge on the flavor profile you're trying to create.

What's the best way to get all the juice out of a lime or lemon?

We think it's worth investing in a special gadget for this task.

We've squeezed our way through literally thousands of lemons and limes, so we've had a chance to test all kinds of different methods for getting as much juice as possible from these fruits. We tested squeezing against a citrus juicer, in which a fruit half is twisted over a ridged, conical head set over a bowl; a simple wooden reamer, which is manually turned inside the fruit half; and a citrus squeezer, a device that presses the fruit half inside out to extract the juice.

Each method yielded the same amount of juice, about twice as much as by hand squeezing alone. But when we factored in ease of use and speed, the squeezer pressed ahead of the competition. An added bonus: All the bits of pulp were contained in the well of the press rather than dropping down into the juice.

Are there any tricks for yielding more juice? We tried rolling the fruits on the counter, heating them in the microwave, and poking them with a fork; while these tips may help when squeezing by hand or using a reamer, none made a bit of difference in yield (or ease) when using a hand-held squeezer. In fact, we found that cold lemons and limes straight out of the refrigerator yielded the most juice—the firm flesh split open more readily than when warm and more pliable.

What is the best way to revive wilted produce?

Cold water is the answer to all your wilted produce woes.

S oft leafy greens like lettuce, spinach, and arugula can be revived by simply soaking them in a bowl of ice water for 30 minutes. We wondered if a similar technique might be used to revive other types of produce.

Vegetables like broccoli, asparagus, celery, scallions, and parsley absorb water best through their cut bases (not along their waxy stalks and stems). We found that the best way to revive these vegetables was to trim their stalks or stems on the bias and stand them up in a container of cold water in the refrigerator for about an hour. This exposes as many of their moisture-wicking capillaries as possible to water.

I know that I'm supposed to soften kale if I'm going to eat it raw, but I'm not sure how—do I really have to massage it?

Don't be weirded out by the idea of massaging kale—it's easy and effective.

O nce just a garnish, raw kale has recently become a star addition to salads. While we love the bright, nutty flavor of the uncooked vegetable, unless we're using baby kale, its texture can be a little tough. You can soak the kale in hot water for about 10 minutes to tenderize it, but there's a way to soften these greens without subjecting them to heat: After removing the ribs, cut the leaves into ¼-inch ribbons and "massage" them. Kneading and squeezing breaks down the kale's cell walls much the way that heat does, darkening the leaves and turning them silky. We found that it takes a rubdown of at least 5 minutes to soften a bunch of coarse green curly kale, but the more delicate leaves of Tuscan kale (also known as dinosaur or Lacinato kale) or red kale need just a minute of massaging.

Do you have any suggestions for getting rid of the irritating burn that can happen when you accidentally touch a fresh hot chile?

Relief is on the way—just make sure you have hydrogen peroxide on hand.

Capsaicin is the chemical in chiles responsible for their heat. It binds to receptors on the tongue or skin, triggering a pain response. To find out if anything could be done to lessen this burn, we rounded up some brave testers to seed chiles without gloves, smear chile paste onto patches of their skin, and eat scrambled eggs doused in hot sauce. We then tested some home remedies. For the skin, we washed with soap and water and rubbed the affected area with oil, vinegar, tomato juice, a baking soda slurry, and hydrogen peroxide. For the mouth, we swished with (but did not swallow) water, milk, beer, and a mixture of hydrogen peroxide and water.

Soap and water helped lessen the burn on skin a bit, but oil, vinegar, tomato juice, and baking soda didn't help at all. As for a mouthwash, water and beer failed, and milk had only a slight impact. What worked well both on the skin and in the mouth? Hydrogen peroxide.

It turns out that peroxide reacts with capsaicin molecules, changing their structure and rendering them incapable of bonding with our receptors. Peroxide works even better in the presence of a base like baking soda: We found that a solution of ⅛ teaspoon of baking soda, 1 tablespoon of water, and 1 tablespoon of hydrogen peroxide could be used to wash the affected area or to rinse the mouth (swish vigorously for 30 seconds and then spit out) to tone down a chile's stinging burn to a mild warmth. (Toothpaste containing peroxide and baking soda is a somewhat less effective remedy.) Always keep peroxide, baking soda, and toothpaste away from your eyes. To avoid these issues in the first place, it's a good idea to wear gloves when working with very hot chiles. If you don't have gloves, avoid touching your eyes, nose, or mouth with your fingertips and make sure to wash well as soon as chile prep is completed.

When I make chicken, it always comes out dry and bland. How can I make it juicy and tender like the stuff I get at good restaurants?

Here in the test kitchen, one of our favorite tricks for lean meats is to brine them to improve both flavor and texture.

We find that soaking chicken (as well as turkey and even pork) in a saltwater solution before cooking is the best way to protect the delicate meat. Whether we are roasting a turkey or grilling chicken parts, we have consistently found that brining keeps the meat juicier. Brining gives delicate poultry a meatier, firmer consistency and seasons the meat down to the bone. We also find that brining adds moisture to pork and shrimp and improves their texture and flavor when grilled.

Brining promotes a change in the structure of the proteins in the muscle. This rearrangement of the protein molecules compromises the structural integrity of the meat, reducing its overall toughness. It also creates gaps that fill up with water. The added salt makes the water less likely to evaporate during cooking, and the result is meat that is both juicy and tender.

In many cases, we also add sugar to the brine. Sugar has little if any effect on the texture of the meat, but it does add flavor and promote better browning of the skin, which results in even more flavor. Just be sure to pat the meat dry after removing it from the brine.

I've read that tenting meat with aluminum foil can ruin its crust. Is this true?

For most meats (but not poultry), just make sure you tent the foil loosely and there shouldn't be any problems.

Here in the test kitchen, we often call for tenting meat with foil to keep it warm while it rests. And because meat's temperature continues to rise for a few minutes after it's pulled from the oven (known as carryover cooking), we often build the tenting step into our recipe times.

We tested different cuts of meat not tented, tented, and with the foil tightly crimped around the plate the meat was resting on. Our results depended on the meat in question. We do not recommend tenting chicken or turkey when you're looking for crispy skin, because tenting traps steam and leaves the skin soggy. We do, however, suggest tenting steaks, beef roasts, and pork roasts, so long as they don't have a glaze. These meats are often cooked to lower temperatures, so the foil plays a bigger role in keeping the temperature of the meat from dropping. In our tests, the crusts on these meats did not soften significantly when tented. When the meats were glazed, however, the foil often hit and damaged the glaze, and the trapped steam compromised the glazy texture.

Unless a recipe calls for something more specific, we found that tenting works best when the foil is loosely placed on top of the meat in an upside-down V. Don't crimp the edges of the foil around the meat or the plate that the meat is resting on, because air needs to be able to circulate under the foil.

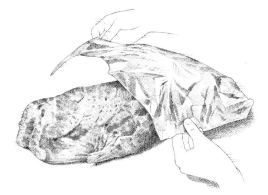

Should I take the rubber bands off a lobster's claws before I boil it?

Don't risk your fingers.

For safety reasons, we've always left the rubber bands on lobster claws when adding lobsters to a pot of boiling water. But after a test kitchen photo of rubber-banded lobsters going into a pot appeared on our website, we received a number of emails and letters from readers stating that the rubber bands would affect the flavor of the cooked lobster. To find out if this is true, we decided to run a test.

We cooked lobsters with and without rubber bands in separate pots of boiling water and then tasted both the lobster meat and the cooking water. While a few tasters claimed they noticed a subtle difference in the cooking water taken from the pot in which we cooked the banded lobsters, no one could detect any flavor differences between the lobster meat samples. Our takeaway? We'll keep our fingers safe and continue to leave the rubber bands in place until after the lobsters are cooked.

Is there a way to use one measuring cup for all different types of ingredients? Do I really need liquid cups and dry cups?

>< ><

*Using the same measuring cup for all
kinds of ingredients is a recipe for disaster.*

To prove how important it is to use the right measuring tools for a particular ingredient, we asked 18 people, both cooks and non-cooks, to measure 1 cup of all-purpose flour in both dry and liquid measuring cups. We then weighed the flour to assess accuracy (a properly measured cup of all-purpose flour weighs 5 ounces). With the dry measuring cup, the measurements were off by as much as 13 percent. This variance can be attributed to how each person dipped the cup into the flour; a more forceful dip packs more flour into the same volume. Measuring flour in a liquid measuring cup, where it's impossible to level off any excess, drove that variance all the way up to 26 percent.

The same people then measured 1 cup of water (which should weigh 8.345 ounces) in both dry and liquid measuring cups. The dry cup varied by 23 percent, while the liquid cup varied by only 10 percent. There was a greater variance when measuring water in a dry cup because it was so easy to overfill, as the surface tension of water allows it to sit slightly higher in this type of vessel.

When measuring a dry ingredient, it is best to scoop it up with a dry measuring cup and then sweep off the excess with a flat utensil, a method we call "dip and sweep." To fill a liquid measuring cup, we recommend placing it on the counter, bending down so that the cup's markings are at eye level, and then pouring in the liquid until the meniscus (the bottom of the concave curve of liquid) reaches the desired marking. And whenever you want to be closer to 100 percent accurate, use a scale.

How should I measure sticky ingredients that aren't quite wet but definitely aren't dry?

If you don't have a special measuring cup for ingredients that fall between wet and dry, your best bet is to use a dry measuring cup.

Measuring semisoft "in-between" ingredients such as honey, peanut butter, mayonnaise, and ketchup can be a challenge: Do you use a dry measuring cup? A liquid measure? And how do you get every last bit out of the cup? In the test kitchen, we use an adjustable measuring cup because it provides us with the most accurate and consistent results. Our favorite features a plastic barrel with clear measurement markings and an easy-to-use plunger insert.

The next-best option is to use a dry measuring cup. If the item you're measuring is thick, you can slide the back of a butter knife across the top of the cup to get a more accurate measurement. We recommend spraying the measuring cup lightly with vegetable oil spray before filling it. When emptied, the ingredient should slide right out of the cup, but make sure you also carefully scrape out the cup. Leaving traces of sticky ingredients behind in the cup can negatively affect a recipe. All that being said, if a weight is listed in the ingredient list and you have a scale, rely on that for the most accurate measurement.

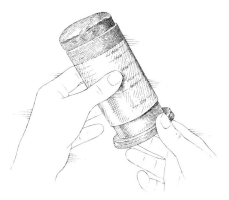

How do I measure "packed brown sugar"? What exactly does that mean?

>≫≪

When we say "packed brown sugar," we really do mean packed.

When a recipe calls for "packed brown sugar," that means firmly packed. Packing is necessary because the moist brown sugar naturally clumps together. But as we learned after asking five test kitchen staffers to pack brown sugar into a 1-cup dry measure, "firmly packed" can mean different things to different people. The five packed cups of brown sugar ranged in weight from 6¾ ounces to 8 ounces, although on average they weighed 7 ounces, the same as 1 cup of granulated sugar.

For those readers who do not own a kitchen scale, we thought it would be helpful to describe the act of packing brown sugar: Fill the cup with sugar until mounded and then use your fingers, a spoon, the back of another measuring cup, or the flat part of an icing spatula to compress the sugar until no air pockets remain and the sugar can be compressed no more (but be reasonable—don't strain a muscle). If the cup isn't completely filled, add more sugar and compress again; if it is then mounded, scrape off the excess so that the sugar is level with the sides of the cup.

What's the best way to measure grated cheese? Should I be packing it into the measuring cup or not?

>≫≪

Be gentle when measuring fluffy ingredients like grated cheese.

Whether it's shredded mozzarella or finely grated Parmesan, you want a measure of cheese that's more fluffy than not. Simply grate the cheese over a piece of waxed paper and then pile it into the cup, tamping down on the cheese very gently to make sure there are no air pockets that will give you a false reading. Packing the cheese—as you would brown sugar—would undo all the work of grating it.

What's the best way to measure lettuce?

><

*Be gentle with the greens and keep in mind that
different types might need slightly different treatments.*

We always give both an ounce measure and a cup measure for greens. But when we tried to convert our usual formula of 2 ounces (or 2 cups) of lightly packed greens per serving to arugula, we ended up with more greens than we could eat. That's because our calculation was based on head lettuce, which is heavier than arugula. For lighter greens such as baby spinach, mesclun, and arugula, less is more: One ounce of lightly packed baby greens yields roughly 1½ cups, just enough for one serving.

But what exactly does "lightly" packed mean? The reason we don't just call for a more accurate measure of "tightly" packed greens pressed firmly into the cup is that this method would bruise delicate leafy greens. To lightly pack greens, simply drop them by the handful into a measuring cup and then gently pat down, using your fingertips rather than the palm of your hand. This method also applies to fresh herbs.

Does it matter whether I drink beer from the bottle or from a glass?

><

If you care what your beer tastes like, always go for the glass.

We sampled three styles of beer—lager, IPA, and stout—straight from the bottle and in a glass and evaluated the differences, if any, in bitterness, maltiness, and aroma. We expected that a glass might make a difference for the aromatic, hoppy IPA, but we were surprised that tasters noticed that all three beers were more aromatic when sipped from a glass, even the lager. In addition, the IPA was perceived as less bitter and more balanced when sipped from a glass, while the stout tasted fuller and maltier. Why? The glass allows more of a beer's aromas to be directed to your nose than does the narrow opening of a bottle. Our recommendation: No matter the beer, using a glass will improve the drinking experience.

My cast-iron skillet is my favorite
tool for cooking fish, but the fish
leaves a smelly mess behind. How
can I totally clean and deodorize
the skillet without damaging
the pan's seasoning?

*There's a simple way to remove all traces of fish
from your cast-iron skillet: Just use your oven.*

A cast-iron skillet is a great tool for searing salmon and tuna, but you can end up with a lingering fishy taste and odor that make it unpleasant to cook other ingredients in the same pan. After frying up more than 3 pounds of salmon and trying several ways to eliminate the smelly evidence—using kosher salt, baking soda, lemon juice, and various combinations thereof—we were stumped.

Scrubbing with baking soda and rubbing with lemon juice and kosher salt helped diminish the smell, but not enough to keep an egg subsequently fried in the pan from smelling like fish oil. Dish soap helped, but since some cooks don't like to use soap in cast-iron pans since they're afraid it will strip the valuable seasoning, we wanted to find an alternative. (For the record, a well-seasoned pan shouldn't be damaged by a small amount of dish soap as long as you rinse and dry it well afterward—see page 47.)

One last thought we had was to heat the pan up again. The two sources of fishy funk are compounds called trialkyamines, which evaporate at around 200 to 250 degrees, and oxidized fatty acids, which vaporize at temperatures above 350 degrees. We heated the empty pans over a medium flame on the stovetop for 15 minutes and in a 400-degree oven for 10 minutes. Sure enough, both methods worked equally well at eliminating odors. We particularly liked the oven method: It's fast and doesn't stink up the kitchen.

How can I clean off really baked-on, built-up messes in my pans without damaging the pans themselves?

Sometimes there's nothing like soap and water for cleaning a really dirty pan.

In the test kitchen, our stainless pots and pans get a daily workout in many high-heat applications. Over time, a layer of baked-on oil and grease often develops that is difficult to remove without the aid of harsh, toxic cleansers. This scorched residue is the result of heating oil or other fats to high temperatures. When oil or other fats are heated to or above their smoke point, their triglycerides break down into free fatty acids, which then polymerize to a resin that is insoluble in water.

Is there a way to remove this residue without resorting to caustic chemical cleansers? To find out, we let four seriously damaged pans sit overnight with the following treatments: one coated with a thick paste of baking soda and water, one filled with straight vinegar, one soaked in a 20 percent vinegar solution, and one soaked in hot, soapy water. (Baking soda, vinegar, and soap all contain compounds that help dissolve fatty-acid resins and help them release from metal.) None of these treatments was 100 percent effective; we still needed scouring powder and a metal scrubbing pad to remove the most tenaciously burnt-on bits of oil. But somewhat surprisingly, the hot, soapy water was the best treatment of the bunch, loosening the residue enough so that it required the least amount of elbow grease and a minimum of scratching of the pan's finish to fully release.

There are stains on the inside of my enameled pans that I just can't get rid of—do you know any tricks?

No matter how dirty they are, you can still get your enameled pans looking as good as new.

We are very fond (culinary pun intended) of Le Creuset enameled cast-iron Dutch ovens; the 12 or so we have in the test kitchen get a lot of use. The downside to these workhorses is that their light-colored enamel interiors become discolored and stained with use. While the staining doesn't affect your ability to use the pot, it can be aesthetically undesirable.

We took a couple of stained pots from the kitchen and filled them with Le Creuset's recommended stain-removal solution of 1 teaspoon of bleach per 1 pint of water. The pots were slightly improved but still far from their original hue. We then tried a much stronger solution (which was OK'd by the manufacturer) of 1 part bleach to 3 parts water. After standing overnight, a lightly stained pot was just as good as new, but a heavily stained one required an additional night of soaking before it, too, was looking natty.

What's the best way to keep my butcher-block countertop clean?

Your butcher-block counter needs to be treated differently from the other work surfaces in your kitchen.

Butcher-block tables, which function not only as a work space but as a cutting surface, must be cared for and treated in a manner similar to cutting boards. To reduce the growth of bacteria on your butcher block, be sure to scrub it with hot, soapy water after each use. The U.S. Department of Agriculture also recommends the periodic application of a solution of 1 teaspoon of bleach per quart of water to sanitize the surface, which should then be rinsed off with cold water.

To maintain the appearance of the wood surface, some manufacturers suggest applying a food-safe oil every few weeks using a clean cloth. The oil soaks into the fibers of the wood, acting as a barrier to excess moisture. The experts we consulted recommend using mineral oil (make sure the container is labeled "food-grade") rather than more volatile oils like vegetable oil and olive oil, which can turn rancid over time. For day-to-day use, we suggest reserving your butcher block for applications that don't involve fish, meat, or poultry. Instead, use a separate cutting board for these tasks, which will make cleaning much easier while reducing the risk of cross-contamination.

How should I wash my blender jar?

To extend the life of your blender,
we recommend hand-washing whenever possible.

Even blenders that are deemed dishwasher-safe may not be immune to shrinking or warping after enough trips through the dishwasher; especially vulnerable are the rubber gaskets, which when damaged can cause leaking.

To make hand-washing easier, particularly when cleaning sticky or pasty ingredients such as peanut butter and hummus, we recommend an initial 20-second whir with hot tap water (enough to fill the bottom third of the jar) and a drop or two of dish soap to loosen any material trapped underneath the blades, and then repeating once or twice with hot water only. To finish the job, unscrew the bottom of the jar and hand-wash each piece using a soapy sponge. For one-piece jar models, use a long, plastic-handled wand-style sponge to reach food stuck on the bottom or sides.

What's the best way to avoid getting beet stains on my cutting board?

We have a simple trick: Use vegetable oil spray.

Prepping beets usually leaves your cutting board with dark stains that discolor other foods you put on it. If you need to keep using a beet-stained board for the rest of a recipe, try this trick: Give its surface a light coat of nonstick cooking spray before chopping the beets. This thin coating adds no discernible slickness under your knife and allows you to quickly wipe the board clean with a paper towel before moving on to your next task.

What's the best way to clean stained silicone spatulas?

You can spruce up stained silicone with a little chemical intervention.

After staining one set of white silicone spatulas bright yellow with a turmeric-and-water paste and another set red with tomato sauce, we soaked each one in potential stain fighters: white vinegar, a slurry of dish soap and baking soda, 3 percent hydrogen peroxide, a bleach solution (made by diluting 2½ tablespoons of bleach in 2 cups of water), and a control mixture of soapy water. After 24 hours of soaking, only the spatulas soaked in hydrogen peroxide or the bleach solution were back to their original white.

It turns out that while soap can help break up and wash away oil, to remove intensely colored stains, the compounds that provide the color need to be broken down into colorless molecules. Hydrogen peroxide and bleach are both oxidants, a type of compound that excels at this task. Just remember to wash your stain-free spatulas in warm soapy water before use.

Is there a way to fully clean a wooden spoon? Mine always seem to hold on to odors and flavors.

Baking soda is the key to keeping your wooden utensils odor-free.

We love wooden spoons, but because of their tendency to retain odors and transfer flavors, a hint of yesterday's French onion soup can end up in today's cake batter. Since it isn't advisable to put wooden utensils in the dishwasher, what's the best way to remove odors?

To find out, we stood six brand-new wooden spoons in a container of freshly chopped raw onions for 30 minutes, rinsed them with water, then cleaned them with the following substances: dish soap and water, vinegar and water, bleach and water, a lemon dipped in salt, a tablespoon of baking soda mixed with a teaspoon of water, and more plain water as a control.

The only spoon that our panel of sniffers deemed odor-free was the one scrubbed with baking soda. Here's why: Odors left behind in the porous surface of a wooden spoon are often caused by weak organic acids. Baking soda neutralizes such acids, eliminating their odor. Furthermore, since baking soda is water soluble, it is drawn into the wood along with the moisture in the paste, thus working its magic as far as the water is able to penetrate.

Is there a way to really deep-clean a wooden salad bowl?

The answer is sandpaper.

Years of exposure to oily salad dressings can leave wooden salad bowls with a gummy, rancid residue that all the soap and hot water in the world can't wash off. To find a better solution, we hunted around in our cupboards for the most gunked-up wooden bowl we could find and subjected it to several treatments—rubbing it with baking soda, scrubbing it with lemon juice and salt, and wiping it down with alcohol—but the sticky buildup wouldn't budge.

In the end, we decided to get tough and found that the best way to restore our bowl to good-as-new condition was to completely remove the accumulated layers of oil with sandpaper and start fresh. Using medium-grit sandpaper (80 to 120 grit), gently rub the bowl's surface until it turns matte and pale; thoroughly wash and dry the bowl; and give it a new coat of food-grade mineral oil (don't use vegetable oil or olive oil, which quickly turn rancid and sticky). With a paper towel, liberally apply the oil to all surfaces of the bowl, let it soak in for 15 minutes, and then wipe it with a fresh paper towel. Reapply oil whenever the bowl becomes dry or dull.

It's fine to use mild dish soap and warm water to clean well-seasoned wooden bowls; doing this will help maintain the seasoning and prevent oil buildup. Dry the bowl thoroughly after cleaning and never put it in the dishwasher or let it soak in water; otherwise, it can warp and crack.

I've heard that sponges are breeding grounds for bacteria, but I have no idea how to clean something that's always cleaning other things—can you help?

Your sponge is one of the dirtiest things in your kitchen, but you can fix that with simple boiling water.

Whenever possible, use a paper towel or a clean dishcloth instead of a sponge to wipe up. If you do use a sponge, disinfect it. We tried microwaving, freezing, bleaching, and boiling sponges that had seen a hard month of use in the test kitchen, as well as running them through the dishwasher and simply washing them in soap and water. Lab results showed that microwaving and boiling were most effective, but since sponges can burn in a high-powered microwave, we recommend boiling them for 3 minutes.

Is there any way to quickly cool a whole pot of soup so I can package it up and put it in the fridge faster?

We like a quick ice bath to help speed up the cooling process.

P utting hot food directly into the fridge after cooking isn't a good idea—it can give off enough heat to raise the temperature in your refrigerator, potentially making it hospitable to the spread of bacteria. The U.S. Food and Drug Administration (USDA) recommends cooling foods to 70 degrees within the first 2 hours after cooking, and to 40 degrees within another 4 hours. We usually cool food on the counter for about an hour and then put it in the fridge. If you're in a rush to cool off a sauce, soup, or stew so that you can put it in the fridge for storage, the best thing to do is get it out of the pot that it was cooked in and into a wide, shallow receptacle, such as a baking dish or large bowl. This increases the surface area, thereby speeding cooling.

If you care to further fast-forward cooling, fill a large cooler or the sink with cold water and ice packs. Place the saucepan or stockpot in the cooler or sink and stir the contents occasionally to speed the chilling process. Refill the cooler or sink with cold water if necessary. Once cooled, the food can be transferred to a storage container and put into the fridge.

Sometimes I forget to take meat out of the freezer to defrost; is there a way to thaw it quickly without compromising quality or safety?

Small cuts can be quick-thawed using hot water, but with large cuts you might be out of luck.

To prevent the growth of harmful bacteria when thawing frozen meat, we use one of two methods: We defrost thicker (1 inch or greater) cuts in the refrigerator and place thinner cuts on a heavy cast-iron or steel pan at room temperature, where the metal's rapid heat transfer safely thaws the meat in about an hour.

But an article by food scientist Harold McGee in the *New York Times* alerted us to an even faster way to thaw small cuts—a method that's been studied by and won approval from the USDA: Soak cuts such as chops, steaks, cutlets, and fish fillets in hot water.

Following this approach, we sealed chicken breasts, steaks, and chops in zipper-lock bags and submerged the packages in very hot (140-degree) water. The chicken thawed in less than 8 minutes, and the other cuts in roughly 12 minutes—both fast enough that the rate of bacterial growth fell into the "safe" category, and the meat didn't start to cook. The chicken breasts turned slightly opaque after thawing. Once cooked, however, the hot-thawed breasts and other cuts were indistinguishable from cold-thawed meat.

Large roasts or whole birds are not suitable for hot-water thawing because they would need to be in the bath so long that bacteria would proliferate.

What's the correct way to measure the doneness of poultry? I'm never quite sure where to put the thermometer, so I just poke random parts of the bird until I get a reading of 160 degrees.

The short answer is "by sticking the thermometer in the thickest part of the chicken," but there's a little more to it than that.

The doneness of poultry is determined by taking its temperature in the thickest part of the breast and/or thigh. If you're taking the temperature of the breast on a whole chicken, aim for the meat just above the bone by inserting the thermometer low into the thickness of the breast. Insert the thermometer horizontally from the top (neck) end down the length of the breast. Because the cavity slows the cooking, the coolest spot sits just above the bone. If you're taking the temperature of a single breast (bone-in or boneless), aim for the dead center of the meat by inserting the thermometer at the midpoint of the thickness.

On a single thigh or leg quarter, the meat is relatively thin and of even thickness, which simplifies the task of taking the temperature. When the leg is part of a whole chicken, the best way to take the temperature of the thigh is to insert the probe down into the space between the tip of the breast and the thigh. Angle the probe outward ever so slightly so that it pierces the meat in the lower part of the thigh. To be certain that it isn't inserted too far, push the probe until it pokes through the bottom side of the chicken, then slowly withdraw it, looking for the lowest registered temperature.

Even if you follow the above guidelines to the letter, the process of testing for doneness remains by and large one of trial and error. Make sure you poke the bird a couple of times to find the lowest temperature.

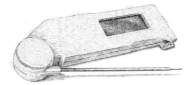

Is it possible to bring home leftover French fries from a restaurant and reheat them successfully?

Reheating restaurant French fries in a preheated, lightly oiled skillet yields the crispest results.

Common wisdom says that French fries must be eaten right away; old, cold fries are fit only for the trash bin. But is this really true? We hoped not. We brought in French fries from a few local restaurants, let them cool, and tried several methods of reviving them with a goal of crisp, hot fries that, if they didn't taste exactly the same as those straight out of the fry basket, came close.

Microwaving them, unsurprisingly, resulted in soggy fries. And even at a variety of temperatures, the oven left fries dry, leathery, and decidedly uncrisp. We turned our attention to the stovetop. We tried heating the cold fries through in a dry skillet, in ½ inch of oil, and in a lightly oiled skillet. In a side-by-side tasting, this last method worked especially well.

To use our method, heat 1 tablespoon of vegetable oil in a 12-inch nonstick skillet until nice and hot (it should just start smoking). Add the fries in a single layer just covering the bottom of the skillet and stir frequently until they darken slightly in color and are fragrant, 2 to 3 minutes. Drain them on a paper towel–lined plate to absorb any excess oil. If you'd like, sprinkle them with a little salt for extra seasoning.

When using a 12-inch skillet, we were able to effectively reheat 6 ounces of fries, or about the amount in a large order of McDonald's fries. This method worked equally well for standard, shoestring, and steak fries.

What's the best way to reheat leftover steak?

*Our favorite reheating method for steak
mirrors our favorite cooking method.*

The best method we have found for cooking steaks is to slowly warm them in the oven and then sear them in a hot skillet. This produces medium-rare meat from edge to edge, with a well-browned crust. When we rewarmed leftover cooked steaks in a low oven and then briefly seared them, the results were also remarkably good. The reheated steaks were only slightly less juicy than freshly cooked ones, and their crusts were actually more crisp.

Here's the method: Place leftover steaks on a wire rack set in a rimmed baking sheet and warm them on the middle rack of a 250-degree oven until the steaks register 110 degrees (roughly 30 minutes for 1½-inch-thick steaks, but timing will vary according to thickness and size). Pat the steaks dry with a paper towel and heat 1 tablespoon of vegetable oil in a 12-inch skillet over high heat until smoking. Sear the steaks on both sides until crisp, 60 to 90 seconds per side. Let the steaks rest for 5 minutes before serving. After resting, the centers should be at medium-rare temperature (125 to 130 degrees).

Is there a way to reheat leftover fish so it isn't terrible?

You can use a low, gentle oven to reheat thick cuts of leftover fish, but you're probably out of luck with thinner cuts.

Fish is notoriously susceptible to overcooking, so reheating previously cooked fillets is something that makes nearly all cooks balk. But since almost everyone has leftover fish from time to time, we decided to figure out the best approach to warming it up.

We had far more success reheating thick fillets and steaks than thin ones. Both swordfish and halibut steaks reheated nicely, retaining their moisture well and suffering no detectable change in flavor. Likewise, salmon reheated well, but thanks to the oxidation of its abundant fatty acids into strong-smelling aldehydes, doing so brought out a bit more of the fish's pungent aroma. There was little we could do to prevent trout from drying out and overcooking when heated a second time.

To reheat thicker fish fillets, use this gentle approach: Place the fillets on a wire rack set in a rimmed baking sheet, cover them with foil (to prevent the exterior of the fish from drying out), and heat them in a 275-degree oven until they register 125 to 130 degrees, about 15 minutes for 1-inch-thick fillets (timing varies according to fillet size). If you have leftover cooked thin fish, we recommend serving it in cold applications like salads.

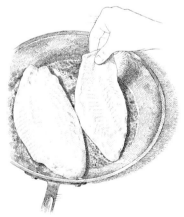

Leftover turkey is always so disappointing—is there any way to save it?

Our gentle method helps ensure that as much moisture as possible stays in the meat and crisps the skin.

Leftover turkey is a fact of life during the holidays, but when you reheat the meat (especially lean breast meat), it rarely comes out well. Here's the best method we've come up with to avoid next-day turkey disappointment.

Wrap the leftover portions in aluminum foil, stacking any sliced pieces, and place them on a wire rack set in a rimmed baking sheet. Transfer them to a 275-degree oven and heat them until the meat registers 130 degrees, a temperature warm enough for serving but not so hot that it drives off more moisture. (Sliced turkey should be warm throughout; if the slices are relatively thick, you can insert the probe into the meat just as you would with bone-in pieces.) This gentle oven temperature also means that the meat comes up to temperature slowly and evenly. Timing will vary greatly based on the shape and size of the leftover turkey pieces. For a crosswise-cut half breast, we found 35 to 45 minutes to be sufficient. Finally, place any large skin-on pieces skin side down in a lightly oiled skillet over medium-high heat, heating until the skin recrisps.

Memorize This!

How to Know When Food Is Done

SINCE THE TEMPERATURE OF COOKED MEAT WILL CONTINUE TO rise as it rests, it should be removed from the oven, grill, or pan when it is 5 to 10 degrees below the desired serving temperature. The temperatures in the following charts should be used to determine when to stop the cooking process. A thin steak or chop should then rest for 5 to 10 minutes, a thicker roast for 15 to 20 minutes. And when cooking a large roast like a turkey, the meat should rest for about 40 minutes before it is carved. To keep meat warm while it rests, tent it loosely with foil (except skin-on chicken and turkey or glazed roasts—see page 158 for more details).

Our doneness recommendations represent our assessment of palatability weighed against safety. The basics from the USDA differ somewhat: Cook whole cuts of meat to an internal temperature of at least 145 degrees and let rest for at least 3 minutes. Cook ground meat to an internal temperature of at least 160 degrees. Cook all poultry, including ground poultry, to an internal temperature of at least 165 degrees. For more information on food safety from the USDA, visit www.fsis.usda.gov.

For This Ingredient	Cook to This Temperature
BEEF/LAMB/VEAL	
Rare	115 to 120 degrees
Medium-Rare	120 to 125 degrees
Medium	130 to 135 degrees
Medium-Well	140 to 145 degrees
Well-Done	150 to 155 degrees

For This Ingredient	Cook to This Temperature
PORK	
Chops and Tenderloin	145 degrees
Loin Roasts	140 degrees
CHICKEN AND TURKEY	
White Meat	160 degrees
Dark Meat	175 degrees
FISH	
Rare	110 degrees (for tuna only)
Medium-Rare	125 degrees
Medium	140 degrees (for white-fleshed fish)

WE RELY ON TEMPERATURE TO PROPERLY PREPARE ALL KINDS OF foods, not just meat, poultry, and seafood. Here's a partial list of other times when temperature is particularly useful.

Ingredient/Food	Ideal Temperature
Oil, for frying	325 to 375 degrees
Sugar, for caramel	350 degrees
Yeast bread, rustic and lean	195 to 210 degrees
Yeast bread, sweet and rich	190 to 200 degrees
Custard, for ice cream	180 degrees
Custard, for crème anglaise or lemon curd	170 to 180 degrees
Custard, baked (such as crème brûlée or crème caramel)	170 to 175 degrees
Water, for bread dough	105 to 115 degrees (dependent on recipe)

How can I tell if my grill fire is "medium-hot"? Does that correspond to a particular temperature? What if I don't have a thermometer?

Even if your grill doesn't have a thermometer, there is an easy way to determine the intensity of a fire's heat, and it works for both charcoal and gas grills: Just use your hand.

With charcoal, once you have started the coals and they are covered with a layer of gray ash, distribute the coals on the grill bottom, put the cooking grate in place, and allow the grate to heat up for about 5 minutes. On a gas grill, preheat with the lid down and all burners on high for about 15 minutes.

Take the temperature of either type of fire by holding your hand 5 inches above the cooking grate and counting the number of seconds you can leave it there comfortably. Yes, really: your hand. With a hot fire (about 500 degrees), you'll be able to hold your hand above the grate for only 2 seconds. With a medium-hot fire (about 400 degrees), you'll be able to keep your hand there for 3 to 4 seconds; a medium fire (about 300 degrees), 5 to 6 seconds; and a medium-low fire (about 250 degrees), 7 seconds.

When using a gas grill, you may just as well ignore the built-in thermometer with its general readings of medium, medium-high, or high in favor of the hand-testing method, which is much more accurate.

What's the best way to figure out if my oven is running hot or cold? Do I have to buy a special oven thermometer?

A properly calibrated oven is essential for ensuring consistent cooking results, but you don't need an oven thermometer to check yours.

Because many people don't have an oven thermometer, we developed an easy method to test for accuracy using an instant-read thermometer. We tested this method in multiple ovens, both gas and electric, and it worked well in all of them. Here's how to do it.

Set an oven rack in the middle position and heat your oven to 350 degrees for at least 30 minutes. Fill an ovensafe glass 2-cup measure with 1 cup of water. Using an instant-read thermometer, check that the water is exactly 70 degrees, adjusting the temperature with hot or cold water as necessary. Place the cup in the center of the rack and close the oven door. After 15 minutes, remove the cup and insert the instant-read thermometer, making sure to swirl the thermometer around in the water to even out any hot spots. If your oven is properly calibrated, the water should be at 150 degrees (plus or minus 2 degrees). If the water is not at 150 degrees, your oven is running too hot or too cold and needs to be adjusted accordingly. (Note: To avoid shattering the glass cup, allow the water to cool before pouring it out.)

What's the proper technique for whisking? I've heard it's all in the wrist, but I'm not sure I'm doing it right; sometimes I feel like I'm just stirring with the whisk.

Most of the time, side-to-side movement is most effective, but whipping egg whites is a different story.

We've noticed that different cooks seem to favor different motions when using a whisk. Some prefer side-to-side strokes, others use circular stirring, and others like the looping action of beating that takes the whisk up and out of the bowl. That got us wondering: Is any one of these motions more effective than the others? We compared stirring, beating, and side-to-side motions in three applications: emulsifying vinaigrette and whipping small amounts of cream and egg whites. We timed how long the dressing stayed emulsified and how long it took to whip cream and egg whites to stiff peaks.

In all cases, side-to-side whisking was highly effective. It kept the vinaigrette fully emulsified for 15 minutes, and it speedily whipped cream to stiff peaks in 4 minutes and egg whites to stiff peaks in 5 minutes. Circular stirring was ineffectual across the board. Beating was effective only at whipping egg whites, creating stiff peaks in a record 4 minutes, surpassing the timing of side-to-side strokes.

Side-to-side whisking is an easier motion to execute quickly and aggressively, allowing you to carry out more and harder motions per minute than with the other strokes. This action also causes more of what scientists call "shear force" to be applied to the liquid. As the whisk moves in one direction across the bowl, the liquid starts to move with it. But then the whisk is dragged in the opposite direction, exerting force against the rest of the liquid still moving toward it. In vinaigrette, the greater shear force of side-to-side whisking helps break oil into tinier droplets that stay suspended in vinegar, keeping the dressing emulsified longer. To create stiff peaks in cream and egg whites, shear force and efficiency are both key. As the tines are dragged through each liquid, they create channels that trap air. Since the faster the channels are created, the faster the cream or whites gain volume, rapid, aggressive side-to-side strokes are very effective. However, because egg whites are very viscous, more of them cling to the tines of the whisk. This allows the whisk to create wider channels to trap air. Since beating takes the whisk out of the liquid during some of its action, these larger channels can stay open longer, thus trapping even more air.

What's the best way to make fried foods at home without creating a giant mess or burning down the house?

Frying stirs fear in many home cooks, but if you follow a few simple guidelines, it's really not that scary.

When done right, frying isn't difficult. It all comes down to the temperature of the oil. If the oil is too hot, the exterior of the food will burn before it cooks through. If it's not hot enough, the food won't release moisture and will fry up limp and soggy.

Use the Right Thermometer A thermometer that can register high temperatures is essential. One that clips to the side of the pot, like a candy thermometer, saves you from dipping it in and out of a pot of hot oil.

Use a Large, Heavy Pot A heavy pot or Dutch oven that is at least 6 quarts in capacity allows plenty of room for the food to fry, ensures even heating, and helps keep the oil hot.

Use Peanut Oil An oil with a high smoke point is a must for frying; we prefer the neutral flavor of peanut oil, but vegetable oil will also work. Fill the pot no more than halfway with oil to minimize any dangerous splattering.

Keep the Oil Hot The temperature of the oil will drop a little when you first add the food to the pot, so we usually increase the heat right after adding the food to minimize the temperature change. If the oil splatters, wipe up as you go.

Fry in Batches Add food to the hot oil in small portions. Adding too much food at once will make the temperature drop too much and will result in soggy–rather than crispy–fried food.

Let the Fried Food Drain Let the finished food drain on paper towels to minimize greasiness.

Is there an easy way to make fried food less greasy (but not less delicious)?

For fried food that's light, crisp, and not greasy, the proper oil temperature is critical, and maintaining that takes effort.

Most deep frying starts with oil between 325 and 375 degrees, but the temperature drops as soon as food is added. Once the oil recovers some heat, it should remain somewhere between 250 and 325 degrees (depending on your recipe) for the duration of cooking. To maintain the proper oil temperature, use a clip-on deep-fry thermometer and keep close watch.

If the oil starts lightly smoking, that's a sign that it's over-heated and starting to break down; remove the pot from the heat until the oil cools to the correct temperature. If the oil has given off a significant amount of smoke, it will impart an off-flavor to foods and should be discarded. (Make sure to thoroughly pat food dry before frying, because water can cause oil to decompose, lowering its smoke point by as much as 30 degrees.)

On the other hand, food fried in oil that's too cool will retain too much moisture and emerge soggy. If the tempera-ture drops too low, bring the oil back up to your target range before frying the next batch.

For many years I have been trying to decipher the instructions typically given for boiling times. Should I boil an item from the time it goes into the water or from the time the water returns to a boil? Does the same formula hold for both blanching vegetables and cooking lobster?

It depends on the kind of cooking, but in most cases you should start counting when the food goes into the water to avoid overcooking.

Hmmm. We realized this was a good question when we turned to a number of our recipes for blanching and found that we don't specify whether the water must return to a boil before you start counting the seconds or minutes. We can't speak for other recipe writers, but in our recipes for blanching, you should start counting from the moment you plunge the fruit or vegetable into the boiling water. The goal in blanching is not to cook foods through but usually to aid in skinning (peaches and tomatoes) or to soften till the food becomes crisp-tender (vegetables for crudités). If you don't start counting till the water returns to a boil, the food will be overcooked.

For foods meant to be cooked all the way through, from lobster to pasta to potatoes, you should generally start counting once the water returns to a boil—at least that's the way it works in our recipes. And if the recipe gives a range (say, 20 to 30 minutes for good-size potatoes), it's always best to start checking for doneness early—once those potatoes are overcooked, there's no going back.

Why do recipes always say to bring liquids to a full boil and then reduce them to a simmer? Why not just slowly work up to a simmer and stay there?

There are two good reasons for this practice: time efficiency and food safety.

Simmering—cooking foods over moderate heat—is an important technique in making soups, stews, braises, sauces, and stocks. But why boil first? First, if you bring a stew or braise up to a simmer over low heat, the total cooking time will be considerably longer. In one recent test here in the kitchen, an osso buco recipe required an extra hour when we failed to bring the liquid to a boil before turning down the heat. Starting from a boil also ensures that all the ingredients (proteins and starches, as well as the liquid) in the pot get up to a safe temperature quickly and evenly. If you let foods come to a simmer very slowly, they are likely to spend more time in the so-called danger zone, between 40 and 140 degrees, which in certain foods promotes the growth of bacteria.

Is it possible to flambé at home without setting my kitchen on fire?

Flambéing is more than just table-side theatrics, and anyone can master it with a few tips.

Yes, it looks incredibly cool, but igniting alcohol also helps develop a deeper, more complex flavor in sauces, thanks to flavor-boosting chemical reactions that occur only at the high temperatures reached in flambéing. But accomplishing this feat at home can be daunting. Here are some tips for successful—and safe—flambéing at home.

Be Prepared Turn off the exhaust fan, tie back long hair, and have a lid ready to smother dangerous flare-ups.

Use the Proper Equipment A pan with flared sides (such as a skillet) rather than straight sides will allow more oxygen to mingle with the alcohol vapors, increasing the chance that you'll spark the desired flame. If possible, use long, wooden chimney matches, and light the alcohol with your arm extended to full length.

Ignite Warm Alcohol If the alcohol becomes too hot, the vapors can rise to dangerous heights, causing large flare-ups once lit. Inversely, if the alcohol is too cold, there won't be enough vapors to light at all. We've found that heating alcohol to 100 degrees produces the most moderate yet long-burning flame. It usually takes about 5 seconds over medium heat to get alcohol to the right temperature. You can tell it's ready when vapors start to rise up from the pan.

Light the Alcohol off the Heat If using a gas burner, be sure to turn off the flame to eliminate the chance of accidental ignitions near the side of the pan. Removing the pan from the heat also gives you more control over the alcohol's temperature.

If a Dangerous Flare-Up Should Occur Simply slide the lid over the top of the skillet (coming in from the side of, rather than over, the flames) to put out the fire quickly. Let the alcohol cool down and start again.

If the Alcohol Won't Light If the pan is full of other ingredients, the potency of the alcohol can be diminished as it becomes incorporated. For a more foolproof flame, ignite the alcohol in a separate small skillet or saucepan; once the flame has burned off, add the reduced alcohol to the remaining ingredients.

Can you explain the differences between sautéing and searing? How do I know which technique to use?

Sautéing and searing both involve cooking food in a shallow pan on the stovetop, but their similarities end there.

Sautéing and searing are both techniques that are used to develop browning, but they work best with very different types of ingredients.

Sautéing, which relies on cooking food in a small amount of fat over moderately high heat, is best for thin, lean cuts of meat like cutlets or medallions, and for smaller pieces of delicate foods like chopped vegetables. The use of moderate heat extends the time window for browning, allowing these quick-cooking ingredients to brown before they overcook. Sautéing is also characterized by shaking the pan or stirring to make sure all the ingredients are equally exposed to the heat (the verb *sauté* in French means "to jump," which describes the way the food should move in the pan). Using a slope-sided skillet facilitates flipping and stirring.

Searing is a surface treatment used to produce a flavorful brown crust on thick cuts of protein and vegetables, such as chops, cauliflower steaks, or tofu. In most cases, searing is the first step in the cooking process, followed by a gentler cooking method to finish the interior of the food. It uses high heat in a conventional, rather than nonstick, skillet. This helps develop the fond (brown bits that stick to the pan) and build flavor. Unlike in a sauté, food that is being seared should be left alone and not moved or flipped until it has had a chance to build a crust. Note that searing does not "seal in" juices in meat, as is commonly believed (see page 6).

When I sear meat on the stovetop, it always gets stuck to the pan and makes a huge mess! Is there a better way to do it?

The key ingredient for making sure meat doesn't stick to the pan when you sear it is patience.

Meat sticks during cooking thanks to the adhesion of dissolved proteins to the cooking surface in a process known as adsorption. While the mechanisms by which proteins adsorb onto a skillet are complicated and not fully understood, we do know that once the pan becomes hot enough, the link between the proteins and the pan will loosen, and the bond will eventually break.

To prevent steak from sticking, follow these steps: Heat oil in a heavy-bottomed skillet over high heat until it is just smoking (on most stovetops, this takes 2 to 3 minutes). Sear the meat without moving it, using tongs to flip it only when a substantial browned crust forms around the edges. If the meat doesn't lift easily, continue searing until it does.

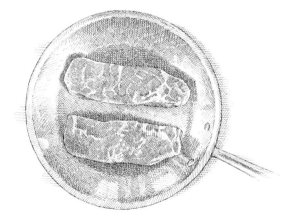

I can't figure out how to use my broiler—sometimes it burns my food but other times it seems to be barely working. What's going on in there?

Almost all broilers heat unevenly, but you can make a map of yours in order to make it easier to use it effectively.

Uneven broiler heat is a fact of kitchen life; even with identical oven models, we've found individual quirks. But in general, most broilers tend to heat up the center and back of the oven, leaving the sides and front cool. To test your oven's heating pattern, make a "map" by lining a baking sheet with slices of white bread and toasting it under the broiler. The different degrees of browning will provide an accurate representation of the oven's hot spots and cooler regions, so you can position food accordingly (and, if necessary, move it partway through cooking).

How to Make a Broiler "Map"

1 Position the oven rack 4 inches from the broiler element and heat the broiler. Line the entire surface of a large baking sheet with a single layer of white bread slices.

2 Place the baking sheet in the oven under the heated broiler. Cook until all the bread slices have started to brown (some pieces may turn black—if the bread starts to smoke, remove the baking sheet immediately). Remove the baking sheet from the oven, being careful to maintain its orientation.

3 Take a photo of your broiler map and keep it near your oven.

What size pieces should I aim for when a recipe calls for "chopped" vegetables? And what's the difference between "chopped" and "diced"?

There are some basic rules of thumb for common descriptive terms you'll encounter in recipe prep.

Cutting ingredients to the correct size is important to the success of a recipe. Uniformity of size is the top concern, since ingredients cut to different sizes will have different cooking times: Some smaller pieces of vegetables might burn, for instance, while the bigger chunks continue to cook. In the test kitchen, a ruler is a necessary tool for all our test cooks to ensure that ingredients are cut to the proper size and will cook for the same amount of time, every time. See page 204 for guidelines on how to prep food to different specifications. (And if you don't have a ruler on hand, keep in mind that for most people, the length between the thumb's knuckle and its tip is almost exactly 1 inch.)

While "chopping" is a general word for cutting food into small pieces, dicing is a much more specific designation. Diced food is cut into uniform cubes, the size of which will be specified in the recipe. Of course, most ingredients do not have right angles, so not every piece will be a perfect cube; just do your best.

Does it matter which way I slice an onion? Once it's cut up, it's all the same, right?

Slicing with the grain of the onion will make it taste less pungent, while cutting against the grain makes for more pungent onions.

We took eight onions and sliced each two different ways: pole to pole (with the grain) and parallel to the equator (against the grain). We then smelled and tasted pieces from each onion cut each way. The onions sliced pole to pole were clearly less pungent in taste and odor than those cut along the equator. Here's why: The intense flavor and acrid odor of onions are caused by substances called thiosulfinates, created when enzymes known as alliinases contained in the onion's cells interact with proteins that are also present in the vegetable. These reactions take place only when the onion's cells are ruptured and release the strong-smelling enzymes. Cutting with the grain ruptures fewer cells than cutting against the grain, leading to the release of fewer alliinases and the creation of fewer thiosulfinates. We have also found that slicing onions pole to pole helps them retain their shape and texture and makes them more pleasing to the eye in the finished dish.

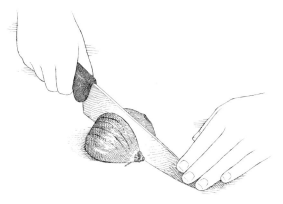

Is there an easy way to deal with fresh thyme? I find it so fussy to work with.

Stop going leaf by leaf and use the stems to your advantage.

Picking minuscule leaves of fresh thyme off the stem can really pluck at your nerves, especially if a recipe calls for a good deal of it. In the test kitchen, we rely on some tricks to make this job go faster. If the thyme has very thin, pliable stems, just chop the stems and leaves together, discarding the tough bottom portions as you go. If the stems are thicker and woodier, hold the sprig of thyme upright, by the top of the stem; then run your thumb and forefinger down the stem to release the leaves and smaller offshoots. The tender tips can be left intact and chopped along with the leaves once the woodier stems have been sheared clean and discarded.

How do I know when my knives need to be sharpened?

Give them the paper test.

Owning a knife sharpener makes tuning up your knives easy, but how do you know when it's time? The best way to tell if a knife is sharp is to put it to the paper test. Holding a sheet of paper (basic printer paper is best) firmly at the top with one hand, draw the blade down through the paper, heel to tip, with the other hand.

The knife should glide through the paper and require only minimal pushing. If it snags, try realigning the blade's edge using a honing, or sharpening, steel and then repeat the test.

To safely use a steel, hold it vertically with the tip firmly planted on the counter. Place the heel of the knife blade against the top of the steel and point the knife tip slightly upward. Position the blade at a 15-degree angle away from the steel. Maintaining light pressure and a 15-degree angle between the blade and the steel, slide the blade down the length of the steel in a sweeping motion, pulling the knife toward your body so that the middle of the blade is in contact with the middle of the steel. Finish the motion by passing the tip of the blade over the bottom of the steel. Repeat this motion on the other side of the blade. Four or five strokes on each side of the blade (a total of eight to ten alternating passes) should realign the edge. If the knife still doesn't cut the paper cleanly, use an electric or manual sharpener. You can minimize the amount of metal removed by focusing on just this section of the blade to fine-tune the sharpening.

How do I dispose of an old knife?

Never just throw an old knife in the trash.

Many home cooks have old or unused knives lurking in the back of kitchen drawers, taking up space and posing a safety risk. Just tossing knives in the trash creates a hazard for sanitation workers, so we contacted a few professional knife manufacturers and waste disposal companies for advice on getting rid of them safely. Many suggested donating the knife if there's still life in it. You could take it to a thrift store or soup kitchen in your area.

If donating isn't possible, carefully wrapping the knife for disposal is important for the safety of waste management workers. Use two 9-inch strips of 2-inch-wide electrical tape to cover the tip end and butt end of the blade in a double layer. Then fold an 8 by 10-inch piece of cardboard lengthwise around the blade to cover it entirely. Secure this in place with more heavy-duty tape and write "SHARP KNIFE" on both sides of the package. From there you can hand-deliver it to a waste management or recycling center for safe disposal and/or recycling.

What's the difference between "processing" ingredients in the food processor and "pulsing" them? Why would a recipe call for one technique or the other?

>
> *The food processor is a great tool for chopping ingredients—as long as you use it correctly.*

Pulsing food offers more control than simply processing it; the food is chopped more evenly because the ingredients are redistributed—akin to stirring—with every pulse. To test this theory, we made two batches of tomato salsa. We made one batch pulsing the ingredients three times and another batch in which we let the processor run for 3 seconds. We repeated this test with shelled pecans.

The tomato salsa that had been processed was significantly more pureed and had the consistency of a tomato sauce, while the pulsed salsa was pleasantly chunky, as a salsa should be. The processed pecans featured an uneven mix of very small and large pieces; the pecans that were pulsed for the same amount of time were chopped much more evenly.

This proved to us that pulsing produces more evenly chopped food than processing does. For that reason, we call for pulsing when we want foods to be evenly chopped.

When a recipe calls for "one-second pulses" in the food processor, should you hold down the button for a full second and then release it? Or just press it for a microsecond, release it, and wait a full second before pressing down again? The answer depends on your machine. Some instantly spin and continue to rotate for a second after you lift your finger off the button. Others come to a halt as soon as you lift up, requiring you to keep the button depressed to complete a "pulse." You want the blade to be in motion for about 1 second for each pulse. To ensure that you get the right results when a recipe calls for a certain number of pulses, observe your processor to determine what exactly happens to the blade.

What's the best way to prepare cake pans so my cakes won't stick?

It depends on what kind of pan you're using, but you definitely do need to prepare the pans.

Different cooks in our test kitchen have championed various methods for preparing pans over the years. To find out which strategies are best, we baked a few dozen butter cakes, pound cakes, sponge cakes, and Bundt cakes, using all manner of pan preparations.

With their bumps and ridges, Bundt cakes proved the trickiest. Greasing with softened butter and then dusting the pans with flour left us with a streaky, frosted look on our finished cakes (think bad dye job). A paste made of melted butter and flour (or cocoa for chocolate Bundt cakes), or just plain baking spray (which is vegetable oil spray with flour added), produced clean, perfectly released cakes every time.

The best way to coat a loaf pan for a pound cake turned out to be applying a thick coating of softened butter followed by an even dusting of flour; the flour provided an added layer of protection against sticking and made for an easy and clean release.

As for regular nonstick cake pans, the traditional parchment lining called for in most recipes wasn't necessary—even when making sponge cakes. The same buttered-and-floured pan method we used for the loaf pans produced the cleanest release.

Is folding the same as stirring? What are the best practices for this technique?

Folding is gentler and more gradual than stirring, which makes it ideal for delicate mixtures.

The goal of folding is to incorporate delicate, airy ingredients such as whipped cream or beaten egg whites into heavy, dense ingredients such as egg yolks, custard, or chocolate without causing deflation. The tools required for folding are a balloon whisk and a large, flexible rubber spatula.

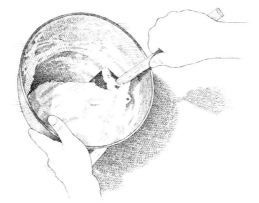

In the test kitchen, we like to start the process by lightening the heavier ingredients with one-quarter or one-third of the whipped mixture. A balloon whisk is ideal for the task: Its tines cut into and loosen the heavier mixture, allowing the whipped mixture to be integrated more readily. Next, the remaining whipped mixture can be easily incorporated into the lightened mixture. For this round of folding, we preserve the airiness of the dessert by using a rubber spatula, which is gentler than a whisk.

To demonstrate the importance of folding, we made two kinds of lemon soufflés and a chocolate mousse cake using three methods: incorporating the whipped ingredients in two additions as specified in the recipes; folding in the whipped ingredients all at once; and finally, vigorously stirring in the whipped ingredients in one addition. The results were not surprising. When the beaten egg whites or whipped cream was incorporated in two batches, the soufflés and mousse were perfectly smooth and light. When we ignored the two-step process and folded everything together at once, the desserts were not quite as ethereal. Finally, strong-armed stirring produced a lumpy, dense end product.

Our recommendation: Don't cut corners when it comes to folding. Take your time and use a light hand to gradually incorporate beaten egg whites or whipped cream into heavier ingredients. To fold properly and avoid deflating your mixture, start with your spatula perpendicular to the batter and then cut through the center down to the bottom of the bowl. Holding the spatula blade flat against the bowl, scoop along the bottom and then up the side of the bowl. Fold over, lifting the spatula high so that the scooped mixture falls without the spatula pressing down on it.

What's the best way to toast nuts? Can I use the microwave?

We prefer to toast small amounts of nuts on the stovetop and large amounts in the oven, but the microwave is also an option.

We toasted a range of different-size nuts (slivered almonds, sliced almonds, walnut halves, pecan halves, and whole pine nuts) in a 10-inch skillet over medium heat until lightly browned and fragrant, 3 to 8 minutes, and on a baking sheet in a 350-degree oven until lightly browned and fragrant, 5 to 10 minutes. After comparing the cooled nuts, we found no color or flavor differences. (Note: Properly toasted whole nuts are browned not just on the outside, but all the way through the nut flesh. Cut one in half to check for light browning.) As for technique, toasting nuts on the stovetop requires more attention from the cook; frequent stirring is a necessity. Another strike against the stovetop is that large amounts of nuts can crowd a skillet, preventing thorough toasting. The bottom line: For more than 1 cup of nuts (or if you happen to have the oven on already), use your oven. For smaller quantities, pull out a skillet; just remember to stir the nuts often to prevent them from burning.

But there's another option: toasting nuts in the microwave. Simply spread out the nuts in a thin, even layer in a shallow microwave-safe bowl or pie plate. Cook on full power, stopping to check the color and stir every minute at first. As the nuts start to take on color, microwave in 30-second increments to avoid burning.

The cooking is more even in the microwave, so less stirring is required. This approach works well not only with nuts but also with other ingredients that need a quick toasting before use, such as bread crumbs, seeds (like pepitas or sesame seeds), shredded coconut, and whole spices like coriander or cumin seeds. Whole spices need only a couple of minutes, while most other ingredients need about 5 minutes (your timing may vary depending on your microwave, of course).

What's the easiest way to remove all the papery skin from hazelnuts?

Our favorite trick for this fussy task uses baking soda.

The most common method for removing hazelnut skins—toasting them and then rubbing them in a towel—can still leave some skins stubbornly hanging on. Here's a better approach: In a saucepan, bring 2 cups of water and 3 tablespoons of baking soda to a boil. Add 1 cup of untoasted hazelnuts and boil for 3 minutes. Transfer the nuts to a bowl of ice water with a slotted spoon, drain, and slip the skins off with a towel. The hot alkaline water quickly breaks down the pectin, the primary component in the skins, allowing them to peel off not only more easily but also more completely.

A similar trick is helpful for removing the skins of canned chickpeas. Toss the rinsed and drained chickpeas with baking soda (1½ teaspoons per 14-ounce can) and then heat them in the microwave or in a skillet over medium heat for 2 to 3 minutes, until the beans are hot. Transfer the beans to a large bowl and wash with three or four changes of cold water, all the while agitating the beans vigorously between your hands to release the skins, which will float away easily.

What's the best way to melt chocolate? I always seem to mess it up.

You can use either the stovetop or the microwave—the key is to employ gentle heat.

Melting chocolate can be a dangerous game—let it get too hot and it will break, becoming irreparably grainy. A heavy-bottomed skillet over very low heat does the trick, but not every burner is capable of maintaining a low enough flame. Here are two melting techniques we've tested again and again and found to be foolproof.

Double-Boiler Method

1 Bring a pot of water to a near simmer over low heat; set a large heatproof bowl (the edges should be higher than the pot for easier removal) over it, making sure that the water does not touch the bottom of the bowl (to avoid overheating the chocolate).

2 Add 8 ounces of chocolate chips (or bar chocolate chopped into ½-inch pieces) and heat, stirring occasionally with a rubber spatula, until uniformly smooth and glossy, about 10 minutes (adjust the cooking time as necessary for larger or smaller amounts of chocolate). If the recipe calls for melting the chocolate with butter, add both to the bowl at the same time.

Microwave Method

1 Put 8 ounces of chocolate chips (or bar chocolate chopped into ½-inch pieces) in a large microwave-safe bowl. Microwave on high power for 45 seconds.

2 Stir with a rubber spatula, scraping down the sides of the bowl, and then heat 30 seconds more. Continue heating and stirring in 15-second intervals until the chocolate is uniformly smooth and glossy. (To melt smaller or larger amounts, decrease or increase the initial microwaving time by 10 seconds for every 2 ounces of chocolate.) If the recipe calls for melting the chocolate with butter, do not add the butter until the chocolate is almost completely melted, as adding the butter earlier will cause it to splatter.

How soft does "softened" butter actually have to be?

Butter temperature can dramatically affect the texture of baked goods so it's important to understand what the lingo means.

Terms like "chilled," "softened," or "melted and cooled" are imprecise ways to describe butter, but they're also very common in recipes. To clarify the nomenclature in our recipes, we came up with the following temperature ranges and tactile clues. (For best results, check the temperature with an instant-read thermometer.)

Chilled (about 35 degrees)
Tactile Clue Unyielding when pressed with a finger and cold to the touch
Common Application Pie dough
Method Cut into small pieces and freeze until very firm, 10 to 15 minutes.
Result Cold butter melts during baking, leaving behind small pockets that create flaky layers.

Softened (65 to 67 degrees)
Tactile Clue Easily bends without breaking and gives slightly when pressed
Common Application Cake
Method Let refrigerated butter sit at room temperature for about 1 hour.
Result Properly softened butter is flexible enough to be whipped but firm enough that it retains the air incorporated during creaming.

Melted and Cooled (85 to 90 degrees)
Tactile Clue Fluid and slightly warm to the touch
Common Application Cookies and bars
Method Melt in small saucepan or microwave-safe bowl and cool for about 5 minutes.
Result Melted butter is the key to chewy cookies and bars.

I was recently softening butter in the microwave to make cookies when part of the stick melted. It was my last stick, so I tried to harden it a little in the fridge, but my cookies didn't turn out right. Could I have done something different?

You can save oversoftened butter, but you have to act fast.

The fat in butter is partially crystalline and highly sensitive to temperature changes. When butter is properly softened, the tiny crystals can effectively surround and stabilize the air bubbles that are generated during creaming. When heated to the melting point, however, these crystals are destroyed. They can be reestablished, but only if the butter is rapidly chilled. (Returning it to the refrigerator will cool it too slowly and fail to reestablish the tiny crystals.)

To quickly cool down partially melted butter, we mixed in a few ice cubes. After less than a minute of stirring, the butter had cooled to a softened stage, so we extracted the ice and prepared a couple of recipes. (The amount of icy water that leaked into the butter was negligible.)

Our fix worked: Sugar cookies made with our rehabilitated butter were nearly identical to those made with properly softened butter, and buttercream frosting was also acceptable, if slightly softer than a control batch.

If you're worried about overdoing it in the microwave but still don't have an hour to wait for butter to soften on its own at room temperature, try this trick: For baking applications where butter is creamed, cut the stick into 1-tablespoon pieces (more exposed surface area helps the butter warm evenly) and stand them on a plate. The pieces will soften in about 20 minutes.

How can I crack and separate eggs without making a mess?

*You don't need any gadgets to separate eggs,
but we do recommend using multiple bowls.*

We strongly recommend that you separate eggs when they are cold, as yolks are more taut and less apt to break into the whites when cold. Since even a speck of yolk in the whites can prevent them from whipping properly, this is especially important in dishes like soufflés that rely on whipped whites for volume. If a recipe calls for separated eggs at room temperature, separate the eggs while cold, cover both bowls with plastic wrap (make sure the wrap touches the surface of the eggs to keep them from drying out), and let them sit on the counter.

Start by cracking the side of the egg against the flat surface of a counter or cutting board. This gives a cleaner break than using the edge of the counter or a mixing bowl. Then you can either use the broken shell or your hand to separate the eggs. To separate with the shell, hold the broken shell halves over a bowl and gently transfer the egg yolk back and forth between them, letting the egg white fall between the shells and into the bowl. To separate by hand, cup your hand over the bowl, then open the cracked egg into your palm. Slowly unclench your fingers to allow the white to slide through and into the bowl, leaving the yolk intact in your palm. Make sure your hands are clean, especially if you plan on whipping the whites.

Whichever method you use, separate each egg over one bowl and let the white fall in. Then transfer the yolk to a second bowl and pour the white into a third bowl. By using this method, if you happen to get some yolk into the white when separating an egg, you can simply throw out that egg (or use it in another recipe that calls for whole eggs)—much better than separating a dozen eggs only to drop yolk from the last egg into a big bowl of clean whites.

Cheat Sheet

Cooking School At-a-Glance

THERE ARE SOME THINGS THAT PROFESSIONAL COOKS JUST KNOW by heart, including basics like how to prep ingredients and how to use common cooking techniques. For those of us who aren't quite at that level yet, here are some reminders.

Prep 101

What It Says	What You Do
MINCE	Cut into ⅛-inch pieces or smaller.
CHOP FINE	Cut into ⅛- to ¼-inch pieces.
CHOP	Cut into ¼- to ½-inch pieces.
CHOP COARSE	Cut into ½- to ¾-inch pieces.
CUT INTO CHUNKS	Cut into ¾-inch pieces or larger.
SLICE	Cut into pieces with two flat sides (thickness depends on the recipe).
DICE	Cut into uniform cubes (size of dice depends on the recipe).
CUT ON THE BIAS OR DIAGONAL	Cut with the knife held at a 45-degree angle to the food (used for longer, slender items).
CUT LENGTHWISE	Cut with the length of the food, or from end to end.
CUT CROSSWISE OR WIDTHWISE	Cut across the food, perpendicular to its length.
CUT INTO CHIFFONADE	Cut into very thin strips (such as basil leaves).
JULIENNE (OR CUT INTO MATCHSTICKS)	Cut into matchstick-size pieces, usually about 2 inches long and ⅛ inch thick.

Technique 101

What It Says	What You Do
BOIL	Heat liquid until large bubbles break the surface at a rapid, constant rate.
BRAISE	Cook food by gently simmering it in a flavorful liquid in a covered pot.
DEEP-FRY	Cook food in hot oil deep enough to fully surround the food.
POACH	Cook food in hot liquid that is held below the simmering point.
ROAST	Cook food in a pan in a hot oven.
SAUTÉ	Cook food in a small amount of fat over moderately high heat while stirring or shaking pan, usually with the goal of browning the food.
SEAR	Cook food over high heat, usually with the goal of creating a deeply browned crust.
SHALLOW-FRY (OR PAN-FRY)	Cook food in hot oil deep enough to partially surround the food.
SIMMER	Heat liquid until small bubbles gently break the surface at a variable and infrequent rate.
STEAM	Cook food using the steam released from boiling liquid.
STIR-FRY	Quickly cook thinly cut food in oil over high heat.
SWEAT	Cook food over gentle heat in a small amount of fat in a covered pot.
TOAST	Cook or brown food by dry heat, and without adding fat, using an oven or skillet.

Kitchen Science

What's Going On in There?

G ood science makes great food. Of course, you also need quality ingredients and some modest equipment. But success in a home kitchen really does benefit from a basic understanding of biology, chemistry, and physics. Put another way: If you know how and why something works, you are much more likely to get it right the first time— and every time. Something as simple as understanding the way heat and flavor interact on your tastebuds can have an enormous impact on how you think about seasoning—and thus on how good your food tastes. But you don't need to go back to school for a triple grad degree in the hard sciences before making dinner. We've done the kitchen experiments (with lab-level precision) to figure out what's really happening when you cook, and we're here to explain the science you need to make food taste better.

Test Your Cooking IQ

Food Science Fill-in-the-Blank

CHOOSE THE OPTION THAT ACCURATELY COMPLETES EACH OF these food science facts.

1 You should refrigerate peaches only **before/after** they are fully ripe or they can become mealy.

2 If your piece of fresh ginger has a blue-gray tint, it **is/is not** still edible.

3 Cold food needs **less/more** seasoning than hot food because of the way the receptors in our mouths respond to temperature.

4 You should **always/never** store nuts in the freezer.

 A flour with a **high/low** gluten content is the best option for bread with a high rise and good texture.

6

Skim/Whole milk is better for creating milk foam because of the way substances in fat affect the milk's ability to form froth.

7

The darker a roux is, the **less/more** thickening power it has.

9

Most of the flavor in a pot of coffee develops in the **late/early** stages of brewing.

8

Whisky with water added tastes **less/more** flavorful than straight whisky.

10

It's important to heat oil until it's just **shimmering/smoking** for successful searing.

Answers

1 after (page 222)
2 is (page 234)
3 more (page 211)
4 always (page 220)
5 high (page 239)
6 Skim (page 228)
7 less (page 241)
8 more (page 245)
9 early (page 238)
10 smoking (page 225)

The flavor of some dishes seems to improve when they are made in advance. Why do soups and stews taste better the next day?

You're not imagining this—some flavor reactions need more time to develop.

Even after cooking ceases, many chemical reactions continue to take place in foods. In the case of a soup or stew containing milk or cream, the lactose breaks down into sweeter-tasting glucose. Similarly, the carbohydrates in onions develop into sugars such as fructose and glucose. Proteins in meat turn into individual amino acids that act as flavor enhancers. Finally, starches in potatoes and flour break down into flavorful compounds.

To verify this, we made batches of onion soup, cream of tomato soup, beef chili, and black bean soup and refrigerated them. Two days later, fresh batches of each recipe were served hot alongside the reheated soups and stews. Tasters unanimously preferred the onion, tomato, and black bean soups that had been held for two days, calling them "sweeter," "more robust-tasting," and "well rounded." When it came to the chili, most tasters made the same comments, but some preferred the fresh sample—as it sat, the flavors of the chile peppers became sweeter and less sharp. If you like vibrant chile pepper flavor, it's best to serve chili the same day you make it. If a recipe specifically calls for you to let the dish sit so the flavors can meld, do it; it will result in a more balanced dish.

My roast chicken tastes great straight out of the oven, but the refrigerated leftovers are always bland. Why is that?

Temperature affects both your ability to taste and the way flavors interact with your senses.

The explanation is twofold. First, scientists have discovered that our ability to taste is heightened by microscopic receptors in our tastebuds that are extremely temperature-sensitive. These receptors, known as TRPM5 channels, perform far better at warm temperatures than at cooler ones. In fact, studies have shown that when food cooled to 59 degrees and below is consumed, the channels barely open, minimizing flavor perception. However, when food is heated to 98.5 degrees, the channels open up and TRPM5 sensitivity increases more than 100 times, making food taste markedly more flavorful.

Second, most of our perception of flavor comes from aroma, which we inhale as microscopic molecules diffuse from food. The hotter the food, the more energetic these molecules are, and the more likely they are to travel from the table to our nose. Chilling dulls all flavors, making them more difficult for us to perceive.

So, dishes meant to be served hot should be reheated, and dishes served chilled (like gazpacho or potato salad) must be aggressively seasoned to make up for the flavor-dulling effects of cold temperatures. But next time you make a dish to serve cold, don't jump the gun by oversalting while the food is still hot. Instead, season as you would normally. Once the food is chilled, taste and add more salt as needed.

Why does my banana bread smell so fragrant and banana-y right out of the oven but lose most of its aroma as it cools? Does it mean that the cool bread will have less flavor than the warm, fragrant bread?

Yes, that's pretty much true. But that doesn't mean you should try to eat the whole loaf the minute it comes out of the oven.

A little background on the chemistry of bananas may help answer your questions. The dominant aromatic compound in bananas, isopentyl acetate (IPA), also known as banana oil, is very volatile—more volatile than oils such as lemon, cinnamon, and peppermint—and evaporates readily at room temperature, taking with it that great banana aroma. In fact, in tests in which we placed IPA bought from a chemical supply company on preweighed cellulose filter paper and weighed the paper every minute, we found that an average of 85 percent of the IPA had evaporated in less than 10 minutes.

Since flavor is perceived not only by our tastebuds but also by our sense of smell, when the IPA in banana bread evaporates (which may take longer in a real loaf than in our contrived test), the bread won't taste quite as banana-y as a loaf straight out of the oven. But we don't recommend that you tuck into a steaming-hot loaf of banana bread in order to experience 100 percent of its fruity flavor: It's important to let banana bread (and all quick breads) cool before serving for optimal texture.

Why do herbs and spices that are "bloomed" in oil have more flavor than those that are just added during cooking?

The main flavor compounds in many spices and some herbs are fat-soluble, so you can extract tons of flavor by heating them in oil before using them in a dish.

We've long advocated "blooming" spices and certain herbs in oil or fat before adding liquid to the pot. Our tastebuds tell us that this yields more flavor, but we wondered whether we could get at a more objective assessment of blooming's impact.

We steeped crushed red pepper flakes in canola oil and another batch in water, holding both liquids at a constant 200 degrees and steeping for 20 minutes. We then strained out the pepper flakes and sent the oil and water to a lab to test for capsaicin (the compound responsible for a chile pepper's heat). We repeated the experiment with thyme and sent the oil and water samples to the lab to test for its main flavor compound, thymol.

The pepper-infused oil had a stronger flavor than the pepper-infused water, and more than double the amount of heat-producing capsaicin. The results for thyme were even more dramatic: The herb-infused oil contained 10 times as much thymol as the herb-infused water.

So our tastebuds are right: Briefly heating spices and some herbs (including thyme, rosemary, lavender, sage, savory, and bay leaves) in fat before they go into the pot yields far more flavor than simply simmering these ingredients in water.

Why do fattier cuts of meat need more salt in order to taste properly seasoned?

*Fat makes it harder for tastes
to come through, including saltiness.*

Several recent studies have concluded that fat has a dulling effect on taste. To put this to the test, we rounded up five meats ranging in fat content: turkey breast, pork loin, strip steak, and both 80 percent and 90 percent lean ground beef. We cooked the meats and chopped them into pieces. We then tossed 10-gram portions of each meat with increasing amounts of salt (0.1 percent, 0.25 percent, 0.5 percent, 0.75 percent, 1 percent, and 1.5 percent by weight of each sample). We had tasters try the samples in order, starting with an unsalted control, and had them record at what percentage the meat tasted properly seasoned. We also sent samples of each type of meat to a lab to determine fat content.

Sure enough, the fattier the meat, the more salt it needed to taste properly seasoned. Tasters preferred the lean turkey breast (0.7 percent fat) and pork loin (2.6 percent fat) seasoned with 0.5 percent salt by weight. The strip steak (6 percent fat) and 90 percent lean ground beef (10 percent fat) required about 0.75 percent salt by weight to taste seasoned. And finally, the 80 percent lean ground beef (20 percent fat) tasted seasoned to a majority of tasters only when it reached 1 percent salt by weight.

So when you season meat, remember to use a heavier hand on fatty burgers than you would on moderately fatty meats like strip steak and 90 percent ground beef. Use an even lighter hand on lean meats like turkey breast and pork loin.

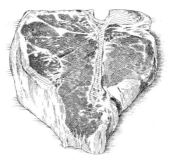

What's so special about dry-aged beef, and can I make my own?

Dry aging is a process used to tenderize and develop flavor in beef, and you can absolutely do it at home.

Beef is aged to develop its flavor and improve its texture. This process depends on certain enzymes that help the animal digest proteins. After the animal is slaughtered, the cells that contain these enzymes start to break down, releasing the enzymes into the beef, where they break down proteins into more flavorful amino acids, and also break down muscle tissue, making it softer. This process can take up to several weeks.

Beef can be either wet-aged or dry-aged. In the former method, the beef is sealed in plastic; in the latter, it is left open and exposed. Wet-aged beef is tender, but it doesn't dehydrate in the same fashion as dry-aged beef and is thus milder in flavor. (Dry-aged beef has nutty, buttery notes that aren't present in wet-aged beef.) Two processes occur in dry aging. In one, called proteolysis, an enzyme turns stiff muscle fibers into tender meat. The other process is simple dehydration. In dry aging, a roast can lose up to 25 percent of its original weight. Less water means more concentrated flavors.

By letting a wet-aged roast from the supermarket age in the refrigerator for just a short period, we found we could approximate the dehydrating effects of dry aging at home, with an eye to improving the flavor of the beef. It's just a matter of making room in the refrigerator and remembering to buy the roast ahead of time, up to one week before you plan on roasting it. (For the sake of safety, meat should not be aged for more than one week at home; beyond that time it must be done under carefully controlled conditions.)

When you get the roast home, pat it dry and place it on a wire rack set over a cake pan or plate lined with paper towels. Set the racked roast in the refrigerator and let it age until you are ready to roast it, up to seven days. (Aging begins to have a dramatic effect on the roast after three or four days, but we also detected some improvement in flavor and texture after just one day of aging.) Before roasting, shave off any exterior meat that has completely dried out. Between the trimming and dehydration, count on a 7-pound roast losing a pound or so during a week of aging.

Why does ice cream make me thirsty? Is it just me, or does this happen to everyone?

You're not imagining that post–ice cream thirst. Go ahead and treat yourself to a tall glass of water.

W e asked around the office to learn whether this was a common affliction, and about half of the people said that yes, ice cream does leave them with a parched mouth. (Most also said that they had thought they were alone in their thirstiness.)

Our research revealed that sweet foods (like ice cream) behave much like salty foods when eaten in quantity. As ice cream is digested and sugar is rapidly absorbed into the blood, the concentration of sugar in the blood becomes higher than the concentration of sugar in the body's other cells. Since nature abhors an imbalance, osmosis kicks in, forcing water out of the cells, through membranes, and into the blood to equalize the relative concentrations of sugar. The brain senses that the cells are losing moisture, resulting in a craving for a glass of water.

I've heard that humidity can affect how baked goods turn out. Is that true? Is there anything I can do to counteract the weather?

Long-term exposure to humidity can mess with flour, but using an airtight container for storage can prevent any problems.

M any baking experts claim that baking on very dry or very humid days can affect flour. We were a little skeptical but thought we'd run some tests. We constructed a sealed humidity-controlled chamber in which we could simulate various types of weather. We made pie crusts at relative humidities of at least 85 percent (more humid than

New Orleans in the wet season) and below 25 percent (drier than Phoenix in midsummer or the average air-conditioned office), leaving the lid to the flour container open for 8 hours beforehand. We found that over the course of the test, the flour's weight varied by less than 0.5 percent between the two samples, and after being baked into pie crusts, the results were indistinguishable.

If an occasional humid day doesn't make a difference, what about long-term exposure to excess humidity? According to the King Arthur Flour Company, flour held in its paper packing bag (even unopened) can gain up to 5 percent of its weight in water after several months in a very humid environment. At this level, humidity might affect baked goods. But this problem is easily avoided by transferring flour to an airtight container (preferably one wide enough to accommodate a 1-cup measure) as soon as you get it home.

Humidity can also affect storage of baked goods, especially those that contain a lot of sugar. Sugar is hygroscopic, meaning that it attracts moisture from the air. For delicate, high-sugar baked goods like meringues, this means that high humidity can turn them sticky and marshmallowy. It's easy to avoid this, though: Just pack the meringues in an airtight container immediately after cooling them, and any humidity in the air won't matter.

When baked goods go stale, why does bread turn hard, while crackers soften?

These are the results of two completely different scientific processes.

Crackers are manufactured to be very dry to make them shelf-stable. Once the package is opened and the crackers are exposed to air, their sugars and starches start to absorb ambient moisture. After a few days, the once-crisp crackers will be soft.

When bread turns stale, an entirely different process takes place. Once exposed to air, bread starch undergoes a process called retrogradation: The starch molecules in the bread begin to crystallize, turning the bread hard and crumbly.

Will meat still taste OK if I refreeze it once I've thawed it?

If you've thawed frozen meat, we don't recommend refreezing it, as the texture will become overly dry and tough. It's best to just go ahead and cook it.

We've all been in the situation of having thawed a piece of meat or poultry only to find that we don't want to cook it that day after all. But then what? Can you refreeze the meat, or is it best to forge ahead and cook it?

We cut a boneless chicken breast into three pieces. We cooked one portion from its fresh state. The second we froze, thawed, and then cooked. The third we froze, thawed, refroze, thawed again, and then cooked. We cooked all the samples to 160 degrees and weighed each piece of chicken before and after cooking to measure moisture loss. We then tasted all three samples, evaluating them for moistness and overall texture. We repeated the test six times, varying which section of the breast was used in each application.

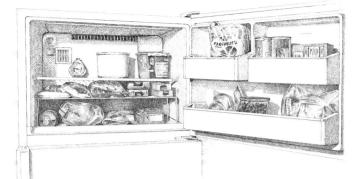

The samples cooked from raw lost approximately 20 percent of their weight when cooked, those frozen once lost around 25 percent, and those frozen twice lost an average of 26 percent. Tasters preferred the samples that had never been frozen, noting moister meat and a more tender texture. This stands to reason, given the significant difference in moisture loss. But the surprising result was that despite the small difference in moisture loss between the once-frozen and twice-frozen samples, tasters noted a dramatic difference between the two: The twice-frozen pieces seemed much drier and tougher than those frozen only once.

Cooking meat causes its muscle fibers to shrink and expel moisture. The process of freezing and then thawing leads to additional moisture loss because the sharp edges of ice crystals created during freezing damage the muscle fibers; this means that when the meat is thawed, water within the fibers is able to escape easily. However, most of this damage is done after just one freeze, so a second freeze can't significantly exacerbate the effect. This explains why the amount of moisture loss was very similar whether the chicken was frozen once or twice.

So why would tasters notice a big difference between the once- and twice-frozen samples? It turns out that freezing water inside the meat's protein cells causes the release of soluble salts. These salts affect some of the proteins, causing them to physically change shape and actually shorten, which leads to a tougher texture. And this effect is more noticeable after each freeze-thaw cycle.

ONE OF THE MOST COMMON QUESTIONS WE GET IS "CAN I FREEZE this?" Freezing ingredients seems like a great idea, but it's not always a smart option. Here is a guide to things you should and should not freeze. (In addition to the items mentioned, we always store whole-grain flours, bread crumbs, coffee beans and ground coffee, cornmeal, oats, grains, yeast, and nuts in the freezer to protect from humidity and rancidity.)

Ingredient	The Rules
ANCHOVIES	Freeze individually. Thawed anchovies can be used just like fresh fillets.
AVOCADOS	Don't do it. Thawed avocados are mushy.
BACON (UNCOOKED)	Roll up individual slices and freeze separately so it's easy to grab a few at a time.
BANANAS	Ripe or overripe frozen bananas are great to have on hand for banana bread or smoothies; peel them before freezing.
BERRIES	Freeze unwashed fresh berries and then transfer to a zipper-lock bag. Use in cooked applications.
BROTH	Freeze small amounts in an ice cube tray, medium amounts in a muffin tin, and large amounts in a zipper-lock bag.
BUTTER	Keep it frozen and transfer to the fridge one stick at a time to avoid off-odors.
BUTTERMILK	Thawed buttermilk is fine as is in baking recipes, but you will need to re-emulsify it for use in salad dressings or dips.
CHEESE	Wrapped tightly in plastic wrap, most types of hard and semifirm cheese will keep for up to two months in the freezer.

Ingredient	The Rules
CITRUS ZEST	Place grated zest in ½-teaspoon piles on a plate and freeze; transfer to a zipper-lock bag. Do not freeze whole citrus.
CREAM CHEESE	Thawed cream cheese has a gritty texture, so it's no good for bagels but can work in baking recipes.
EGG WHITES	Freeze egg whites individually in an ice cube tray. Use in applications that call for small amounts (egg wash) or that don't depend on volume (omelet).
EGG YOLKS	Make a syrup of 2 parts sugar to 1 part water and stir it into the yolks before freezing (¾ teaspoon syrup per 4 yolks); this prevents ice crystals that can affect the yolks' protein structure.
GARLIC	Mix minced garlic with neutral-flavored oil and freeze in teaspoon-size portions. Don't freeze whole cloves.
GINGER	Not recommended. Fresh ginger becomes mushy when thawed.
HEAVY CREAM	Use thawed heavy cream in cooked recipes; it doesn't whip well.
HERBS	Cover chopped fresh herbs with water in an ice cube tray and then freeze until needed for sauces, soups, or stews.
ONIONS	Chopped onions can be frozen and used for cooking but not in raw dishes.
SOUR CREAM/ YOGURT	Thawed sour cream or yogurt is OK for baking but not for uses such as dips or sauces.
TOMATO PASTE	Remove paste from can, wrap in plastic, and freeze. Cut off as much as needed and return frozen log to freezer.
WINE	Freeze wine in 1-tablespoon increments in an ice cube tray. Use for cooking and sauces (but not drinking).

Can refrigerating peaches make them mealy?

Only if you refrigerate them before they get a chance to fully ripen.

Storage at temperatures at or below 40 degrees can destroy the activity of certain enzymes in a peach that normally break down pectin in its cell walls during the ripening process. If these enzymes are deactivated before the fruit is ripe, the pectin will remain intact and the peach will have a mealy texture.

To illustrate this process, we divided a case of peaches into two batches, allowing half to ripen immediately without refrigeration and storing the other half for a week in the fridge before allowing them to finish ripening for a couple of days at room temperature. Both sets of peaches were placed in containers sealed with plastic wrap in order to prevent moisture from evaporating. As expected, our tasters found that despite being soft and ripe to the touch, the peaches that spent time in the fridge were significantly mealier than those kept at room temperature. Moral of the story: Don't refrigerate your peaches unless you're sure they're ripe. You may prolong their shelf life, but the loss of quality isn't worth it.

Is there any way to speed up the process of ripening fruit?

There is a trick for some types of fruit, and all you need is a paper bag—and maybe a ripe banana.

In some fruits, known as climacteric, ripening continues after harvest. In others, known as nonclimacteric, ripening occurs only on the plant; it stops once the fruit is picked. Bland, rock-hard climacteric fruits all have a shot at becoming sweet and juicy (that is, ripe) someday. In contrast, nonclimacteric fruits may get softer over time, but they will not ripen further once picked.

The ripening process in many fruits is controlled by ethylene, a colorless, odorless gas produced in minute quantities by the plant and its fruit. For climacteric types, once the amount of ethylene reaches a certain threshold, the fruit bursts into ripeness; in nature, this process takes some time. But what if we hastened the process by exposing unripe climacteric fruit to ripe fruit already producing copious amounts of ethylene? To test this idea, we purchased a basketful of hard, unripe supermarket pears along with a few ripe bananas. The experiment was simple: We placed three unripe pears and two very ripe bananas in a tightly rolled-up brown paper bag (to concentrate the ethylene) and three more unripe pears in a tightly rolled-up paper bag without bananas. (Don't try to ripen fruit in plastic bags; it will spoil first. Moderately porous paper bags allow a small amount of oxygen to enter, helping the pears produce enzymes that prevent them from spoiling as they ripen.)

Three days later, we checked the progress. The pears stored by themselves (no bananas) were slightly softened but still tasted tart and astringent. The pears stored with the ripe bananas? Soft and deliciously sweet. When we gave the banana-less pears another full day, however, they reached full ripeness. So a simple paper bag works; including ethylene-bloated bananas merely speeds the process along. Our recommendation is to ripen pears in a bowl on the counter. If you need them sooner, ripen them in a bag with bananas. But check them frequently— they can go from just right to mush in a matter of hours.

Climacteric Fruit (will ripen on the counter)	Nonclimacteric Fruit (will not ripen further)
apples, apricots, avocados, bananas, kiwis, mangos, melons, peaches, pears, plums, tomatoes	berries, cherries, grapes, lemons, oranges, pineapples, watermelons

I have some Parmesan cheese in my fridge that has dried out and is now rock-hard. Is there a way to revive it?

There's no way to revive dried-out Parmesan, but it will still have lots of flavor.

The humidity inside a refrigerator is quite low, so the longer cheese sits in there, the more it dries out and hardens. Once cheese loses moisture, there's no effective way to get it back (we tried steaming, microwaving, coating it in butter, and wrapping it in wet towels). But smart storage can help prevent your cheese from drying out. The cheese should be allowed to breathe—but just a little. Our preferred method for storing Parmesan cheese is to wrap it in parchment paper (to allow it some airflow) and then wrap it in aluminum foil or place it in a small zipper-lock bag (be sure to squeeze out as much air as possible before sealing the bag).

If your Parmesan has dried out, it can be added to soups and stews for extra flavor and body. If it's not too hard, it can be cut into 1-inch pieces, processed in a food processor (no more than 1 pound at a time) for about 20 seconds, and sprinkled over pasta, salads, and the like.

A friend told me that storing potato chips in the refrigerator would keep them fresher longer. Is this true?

If you have leftover chips in an open bag, this trick can help keep them fresh.

Stale potato chips make us sad, so we were excited to put this theory to the test. We opened several bags of chips, removed half of the chips from each bag, sealed the bags securely with bag clips, and stored half of the bags in the refrigerator and half in the pantry.

After two weeks, tasters could detect a slight difference, noting that the refrigerated chips were crisp and fresh-tasting, while the pantry chips were a bit stale. Not surprisingly, after a month this difference was more pronounced. After two months—longer than most of us can make a bag of chips last—tasters noted stale flavors in both samples but strongly preferred the crunchy texture of the refrigerated chips to the softer texture of the chips from the pantry.

Why does this work? First, the low-humidity environment in the fridge means that there's not as much moisture in the air for the chips to absorb and become soft. Second, potato chips are starchy; as starch molecules cool (as they would when refrigerated), they crystallize, becoming firm and hard. This makes for crunchier chips.

What will happen if I don't wait until the oil in the pan is smoking before adding food?

There's more than 100 degrees difference between shimmering oil and smoking oil, so this can make a big difference in your cooking.

When searing or pan-frying, we often call for heating oil until just smoking. What happens if you add your food to the pan too soon, before it's actually smoking? We ran an experiment to find out.

We cooked two sirloin strip steaks in identical 12-inch skillets. For one steak, we heated 1 tablespoon of vegetable oil until shimmering, which took about 2 minutes. In the other pan, we heated 1 tablespoon of oil until it reached the smoke point, which took 6 minutes. We cooked both steaks until well browned on both sides. The steak cooked in the oil heated to the smoke point browned quickly and evenly, in about 6 minutes, with a minimal overcooked gray band beneath the surface. The steak cooked in the shimmering oil took 10 minutes to brown, and the meat just beneath the surface overcooked, leaving a larger gray band.

Shimmering oil reaches only about 275 degrees, rather than the 400 degrees of vegetable oil at its smoke point. Making sure the oil is sufficiently hot helps keep the pan from cooling down too much once the food is added and guarantees quick, even browning. If the oil is below the smoke point when the food is added, browning will take too long and the food will overcook. So make sure to heat the oil until just smoking. Oil that has actually hit the smoke point is unmistakable—you'll see multiple wisps of smoke rising from the pan. Don't worry too much about overheating the oil; as long as you have your food at the ready, there is little risk since the oil will cool quickly once you add the food. (If you have overheated it, you will know because the oil will turn dark. In that case, discard the oil and start over.)

Does basting really do anything?

Tradition might not have it right this time—we didn't find any convincing reasons to baste poultry during cooking.

Basting is a time-honored method for keeping a turkey or chicken moist and helping brown the skin to improve both appearance and flavor. We wondered, though, if tradition has it right, so we ran a few tests. We roasted three turkey breasts simultaneously in three 350-degree ovens until they reached 160 degrees. One breast we left in the oven undisturbed to act as a control. The second we basted every 20 minutes while roasting. The third we didn't baste, but we opened and closed the oven door every time we basted the second breast to evaluate the effect of simply opening the door. We weighed all three turkey breasts before and after cooking to determine the percentage of moisture lost and recorded the total cooking time. We also roasted three whole chickens under the same circumstances and compared the level of browning.

The total cooking time was 59 minutes for the control turkey breast, 66 minutes for the unbasted breast exposed to the opening and closing oven door, and 69 minutes for the basted breast. Most important, the moisture loss of all three was comparable, ranging from 22.4 to 24.0 percent—a statistically insignificant difference—and tasters found all the samples comparably moist. In terms of browning, the basted chicken was evenly bronzed, while the other two exhibited slightly lighter, less glossy browning that was also a bit patchy.

Basting purportedly keeps meat moister by cooling the surface and thus slowing down the rate at which the meat cooks. And the more gently the meat cooks, the juicier it will remain. Basting did slow the cooking down more than just opening and closing the oven door but not enough to make a difference in moisture loss. In terms of browning, the drippings used for basting contain a lot of fat and protein, which encourage browning because they provide some of the starting materials (amino acids) for the Maillard reaction.

Basting not only makes a negligible difference in moisture loss but also prolongs the cooking time and requires more hands-on work. For really juicy poultry, we prefer a more hands-off approach such as brining or salting, which not only helps poultry retain moisture but also seasons the meat. And while basting did improve appearance, we don't think the difference is significant enough to make it worth it.

If I have to let my roasted chicken rest for 15 to 20 minutes after it comes out of the oven, won't it be too cold to serve?

Large cuts of meat hold on to heat far longer than you would expect, so don't rush the rest.

Think of resting as part of the cooking process. During cooking, the muscle fibers contract and squeeze liquid out of their cells. Resting gives the fibers a chance to relax and draw moisture back inside. Slicing into a roast before it has sufficiently rested will result in that liquid escaping onto your cutting board rather than being reabsorbed. Since heat moves from the hotter exterior to the cooler interior of the meat, we often suggest lightly tenting the roast with foil to keep the exterior warm without trapping too much moisture inside the tent. Since even light tenting can cause crisp skin to become soggy, we don't usually recommend tenting for chicken and turkey (see page 158).

But will the food cool down too much to serve warm? To find out, we roasted a chicken and checked the temperature when we removed it from the oven: 160 degrees in the breast and 175 degrees in the thigh. Then we took the temperature after 20 minutes of (untented) rest on a carving board. The chicken was still over 140 degrees—and almost too hot to carve. Since most meat tastes best when it's above 100 degrees, the chicken was still comfortably within the serving zone.

We recommend resting all large cuts of meat, though resting times vary. Thinner cuts like steaks, pork chops, and chicken parts cool more quickly. In these cases, we usually recommend only about 5 minutes of resting time to ensure that the proteins are still optimal for serving.

When using my milk frother to make cappuccino, I've noticed that skim milk seems to foam up better than whole milk. Why is this?

The less milk fat, the fewer emulsifiers, and thus the foamier the milk.

We poured 4-ounce samples of both nonfat and whole milk into oversize cups, whipped them up with a handheld milk frother, and compared the results. The skim milk indeed frothed better than the whole milk: The foam was thicker and more stable, and rose up higher in the cup. The whole-milk foam took longer to form and deflated in a matter of minutes.

It turns out that milk fat contains monoglycerides and diglycerides, which happen to be good emulsifiers but have a negative effect on the formation of foam. They destabilize the air bubbles introduced into milk when foam is made, impeding the foam's formation. Skim milk contains less of these emulsifiers, thus making frothing easier. Although most baristas wouldn't recommend using skim milk for rich, creamy cappuccinos, if plenty of airy foam is your goal, go with lower-fat dairy.

Why do catfish and tilapia sometimes taste swampy? Is there a way to reduce or remove this unpleasant flavor?

An acidic bath can help eliminate the disagreeable muddiness of some of these fish.

In the test kitchen, we too have noticed a mysterious muddy flavor in some catfish and tilapia. Our research revealed that the flavor comes from a compound called geosmin, which is Greek for "earth smell." Geosmin is abundant in the blue-green algae found in the bottom of the man-made ponds that catfish and tilapia are raised in. When the fish swim in the geosmin-rich water, they consume the compound as they ingest the algae. Some cookbooks claim that soaking the fish in tap water or milk will remove the unpleasant geosmin flavors, but a quick test proved this untrue. After more research, we learned that only acidic compounds can effectively break down geosmin.

Armed with this knowledge, we decided to soak fillets in lemon water and in buttermilk before cooking them. After an hour-long soak, we battered and deep-fried half of the fillets and pan-seared the other half. The acidic baths did the trick, although tasters detected a slightly mushy texture in the fish soaked in lemon water. So if you want to enjoy clean-tasting, firm catfish and tilapia, immerse it in buttermilk for an hour before cooking. When you're ready to cook the fish, rinse off the buttermilk, pat the fish dry, and proceed with the recipe.

Why does my salmon sometimes ooze a white substance when I cook it? Am I under- or overcooking it?

It's completely harmless, but if you don't like it,
you can either wipe it off or pretreat the fish to minimize it.

We occasionally encounter this phenomenon in the test kitchen when cooking salmon and guessed that the unattractive ooze had something to do with overcooking. But after we pan-seared a few salmon fillets, we were surprised to find that even perfectly cooked fillets (those with opaque exteriors and traces of bright orange inside) exuded a few strands of this white material along the unseared sides. Slightly more of this matter showed up on fillets that we over-cooked intentionally.

We turned to Donald Kramer, professor of seafood science at the University of Alaska, Fairbanks, for an explanation. According to Kramer, this "white curd" is composed of fish albumin, soluble proteins that are squeezed out onto the surface of the fish and coagulate once they denature during the cooking process. Most often, this curd is seen when salmon is canned, smoked, or poached.

"There's nothing harmful in it," said Kramer. "There will always be a certain amount that comes out, and how you cook it is probably not going to affect that."

The best way to check for doneness in salmon is not to wait for albumin to appear on the surface but to peek inside the fillet with the tip of a paring knife. A little translucency is a good sign; if the salmon is opaque all the way through, the fish is overdone. If the look of the albumin really bothers you, use a damp paper towel to gently blot it off.

We often advocate brining meat (and sometimes fish and shellfish) before cooking to ensure moist, tender, flavorful results. We recently discovered another good reason to soak fish in a salt solution: A quick exposure can reduce the unsightly white layer of albumin that coagulates on the surface during cooking. Just 10 minutes in our standard 9 percent solution (1 tablespoon of salt per cup of water) is enough to minimize the effect. The method works in a similar fashion to how a longer soak improves moisture retention: The salt partially dissolves the muscle fibers near the surface of the flesh, so that when cooked they congeal without contracting and squeezing out albumin. We tested the method on salmon and saw a dramatic improvement. The brief soak also seasoned the fish's exterior, making it unnecessary to salt it before cooking.

Since buttermilk always smells sour, how will I know whether it has gone bad?

Unless there's visible mold on it, it's probably fine—but it might lose some of its flavor even before it goes truly bad.

When we asked this question of the folks at the dairy farm that produces the buttermilk we use in the test kitchen, they told us to consume their product within seven days after opening. However, guidelines from agricultural programs at various universities extend that period to two weeks. Then there's our experience, which has shown that refrigerated buttermilk won't turn truly bad (signified by the growth of blue-green mold) until at least three weeks after opening. That it can last this long is not surprising, since buttermilk is high in lactic acid, which is hostile to the growth of harmful bacteria. That said, we wondered whether the flavor of buttermilk changes the longer it's stored. To find out, we held a series of tastings, comparing pancakes made with freshly opened buttermilk with those made with buttermilk that had been opened and refrigerated for one week, two weeks, and three weeks. We found that as time went on, the pancakes tasted increasingly bland.

Here's why: The bacteria in buttermilk produce lactic acid and diacetyl, a flavor compound that gives buttermilk its characteristic buttery aroma and taste (diacetyl is also the dominant flavor compound in butter). As time passes, the buttermilk continues to ferment and becomes more acidic. The abundance of acid kills off virtually all the bacteria that produce the buttery-tasting diacetyl. So three-week-old buttermilk will retain its tartness (from lactic acid) but lose much of its signature buttery taste, giving it less dimension. The good news is that there is an effective way to prolong the shelf life and preserve the flavor of buttermilk: Freeze it (see page 220).

What causes oil to develop a fishy odor or flavor when I'm deep-frying?

Oil used over very high heat, reused oil, and oil that's particularly low in saturated fat are all susceptible to this issue.

Oil is composed mainly of triglycerides, or fat molecules containing free fatty acids. When oil is heated, the fatty acids oxidize to form small volatile molecules (mostly peroxides and aldehydes) that produce a strong, rancid odor. The higher the heat and the longer the oil is used, the greater the likelihood that this effect will occur. It's also worth noting that some oils are more susceptible to oxidation than others: Saturated fats are less likely to oxidize than unsaturated fats. Therefore, oils that are very low in saturated fat will deteriorate more quickly than oils with significant amounts of more stable saturated fats. Our taste tests of fried chicken confirmed that canola oil (6 percent saturated fat) and safflower oil (9 percent saturated fat) are more likely to lend a spoiled, "fishy" flavor to fried foods than refined peanut oil (17 percent saturated fat) and vegetable shortening (25 percent saturated fat), which generally produce clean-tasting fried foods.

Why do apples turn brown when they're cut? Is there a way to avoid that?

You can use lemon juice or honey to deactivate the enzyme that causes this reaction.

Cutting damages the cells of apples, allowing enzymes and compounds stored separately within each cell to mix with one another and with the oxygen in the air, creating brown pigments. To determine whether this brown color does anything more than mar the fresh look of the fruit, we compared an apple crumble made with just-cut fruit with crumbles made with apples that we had cut and peeled (and refrigerated in zipper-lock bags) one and two days earlier. The brown apples and the fresh apples baked up equally tender and juicy and were similar in flavor, and surprisingly all had pretty much the same light golden color. It turns out that as the apples' cell walls rupture during baking, acids are released that partially break down the brown pigments, resulting in a lighter color. So if you're going to cook apples, it's fine to prep them a day or two in advance.

However, if you want raw slices that won't get discolored, there's an easy solution. A peptide found in lemon juice and in honey deactivates the enzyme that causes browning in apples. Most people toss cut apples and other fruits prone to browning in lemon juice, but if the acidic flavor puts you off, try honey water. We diluted 2 tablespoons of honey with 1 cup of water, added a sliced apple, and left it to soak. Compared with untreated apple slices, which began to brown after a few minutes, the apples in honey water were kept bright for more than 24 hours. Even better: We found that the fruit needed only a 30-second dunk in the honey water to inhibit browning for a solid 8 hours.

Recently, while I was making beurre blanc, the garlic in the sauce took on a startling blue color. What happened? Is a blue beurre blanc still safe to eat?

This is a normal chemical reaction; as long as you don't mind blue sauce, you can still eat it.

Blue garlic may look off-putting, but it's perfectly safe to consume and tastes just fine. The color change is caused by a reaction between enzymes and sulfur-containing amino acids in the garlic (the same enzymes are responsible for garlic's flavor). When these enzymes are activated by mild acid (such as the vinegar in beurre blanc), they produce blue and green pigments. The compound responsible for this reaction, isoalliin, is formed when garlic is stored at a cool temperature for several weeks, typically in the winter, when pantries are colder.

In short: To avoid discoloration, use fresh, young garlic when making beurre blanc or any recipe that combines garlic with acidic ingredients.

I recently used red onions in a frittata and was surprised to see that they turned bluish-green during cooking. What happened?

This is a simple chemical reaction that doesn't affect flavor—but if it bothers you, there's an easy way to reverse it.

Red onions—as well as other red produce, including cabbage and cherries—are rich in pigments called anthocyanins. When they're cooked with acid, their color intensifies, but when combined with an alkaline component, they can turn a startling bluish-green color. Since eggs—specifically, egg whites—are basic, ranging from 7.6 to 9.5 on the pH scale, they are most likely responsible for the blue color in your frittata. Just for fun, we decided to see whether we could reverse the color change once a fruit or vegetable with anthocyanin turns blue. We sautéed red cabbage and then added a pinch of baking soda to turn it blue. We found that a splash of vinegar brought its red color right back. (This trick may not have a practical application, but you can use it to impress your friends.)

Fresh ginger also contains anthocyanins. When it is stored for a long period of time in a cold environment, ginger becomes less acidic, and this causes some of its anthocyanin pigments to change to a blue-gray color. It is still safe to eat, and while it has a slightly milder flavor than fresh ginger of a normal color, it's unlikely you'll notice the difference when using it in a recipe.

I substituted sunflower seed butter for peanut butter to make allergen-free cookies—but the cookies turned green! Why did this happen? Are the cookies safe to eat?

The cookies will taste fine and are perfectly safe to eat—the color comes from the chlorophyll present in sunflower seed butter.

This was a new one on us, so we made a batch of peanut butter cookies, substituting sunflower seed butter to see whether we'd get green cookies. The cookies came out fine, but after two days they started to develop green spots on their interiors, and by six days their insides were forest green.

We did a little digging to find out why this was happening. It turns out that sunflower seed butter contains chlorophyll, the green pigment present in all green plants. The color is not visible in the jar of sunflower butter because the chlorophyll is bound by other substances. It's released when the chlorophyll is heated in the presence of an alkali, such as baking soda, which is an ingredient in most peanut butter cookie recipes. This combination caused the color to slowly appear. While they may be unappetizing to look at, the green cookies are safe to eat and don't taste any different once they turn green.

I sometimes notice a rainbowlike sheen on raw tuna and beef. Do you know what causes it?

This phenomenon is simply a function of how the meat is cut and has nothing to do with the freshness of the meat.

The rainbow effect is caused by the reflection of light off muscle fibers, technically known as double refraction or birefringence. It occurs when the muscle fibers are cut crosswise at a specific angle relative to the grain of the meat and is visible only when the meat is viewed at a certain angle. Light striking the ends of the fibers is reflected in two different directions, appearing to the eye as a rainbow of colors. This iridescent appearance can be observed for several days after slicing the meat.

While the rainbow effect is harmless and doesn't offer any indication of how fresh the meat is, there is another color change that is a sign of meat that has passed its prime: the development of a green pigment. Meat with a green cast is contaminated with bacteria and should be discarded.

How does a microwave actually cook my food?

Microwave cooking is unlike any other cooking method in the kitchen.

To illustrate the difference between microwave cooking and stovetop simmering, we ran the following experiment: We microwaved a potato on a plate for 3 minutes, sliced it in half, and compared it with a potato that we simmered in water for 3 minutes before slicing. The microwave cooked a large portion of the potato in just 3 minutes, but the heat penetration was very uneven. In contrast, the simmered potato featured a thin, consistent line of cooked potato around the perimeter.

The electromagnetic waves produced by a microwave oven create an electric field that reverses direction 4.9 billion times per second. Water molecules are polar, meaning that they contain a partial positive and a partial negative electrical charge. In the presence of the oscillating electric field, the water molecules in the potato (or any food) change direction at the same incredibly fast rate. This rapid reversal causes the water molecules to bump into one another, effectively increasing their temperature. The problem is that microwaves can't penetrate more than an inch into food (the heat continues to move toward the center via conduction, just as it does in food cooked in an oven). What's more, microwaves hit foods in an unpredictable pattern, so some parts will cook faster than others. Microwave ovens use turntables to help even out cooking to some degree, but only on one axis. To ensure even cooking, stir or flip food often, add a cover to trap steam to provide another form of cooking, and rest foods for a few minutes after cooking to allow hot and cool spots to even out (especially important for foods that can't be stirred).

Sometimes when I'm making coffee, I steal a cup while the coffee maker is still brewing. Is there any reason I shouldn't do that?

It's not what you want to hear, but this is a bad habit and has a negative impact on the rest of the pot of coffee.

We know the temptation: First thing in the morning, the coffee is brewing, and you can't help sticking your mug beneath the spigot on the coffee maker to sneak a cup before the pot has finished. But how much does removing some coffee early influence the flavor of the final pot? Armed with an array of coffee mugs and a coffee refractometer, a tool that measures the amount of soluble flavor compounds, or total dissolved solids (TDS), extracted from the beans, we put that question to the test.

We took samples from the brewing spout of a coffee maker every 30 seconds and measured the TDS in each. The coffee coming out of the spout at the beginning of the brew time was significantly stronger than the last few drops: 3.93 parts per million (ppm) versus 0.44 ppm, or more than eight times as concentrated. It was also more than twice as strong as coffee from a full pot (1.54 ppm). Only at the midway point of the brew cycle did the concentration of the sample come close to that of a full pot. So hold on to your mug. Most of the flavor in a pot of coffee comes during the first half of brewing. If you sneak a cup early on, not only will it be far too strong, but you'll be running off with most of the good stuff and spoiling the pot for others.

What exactly is gluten,
and why is it so important?

The proteins in gluten give baked goods their structure.

Gluten—an elastic protein that has the ability to trap air, much like a balloon—is formed when two important proteins in wheat flour, glutenin and gliadin, bond together in the presence of water. Whether we are trying to create more of it in rustic bread or pizza dough or working to limit its development for tender cakes and muffins, there's no denying gluten's importance. But beyond our conceptual understanding of it, is there a more tangible way to see and feel gluten? We ran a simple experiment to find out.

We made two basic doughs by mixing flour and water in a food processor until a smooth ball formed. For one dough we used cake flour, which contains between 6 and 8 percent protein, and for the other we used bread flour, which usually runs from 12 to 14 percent protein. After making the doughs, we placed each in a mesh strainer and massaged them under running water to wash away all the starch. Once the water ran clear (a sign that the starch was gone), we were left with two mounds of what was essentially pure gluten. The differences in the appearance and texture of the two doughs were a dramatic confirmation of the profound impact of gluten.

Low-protein cake flour formed a very small amount of sticky, weak gluten. This characteristic is a boon to cakes and muffins, in which too much gluten can turn the crumb unappealingly tough. High-protein bread flour formed a large ball of highly resilient, rubbery gluten that could be stretched very thin without tearing. This structure traps air in breads, providing high rise and good texture.

Why do some cheeses melt really well while others stay solid even when you heat them up?

The protein structure of cheese changes as it ages, and this causes lumpy melting in older cheeses.

Anyone who's melted cheese for a sandwich knows that some types melt better than others, turning creamy without releasing fat. We've found that younger cheeses almost always perform better in grilled cheese sandwiches than aged ones. This is partly because aged cheeses have less moisture, making them prone to clump. To see whether there were other factors at play as well, we ran another test and controlled for moisture.

We purchased cheddars aged for 3, 16, and 24 months (all were sealed against evaporation during aging) and placed slices from each block on top of inverted metal cups that had been preheated in a 175-degree oven. We then baked the cheese until each slice had melted.

The three-month-old cheddar melted smoothly, evenly flowing down the cup's sides. The 16-month-old cheddar showed signs of clumping as it slid down the metal, and the 24-month-old cheese actually broke into two large pieces and never melted.

Moisture plays a part in how cheese melts, but the state of its protein—specifically, its network of casein protein—affects it most. In freshly made cheeses, casein proteins are in tightly wound clusters, allowing for little interaction with one another. As cheese ages, it goes through a process called proteolysis, in which bonds between individual casein molecules are "snipped," allowing the clusters to unwind and bind with other casein molecules, forming a matrix. Early in this process, the matrix is flexible, allowing young cheeses to melt smoothly. With time, the proteins bond together more tightly, forming a stronger network that requires more heat to melt and is less flexible when melted. This can result in more separated fat and clumps, as with our older samples.

How is a roux's color related to its thickening power?

The darker a roux, the less thickening power it will have in your dish.

A roux, a cooked mixture of flour and fat, works primarily as a thickener or structural agent for sauces and stews, but it also provides the dish with flavor and color. Notably, the flavoring and thickening properties don't work independently.

Roux are always cooked to a specific shade that can range from beige to dark brown. The darker the color, the more pronounced the roux's flavor. But at the same time that a roux darkens, its thickening power lessens. This is because the intense heat from frying the flour in fat causes its starch chains to break down, and these smaller pieces are less efficient thickeners. So the longer a roux is cooked, the less effective at thickening it will be.

To quantify more precisely how cooking influences a roux's thickening power, we borrowed a specialized tool for measuring viscosity from Brookfield Engineering Laboratories in Middleboro, Massachusetts. We prepared three roux cooked to beige, light gold, and dark brown using 4 tablespoons of unsalted butter and ¼ cup of all-purpose flour for each batch. We then added 2 cups of water to each roux and simmered the mixtures for 20 minutes. Holding each batch at the same temperature, we tested their viscosities with the borrowed viscometer. Using the beige roux (cooked for just 1 minute) as our baseline, we found that the light gold roux (cooked for 3 minutes) had 14 percent less thickening power. The dark brown roux (cooked for 5 minutes) had 26 percent less thickening power.

The takeaway? These aren't small differences; it's important to cook a roux to the right color. Cook the béchamel for a soufflé too long and it won't have the same thickening power or structural integrity—and your soufflé won't rise as much. And if you shortchange the cooking time for the roux in a stew recipe, you could end up with a gloppy, overly thickened dish.

What does the beer in a beer batter coating do? Can I substitute something else?

The important part of beer in this context is carbonation (and pH), not alcohol, so there are some easy substitutions.

Beer batter—made by combining beer (usually a lighter style such as a lager), egg, and flour—is often used to coat fish, onion rings, and other types of pub-style fare before deep-frying. Though we've found that including hard liquor in the batter can lead to more tender results in tempura, the alcohol in most lagers and pilsners is so low (about 5 percent by volume) that its effect would be minimal at best. Far more important is the fact that beer is carbonated, which affects the batter in two ways. First, the bubbles provide lift as they escape from the batter during frying. Second, the carbonation makes the batter slightly more acidic, which limits how much gluten can form when the beer and flour mix, preventing the batter from turning tough. This is because gluten forms most readily in a pH of 5 to 6, while most carbonated beverages have a pH of 4 (unless they contain a strongly acidic ingredient).

In theory, then, any bubbly liquid with a neutral or appropriate flavor profile could serve as a substitute for beer. We fried fish in batters made with beer, nonalcoholic beer, seltzer water, and plain tap water and found that all the batches made with a carbonated beverage did indeed lead to noticeably lighter, lacier crusts than the batter made with plain water. In sum, carbonation and pH are the biggest factors in delivering a better batter-fried crust, so feel free to use bubbly substitutes such as nonalcoholic beer or seltzer.

Why does starch get crispy when you fry it?

Starchy coatings make for the crispiest fried foods thanks to the chemical reactions that occur when water and starch interact at high heat.

While you can certainly fry food in hot oil as is (think skin-on chicken pieces), we often dip food in a coating first. Such coatings provide a few benefits: They help protect the food from moisture loss, and they shield the food from direct contact with the hot frying oil for more gentle cooking. And, perhaps most important, we know that these coatings—starchy coatings, specifically—become deliciously crispy when fried. But until now we'd never really asked ourselves the deeper question: What exactly is happening that makes starch the key?

Here's what we learned. First, the starch granules in the coating absorb water, whether from the wet surface of the food itself or because they are combined with a liquid to make a slurry before coating the food. The hydrated granules swell when they are initially heated in the oil, allowing the starch molecules to move about and separate from one another. As water is driven away during the frying process, these starch molecules lock into place, forming a rigid, brittle network with a porous, open structure.

Furthermore, the two types of starch molecules (amylose and amylopectin) form some cross-links with one another at high frying temperatures, further reinforcing the coating's structure. Thus, the molecules in this porous network have room to compress and fracture, which results in the sensation of crispiness. We also learned why cornstarch works the best for making crispy coatings on fried foods: Cornstarch contains 25 to 28 percent amylose, compared to only 20 to 22 percent in wheat or potato starch.

A chef friend says that letting salt get into my frying oil is bad. Why?

The idea is that salt can cause rancidity and other issues with the oil, but it isn't a big deal for home cooks.

The theory is that ionic substances, such as table salt, can initiate the formation of small amounts of free radicals when heated in oil to high temperatures. These free radicals spur reactions that create impurities in the oil and, as a result, lower the oil's smoke point, which means it can't be reused for frying. The free radicals can also speed the development of rancid aromas and flavors.

To find out how much of a problem it can be, we added ⅛ teaspoon of table salt (an amount you would use to season potatoes before frying) to 2 quarts of peanut oil, heated the oil to 325 degrees, and made French fries. After letting the oil sit overnight, we repeated the process two more times with the same oil. We also prepared a control batch of peanut oil following the same steps but without the salt. After each round, we smelled both samples to see whether we could detect any off or rancid aromas. Next, we fried cubes of white bread in the two oils and tasted them for traces of rancidity. Finally, we heated both samples and noted at what temperature each began to smoke. None of our tasters were able to detect rancid aromas or flavors, and the salted oil started to smoke within a couple of degrees of the unsalted sample, both right around 415 degrees. Problems caused by salt in frying oil are more of an issue in restaurant kitchens, where the oil is held at high temperatures for an extended time and is used heavily. Most home cooks needn't worry about it.

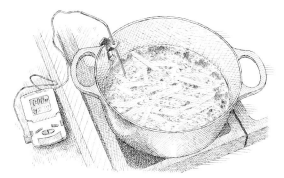

I've heard that adding water to whisky improves its flavor. Is this true, and if so, why?

Adding a little water to whisky will open up the nose and bring out more nuanced flavors, but the ideal amount of water will vary depending on the drinker.

The burning, pungent qualities contributed by the high proportion of alcohol in whisky can make it hard to evaluate nuances. Adding water dilutes the alcohol, which reduces the burn and allows other properties to reveal themselves. But there's also something significant happening on a molecular level. Aroma molecules share more chemical likenesses with alcohol than they do with water, so they tend to bind with alcohol. Adding water frees up more of the aroma molecules to evaporate into the taster's nose. Since appreciation of flavors happens at least as much in the nose as on the tongue, "watered-down" spirits actually seem more flavorful.

To experience the science at work, we had tasters sip 1½-ounce samples of 80 proof whisky neat and then with water added in increasing 1-teaspoon increments. While they noted that the neat sample of whisky had aromas of honey and caramel, flavor comments fell mostly in line with descriptions like "boozy" and "lots of burn." With just 1 teaspoon of water added, the alcohol receded and tasters picked up on sweet, vegetal flavors and subtle aromas like hay and apple. Most tasters preferred the addition of 2 teaspoons (which diluted the alcohol to 65 proof), allowing flavors such as vanilla, apple, and pear to really come to the fore. By 3 teaspoons the whisky began to taste watered down to many tasters, though one found it beneficial to add up to 5 teaspoons.

Is it true that you can make any tea decaf by steeping it twice?

This sort of works, but given how much the flavor suffers, we don't think it's worth it.

Most decaf teas are generic blends that lack complexity, so many tea lovers try to decaffeinate high-quality tea at home. The most common method is to steep the leaves for a few minutes, discard the infusion, and then steep it again to produce a supposedly caffeine-free cup of tea.

When we tried this method using loose-leaf white, green, oolong, and black teas and sent the teas to an independent lab for analysis, we learned that, for the most part, the second infusions did not contain significantly less caffeine than the first, and in fact the green and oolong samples contained more. The exception was the black tea; the second infusion contained about 40 percent less caffeine than the first.

Generally speaking, it was the third infusion of each tea that had a real impact on the caffeine content. White, green, and black all showed a marked drop from their original caffeine content, but the oolong still contained a little more, likely attributable to the fact that these leaves are tightly rolled, and it took the first infusion to start to open them up. However, tasters found all the teas at this point to be noticeably weaker in flavor and body and therefore not really worth drinking.

What's the best way to melt chocolate so that it stays glossy and smooth?

Our favorite method uses the microwave to control the temperature and thus the structure of the cocoa butter crystals.

A bar of good chocolate right out of the wrapper has an attractive sheen and a satisfying snap when you break it in two. But if you melt the chocolate to use as a coating or for drizzling and try to use it immediately, it will set up into a soft, blotchy, dull-looking mess that melts

on your fingers. Why the difference? The short answer is that the crystal structure of the cocoa butter in the chocolate has changed.

Cocoa butter can solidify into any of six different types of crystals, each of which forms at a specific temperature. But only one type—beta crystals—sets up dense and shiny and stays that way even at temperatures well above room temperature. When a chocolate is made up of beta crystals, it is said to be in temper. So how do you put melted chocolate back in temper?

The traditional way is a painstaking process known as tempering. First the chocolate is melted so that all its fat crystals dissolve. It is then cooled slightly, which allows new "starter" crystals to form. Finally, it is gently reheated to a temperature high enough to melt the less stable crystals and allow only the desirable beta crystals to remain (conveniently, both of these occur at around 88 degrees), triggering the formation of more beta crystals that eventually form a dense, hard, glossy network.

We prefer a far simpler approach: Chop the chocolate into fine shards. Microwave three-quarters of the chocolate at 50 percent power until it is mostly melted. Add the remaining chocolate and stir until it melts, returning it to the microwave for no more than 5 seconds at a time to complete the melting. While not quite as shiny as traditionally tempered chocolate, this chocolate will have a nice luster and decent snap once it has cooled and set. This method works because it keeps the temperature of the chocolate close enough to 88 degrees that mostly stable beta crystals form and act as seed crystals. It's a great method when taking the time to carry out true tempering is too much trouble.

Cheat Sheet

The Science of Seasoning

TASTE IS THE MOST OBVIOUS SENSE INVOLVED IN COOKING. There are five primary taste sensations: salty, sweet, bitter, sour, and umami, or savory. The cells in our mouths that respond to taste are located in clusters called tastebuds or taste papillae. Buds for the various tastes are evenly distributed all over the tongue as well as the rest of the mouth. Thanks to genetic variations, different individuals have different numbers and arrangements of receptors and therefore taste things differently.

Toward the end of developing a recipe in the test kitchen, tasters often make comments such as, "It tastes just a bit flat" or "a smidge lean" or "too rich." If you've added too much salt, sugar, or spice to a dish, the damage is usually done. In mild cases, however, the overpowering (or missing) taste can be fixed.

While salt and pepper are always a consideration for final tweaks, our test cooks also look to a range of other pantry ingredients that can help bring a dish into the right balance. Just a small quantity of one of these finishing touches (from a pinch to ½ teaspoon) is a good starting place. Here are a few of our favorites.

Ingredient Type	What It Does	Suggested Uses
SWEET *Granulated or brown sugar, honey, maple syrup, mirin, sweet wine or liqueur, jam or jelly*	Rounds out sharp, bitter, or salty flavors	Salsas, sauces, bitter greens, vinaigrettes, relishes
SOUR *Vinegar, citrus juice, pickled vegetables (such as jalapeños)*	Adds brightness to flat-tasting dishes, cuts through richness or sweetness, balances saltiness	Meaty stews and soups, braised or roasted meats, creamy sauces and condiments
BITTER *Dry or prepared mustard, beer, fresh ginger, chili powder, unsweetened cocoa powder, dark chocolate, horseradish, cayenne pepper, coffee, citrus zest*	Cuts sweetness	Barbecued meats, slaws, chopped salads, chili
UMAMI *Worcestershire sauce, soy sauce, fish sauce, miso, Parmesan cheese, anchovies, tomato paste, mushrooms, sherry*	Adds meatiness, depth, or earthiness; boosts dishes that taste a bit flat	Bolognese or other meaty sauces, hearty vegetarian sauces, soups, deli sandwich fillings such as tuna salad
RICH *Heavy cream, butter, olive oil*	Rounds out flavors, adds viscosity, balances spiciness	Lean vegetable-based soups, sauces

5

Kitchen Speak

What Is That and How Do I Pronounce It?

The first step in the successful completion of a recipe is understanding what it is telling you to do. Cooking has its own special vocabulary; an entire lexicon has evolved to translate what happens in the kitchen to the printed page. Some recipes are precise blueprints, specifying particular sizes, shapes, quantities, and times. Other recipes are rough sketches that leave the cook to fill in the blanks. If you don't talk the talk, you're going to be in trouble. Unfamiliar terms can cause a real problem if you simmer when you're supposed to boil, or chop when you should dice. Specialized vocabulary can also be an issue at the grocery store, where packaging comes covered in jargon and buzzwords. And what about the indecipherable language of restaurant menus? If you aren't sure what a word means, you should always check before proceeding with a recipe or purchasing a product. Start with the helpful notes in this chapter and you'll be fluent in foodie before you know it!

Test Your Cooking IQ

Basic Kitchen Vocabulary

MATCH EACH COOKING TERM TO THE CORRECT DEFINITION.

Cooking Terms

Boil   Sweat   Toast
Deglaze   Fold   Sear
Chop   Poach   Dice
Simmer

1 To heat a liquid until small bubbles gently break the surface at a variable and infrequent rate.

_____

2 To cook food over gentle heat in a small amount of fat in a covered pot.

_____

3 To cook food in hot water or other liquid that is held below the simmering point.

_____

4 To heat a liquid until large bubbles break the surface at a rapid and constant rate.

_____

5 To cook food over high heat, without moving it in the pan, usually with the goal of creating a deeply browned crust.

6 To cut food into uniform cubes (exact size depends on the recipe).

7 To mix delicate batters and incorporate fragile ingredients using a gentle under-and-over motion that minimizes deflation.

8 To use liquid (usually wine or broth) to loosen the brown fond that develops and sticks to a pan during the sautéing or searing process.

9 To cook or brown food by dry heat, and without adding fat, using an oven or a skillet on the stovetop.

10 To cut food into small pieces (⅛ inch to ¾ inch, depending on the recipe).

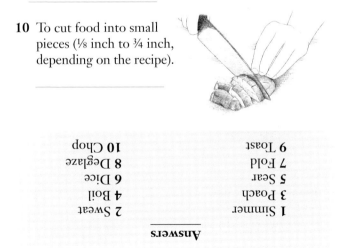

Answers

1 Simmer
2 Sweat
3 Poach
4 Boil
5 Sear
6 Dice
7 Fold
8 Deglaze
9 Toast
10 Chop

Sometimes there isn't a convenient or safe place to put a hot pan. If a recipe says "off heat" or "remove from heat," do I really need to take the pan off the burner, or can I just turn the heat off?

Physically moving the pan off the heat is pretty important, especially if you have an electric stove.

We went into the test kitchen and brought a saucepan of water to a boil several times, recording its temperature change over a three-minute period as it sat on top of the same burner (turned off) as opposed to sitting on a trivet on the countertop. Left on the hot grate of the gas burner, the water in the saucepan remained 10 degrees higher than when the pan was moved to the countertop. When the pan was left on an electric burner, the temperature difference was even greater: The water remained 30 degrees hotter.

While these temperature differences probably won't matter for large pots of stew or pasta sauce, we wondered if they could adversely affect more delicate, heat-sensitive recipes. To find out, we made three batches each of a simple pan sauce and a vanilla custard pie filling, one batch taken completely off the heat when directed by the recipe, one left on the hot grate of a gas burner, and one left on the hot coil of an electric burner. In the 30 seconds that the pans sat on the gas burner while additional ingredients were whisked in, no adverse reaction occurred in either the sauce or the custard. However, when left on the electric burner (which retains heat for a longer period of time), the sauce became darker and clumpier, with a slightly oily rather than rich and glossy texture, and the custard became thick and pasty.

So the next time a recipe calls for adding an ingredient "off heat," don't just turn off the burner (especially if it's an electric burner). Take the extra two seconds to move the pan completely off the heat, onto either a trivet or a cool, unused burner.

How do I measure a "pinch" of an ingredient? What about a "dash"? And a "smidgen" isn't a real thing, right?

Traditionally these measurements were pretty vague, but these days there are slightly clearer rules.

We're pretty particular about measuring—you should always select the appropriate tools for the type of ingredient you're measuring and use them properly (page 160). We also have rules for exactly how to treat tricky ingredients like delicate greens or fluffy grated cheese (pages 162 and 163). And of course, whenever possible, we prefer to use weight instead of volume for maximum accuracy. However, sometimes you need just a tiny amount of an ingredient—a pinch of this, a dash of that, a smidgen of the other thing. While these terms were used pretty vaguely in the past, recently manufacturers have begun offering measuring spoons labeled with them. The general consensus is that a dash is ⅛ teaspoon, a pinch is ½ dash or 1/16 teaspoon, and a smidgen is ½ pinch or 1/32 teaspoon. If you're committed to complete precision, you can use these measurements. However, since they are difficult to achieve without a set of measuring tools exactly calibrated to these rules, and since these are very small amounts in any case, you're probably OK estimating. If we use the word "dash" in a recipe, we usually mean a small splash of a liquid ingredient added to taste, and if we use the word "pinch," we mean the amount of a dry ingredient you can literally pinch between your thumb and forefinger. We don't use the word "smidgen" in recipes.

Many of my favorite recipes include a step where the ingredients are either "caramelized" or "browned." But aren't caramelizing and browning the same thing?

In a word, no: These are two different processes that happen in different circumstances.

Lots of people—even professional chefs—use "caramelize" and "brown" interchangeably, but if you look at the science behind these flavor-boosting techniques, they're actually quite different (though both, of course, lead to a literal "browning" of the food).

Caramelization describes the chemical reactions that take place when any sugar is heated to the point that its molecules begin to break apart and generate hundreds of new flavor, color, and aroma compounds. Consider crème brûlée: After being exposed to high heat, the sugar atop the custard turns golden brown, with rich, complex caramelized flavors. (A similar process takes place when you cook onions, carrots, apples, or any other high-sugar fruit or vegetable; the food's sugars caramelize once most of the moisture has evaporated.)

As for browning, here the process involves the interaction of not just sugar molecules and heat but also proteins and their breakdown products, amino acids. Foods that benefit from browning include grilled and roasted meats and bread. Like caramelizing, browning creates a tremendous amount of flavors and colors, but they're not the same as those created by caramelization, because protein is involved. Another name for browning is the Maillard reaction, after the French chemist who first described these reactions in the 1900s.

I am confused about the meaning of the term "proof" in bread baking. Does it have to do with the yeast or the dough?

No wonder you're confused: The term "proof" has two meanings—one having to do with yeast and the other with dough.

Proofing yeast is a quick way for bakers to determine whether the yeast spores in active dry yeast or cake yeast are active. If these types of yeast have an extended stint in the refrigerator or if their age is unknown, it is a good idea to test them before using them in a recipe. To do so, fill a glass bowl or measuring cup with the amount of lukewarm water (105 to 115 degrees) called for in the recipe, add a pinch of sugar, and whisk until dissolved. Now sprinkle the yeast granules over the surface of the sugar water and whisk again. If active, the yeast will feed on the sugar and begin to foam and swell in five to 10 minutes. At this point, it is safe to proceed with the recipe. If there is no activity, the yeast will not do its work in the recipe and should not be used. Instant yeast, which is what we use in our test kitchen, does not require proofing. Each package is marked with an expiration date and, if used within the specified time, should be active.

The other use of the term "proof" denotes a stage in the rising of dough. After its first rise, dough is deflated, or punched down, and shaped into its final form. The shaped dough is then set out for its final rise and fermentation before baking; this is the step that is referred to as proofing. Fermentation allows flavors to develop for better-tasting bread. Most bread recipes recommend proofing dough at room temperature under plastic wrap or a clean, slightly damp, lightweight towel to prevent dehydration. Some doughs proof quickly; others need to proof overnight. A reliable way to test the dough's progress is to touch it lightly with a moistened finger. At first, the dough will feel firm and will bounce back to the touch. At the halfway mark, it will feel spongy on the surface but firm underneath. It is ready for the oven when it feels altogether spongy and when the indentation left in the dough fills in slowly. If the indentation doesn't fill in at all, the dough has overproofed and is in danger of collapsing in the oven.

I've occasionally seen the word "short" used in articles on baking, as in adding "shortness" to pastry. Can you tell me what this means?

For bakers, "shortness" is a term used to describe the level of tenderness in a dough.

Bakers must be nothing if not precise, so it should come as no surprise that they have a term reserved for a particularly important aspect of pastry: its tenderness. When bakers talk about shortening a pastry, they're essentially talking about increasing its tenderness, making it more crumbly. A shortbread cookie is a perfect example of shortness; it is so tender, so crumbly, so short that it nearly melts in your mouth.

To find out how the term "short" entered the baker's vocabulary, we turned to Ben Fortson, senior lexicographer at the Boston-based *American Heritage Dictionary*. He told us that one of the original meanings of short was "friable," as in easily crumbled or crushed into powder. The first documented use of "short" as applied to baking was in a cookbook in England around 1430, Fortson said, while the term "shortening" as we know it in baking first appeared in America in 1796. Yet another, certainly less pleasant (though no less useful) application of "short" in this sense of crumbly or friable showed up in England in 1618, when farmers were in the habit of adding straw to manure to make it break up more easily when used as a fertilizer. They called their creation "short manure" or "short muck."

I've seen articles on baking that mention the desirability of a "closed crumb" versus an "open crumb." What are bakers talking about when they refer to "crumb"?

These are descriptions of the texture of the baked good; different types of crumb are ideal for different types of baked goods.

Bakers use the terms "closed" (or tight) and "open" (or loose) to describe the texture of a baked good, often in reference to its aeration, or the relative size and concentration of the air pockets. A comparison to knitting may be helpful: A very tightly knit sweater with small stitches that lets little air through (and so keeps you warm) would be comparable to a piece of pound cake or brioche. A shawl with a very open pattern would be comparable to the loose crumb that's typical of an English muffin or a piece of sourdough bread. Crumb is affected by nearly everything that goes into a cake or bread: the type of flour, the amount of yeast or chemical leavener, and the amount of liquid. In general, tenderness is characteristic of a fine, tight crumb, while chewiness goes along with the open crumb of artisan breads such as sourdough.

Is there a difference between "frosting" and "icing"?

There's no hard-and-fast rule, but generally frostings are thick and fluffy, while icings are thin and smooth.

Some food encyclopedias define frosting as the American word for icing, and a handful of culinary dictionaries state that frosting and icing are one and the same, but most other sources differentiate the two. They define frostings as relatively thick, sometimes fluffy confections that are spread over a cake or used to fill it. Icings are considered to have a thinner consistency and are usually poured or drizzled over baked goods as opposed to spread. They form a smooth, shiny coating. Also commonly noted about icings is that they are typically white.

What does it mean to "coddle" an egg? How is it different from poaching?

Coddled eggs are cooked in the shell; poached eggs are not.

Both coddling and poaching refer to cooking something gently in water heated to just below the boiling point. With eggs, the difference comes down to the shell: Poached eggs are cooked without the shell, directly in the simmering water (often with vinegar added to help the whites set). Coddling, on the other hand, involves cooking the eggs still protected by their shell (or by individual covered containers called coddling cups). Lightly coddled eggs (cooked for about 45 seconds, just to thicken the yolks slightly) are commonly used in Caesar salad dressing to provide a more viscous texture. When cooked a few minutes more, to a consistency resembling soft-boiled eggs (the whites are slightly more set), they can be eaten as is.

What is a "bouquet garni," and what does it do for a dish?

A bouquet garni is a bundle of herbs and spices used to flavor a dish; it is removed before serving.

A bouquet garni is a classic combination of fresh herbs used to flavor stocks, soups, and stews. There is no one universal recipe for bouquets garnis, although most variations begin with sprigs of fresh parsley and thyme, plus a dried bay leaf. Possible additions include rosemary, celery, leek, tarragon, savory, fennel, and whole spices, including black peppercorns. All the ingredients are wrapped together, either simply in a bundle tied with kitchen twine or in cheesecloth that's then tied up with twine. One end of the twine is often left long enough to wrap around the handle of the pot; when cooking is finished, the herb bundle is then easily retrieved and discarded.

What are "herbes de Provence"?

This herb mix includes a variety of herbs native to the Provence region of France.

Herbes de Provence, the aromatic blend from the south of France, traditionally combines dried lavender flowers with dried rosemary, sage, thyme, marjoram, and fennel, and sometimes chervil, basil, tarragon, and/or savory. It's a natural partner for poultry and pork (used as a rub or in an herb butter) or in other dishes characteristic of the Provençal region, such as lentil salads or ratatouille. You can find it in the spice aisle of most supermarkets or simply make your own simplified version at home. We like a combination of equal parts dried thyme, dried marjoram, dried rosemary, and toasted fennel seeds. Store homemade herbes de Provence in an airtight container at room temperature for up to 1 year.

What is "kombu"? I've seen it listed as an ingredient in Japanese dishes, but I'm not sure what it is.

Kombu is a form of dried seaweed that's used to enhance savory, umami flavors.

Kombu is a dried kelp, rich in flavor-enhancing glutamic acid, that's used extensively in Japanese cooking. One of its most popular applications is in dashi, Japan's multipurpose base for soups, stews, and sauces. Japanese cooks often add the seaweed to cold water, which is then brought to a simmer, at which point the kombu is removed (since temperatures above a simmer can pull out off-flavors). We've found that kombu can also be used to deepen flavors in nontraditional applications, as when small pieces of it are added to the pot with a vegetable soup's liquid ingredients or with the tomatoes in a pasta sauce. For every quart of liquid (or liquid-like ingredients), add a 2 by 2-inch piece of kombu (which can be found in Asian markets and many ordinary grocery stores), and be sure to remove it just as the liquid begins to simmer.

Why is some olive oil called "extra-virgin"? That seems like an odd term to use for oil.

The term itself might be a little odd, but the meaning is pretty important if you like good olive oil.

Olive oil, which is simply juice pressed from olives, tastes great when it's fresh. Only oil from the very first pressing of olives can be called extra-virgin olive oil. Extra-virgin olive oil is lively, bright, and full-bodied at its best, with flavors that range from peppery to buttery depending on the variety of olives used and how ripe they were when harvested. But like any other fresh fruit, olives are highly perishable, and their pristine, complex flavor degrades quickly, which makes producing—and handling—a top-notch oil time-sensitive, labor-intensive, and expensive.

For all these reasons, olive oil must meet numerous standards in order to achieve official extra-virgin status. These are established by the International Olive Council (IOC), the industry's worldwide governing body. Extra-virgin oil must meet certain chemical standards, be free of off-notes, and contain some positive fruity flavors. Unfortunately, these standards were largely unenforced in the United States until recently, so lower-quality oils were being passed off as extra-virgin. In the past few years, the U.S. Department of Agriculture (USDA) has adopted similar chemical and sensory standards to those used by the IOC in order to better regulate the olive oil most Americans buy at the supermarket. Add extra-virgin olive oil to dishes after cooking, or save it for vinaigrettes; don't use the good stuff for pan-frying, since its delicate flavors break down when heated.

What can labels like "dark" and "light" on ground coffee and coffee beans tell me about how they taste?

Not much, but the roast color can tell you whether the coffee is better black or with milk.

The degree to which coffee beans are roasted has as much of an impact on their final profile as their intrinsic flavors. While coffee roasters use a variety of names to categorize the darkness of their roasts (Italian, French, Viennese), there are no industry standards for this nomenclature. We've found it's more useful to categorize roasts by color. At one end of the spectrum are light roasts, characterized by pale brown color and bright, fruity, more acidic flavors. As roasting continues, color deepens, acids are broken down, and sweeter flavors begin to surface.

Choosing your roast is a matter of preference, but how you take your coffee is also a consideration. We prefer drinking lighter roasts unadulterated; when milk is added, our preference switches to darker roasts. The proteins in milk and cream bind some of the bitter-tasting phenolic compounds in the more deeply roasted beans, reducing both bitterness and intensity of coffee flavor.

Roast	Color/Texture	Flavor
Light	Pale brown with dry surface	Light body and bright, fruity, acidic flavor
Medium	Medium brown with dry surface	Less acidity and the beginnings of richer, sweeter notes
Medium-Dark	Dark mahogany with slight oily sheen	Intense, caramelized flavors with subtle bittersweet aftertaste
Dark	Shiny black with oily surface	Pronounced bitterness with few nuances

I've heard some red wines described as "tannic." Can white wines be tannic, too?

While white wines may contain tannins, their levels are too low to produce the bitterness and astringency that we would characterize as tannic.

Wines that are characterized as tannic are high in tannins, which are chemical compounds known as polyphenols that occur naturally in wood, plant leaves, and the skins, stems, and seeds of fruits like grapes, plums, pomegranates, and cranberries. Tannins have a bitter flavor and astringent quality that has a drying effect on the tongue. One of the challenges of wine making is striking a favorable balance between tannins and sweetness, and wines are manipulated to enhance or suppress either characteristic depending on the varietal. Intense, full-bodied red wines like Malbec or Cabernet Sauvignon are often high in tannins, since the pressed grape juice spends a good deal of time in contact with the grape skins, stems, and seeds before being aged in wood barrels (another source of tannins).

White wines tend to be significantly lower in tannins than red wines since the juice spends so little time exposed to the grape skins. Any tannic characteristics they do exhibit are more likely the effect of oak aging.

What does it mean when a food is "fermented"?

❧

Fermentation is a set of reactions that occur when bacteria and/or yeasts interact with food, changing its flavor, texture, and aroma and helping preserve the food.

Fermentation is a process in which bacteria and/or yeasts consume carbohydrates and proteins naturally present in food, producing alcohols, lactic acid, acetic acid, and/or carbon dioxide as byproducts. Water and salt are often added to the mix because both create a fermentation-friendly environment. (Salt can also keep bad bacteria at bay.) Fermentation helps preserve food and alters its flavor, texture, and aroma. Fermented foods are easy to digest, and their bacteria are thought to offer health benefits—which helps explain their recent uptick in popularity.

Foods like pickles, vinegar, and yogurt have the tang that we often associate with fermentation. And of course beer and wine are fermented. But everyday foods like chocolate, coffee, olives, bread, vanilla, hot sauce, and cheese also get deep flavor from fermentation.

What do "pasteurized" and "ultrapasteurized" mean when it comes to dairy? Is there an advantage to using ultrapasteurized products?

☙

Ultrapasteurization is a version of pasteurization specially designed for dairy that might sit on the shelf longer, such as heavy cream, to help it last longer.

Pasteurization, developed in the 1860s by French scientist Louis Pasteur, is the process of applying heat to a food product to destroy pathogenic (disease-producing) microorganisms and to disable spoilage-causing enzymes. Because cow's milk is highly perishable and an excellent breeding ground for bacteria, yeast, and molds, it and other dairy products are among the most highly regulated and monitored foods in the United States. Heating milk kills 100 percent of existing pathogenic bacteria, yeast, and molds and 95 to 99 percent of other, nonpathogenic bacteria. Rapid cooling and subsequent refrigeration retard the growth of the survivors, which would eventually cause spoilage.

Ultrapasteurization was developed to solve the problem of slow-selling items such as eggnog, lactose-reduced products, and cream. Ultrapasteurized products are heated to 280 degrees or higher for at least two seconds and packaged in an aseptic atmosphere in sterilized containers. This process destroys not only all pathogenic organisms but also those that cause spoilage. Combined with sterile packaging techniques, ultrapasteurization extends shelf life to as much as 14 to 28 days after opening, if properly refrigerated. However, ultrapasteurization also destroys some of the proteins and enzymes that promote whipping, and the higher heat leaves the cream with a slightly cooked taste that our tasters detected, eliminating the more complex, fresh taste of pasteurized cream.

If you take cream in your coffee, or need to keep cream around for more than a few days, reach for ultrapasteurized (organic, if available). Mixed with coffee's strong taste, its flavor deficit will go unnoticed, and the cream will last much longer in your refrigerator. But if you plan to use cream on its own, whether whipped or poured over berries, seek out the pasteurized version—you'll be glad you did.

What make plastics "food grade"?

This term really just means "plastic meant for use with food."

Food-grade plastic is simply plastic that was manufactured with the intent of being used with food. The ingredients in the plastic must be approved by the U.S. Food and Drug Administration to ensure that they do not leach into the food under the intended use. A garbage bag is not intended for storing food, but a zipper-lock bag is. However, note that you can get into trouble if you don't follow manufacturers' recommendations. For instance, excessive heat can promote the leaching of chemicals in plastics into food. Make sure to read labels to see whether (and how) plastic containers can be heated.

What is rose water, and how is it used in cooking?

Rose water is an essence of rose petals commonly used in Middle Eastern and Indian cooking.

Rose water is a floral, perfumelike flavoring made by boiling crushed rose petals and condensing the steam in a still. It is used in Middle Eastern and Indian desserts, sometimes in conjunction with orange blossom water. In Middle Eastern cooking, rose water is often used in cakes, puddings, fruit salads, confections, and baklava. It plays a similar role in sweets from northern India, such as *gulab jamun*, which are deep-fried milk powder balls soaked in a cardamom- and rose-flavored syrup. Rice pudding is another common application.

We purchased three brands of rose water and tasted them in a Middle Eastern rice pudding that calls for 2 tablespoons of the flavoring. Tasters found that the brand containing "natural flavors" had the subtlest flavor, which they liked. The others had stronger profiles that struck our tasters as "fake-tasting" and "overwhelming." Rose water can be found in the international section of some supermarkets and at Middle Eastern and Indian grocers. Rose water is also sold as a beauty product, so make sure to buy a bottle that is labeled for culinary use if you plan to cook with it. If you're not used to its flavor, start out by using slightly less than the recipe calls for. A little goes a long way, and you can always add more.

What are ramps? I keep seeing them at farmers' markets.

Ramps are closely related to onions, leeks, and scallions.

The ramp (also known as wild leek, wild garlic, or ramson) is a member of the onion family that sprouts up in early spring. The bulb looks a little like a scallion, but the leaves are flatter and broader. Both bulb and leaves can be used raw or cooked in applications that call for onions, leeks, or scallions. To prepare ramps, trim off the roots, remove any loose or discolored skin, and rinse well. We sampled ramps sautéed in butter and tossed with pasta, as well as pickled in a simple vinegar mixture. Tasters described the flavor as slightly more pungent than more familiar alliums, with hints of garlic and chive. The raw leaves are slightly grassy, reminiscent of a mild jalapeño.

THERE IS ONE TERM YOU NEED TO KNOW FOR PERFECT PASTA: al dente. This Italian phrase means "to the tooth," and it's used as a doneness instruction for pasta, rice, and other grains. It indicates food that is fully cooked but still firm when bitten into. For perfectly al dente pasta, you can't just use the timing instructions on the side of the box. Several minutes before the pasta should be done, begin taste-testing it—that's really the only way to know when it's ready (see page 22). When the pasta is almost al dente, drain it. The residual heat will finish cooking it. Here are our other tips for getting great pasta every time:

Use Plenty of Water

Use 4 quarts of water for every pound of pasta. You'll need a large pot, but a generous amount of water will ensure that the pasta cooks evenly and doesn't clump.

Salt the Water, but Don't Oil It

Once the water is boiling, add 1 tablespoon of salt. Salt adds flavor—without it, the pasta will taste bland. But forget about adding oil to the pot (see page 22). Adding oil to the boiling water does not prevent sticking; frequent stirring does.

Save Some Water

Before draining, use a liquid measuring cup to retrieve about ½ cup of the cooking water from the pot. Then go ahead and drain the pasta for just a few moments before you toss it with the sauce. (Don't let your pasta sit in the colander for too long; it will get very dry.) When you toss your sauce with the pasta, add some (or all) of the reserved pasta water to help spread the sauce.

Sauce in the Pot

Returning the drained pasta to the pot and then saucing it ensures evenly coated, hot pasta. You generally need 3 to 4 cups of sauce per pound of pasta.

Pairing Shapes and Sauces

There are dozens of shapes of pasta. Our general rule for matching pasta and sauces is that you should be able to eat some pasta and sauce easily with each bite. This means that the texture of the sauce should work with the pasta shape. In general, long strands are best with smooth sauces or sauces with very small chunks. Wider noodles, such as fettuccine, can more easily support slightly chunkier sauces. Sauces with very large chunks are best with shells, rigatoni, or other large, tube-shaped pastas, while sauces with small to medium chunks make more sense with fusilli or penne.

Pasta in Translation

Here are the most common pasta shapes we use in the test kitchen, along with what their names really mean.

Farfalle butterflies, bow ties

Conchiglie conch shells

Orecchiette little ears

Fusilli little springs

Penne pens, quills

Ziti bridegrooms

Gemelli twins	*Spaghetti* little strings
Macaroni elbows	*Spaghettini* little spaghetti
Rigatoni fluted tubes	*Linguine* little tongues
Rotelle wagon wheels	*Fettuccine* little ribbons
Campanelle bellflowers	*Pappardelle* gulping down
Vermicelli little worms	*Bucatini* little holes

What exactly is "prime" beef, and should I pay extra for it?

To grade meat, inspectors evaluate color, grain, surface texture, and fat content and distribution.

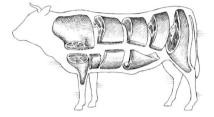

The USDA assigns eight different quality grades to beef, but most of the meat available to consumers is confined to just three: prime, choice, and select. Grading is strictly voluntary on the part of the meat packer. If meat is graded, it should bear a USDA stamp indicating the grade, though the stamp may not be visible to the consumer. To grade meat, inspectors—or, more often today, video image analysis machines—evaluate color, grain, surface texture, and fat content and distribution. Prime meat (often available only at butcher shops) has a deep maroon color, fine-grained muscle tissue, and a smooth surface that is silky to the touch. It also contains fat that is evenly distributed and creamy white instead of yellow, which indicates an older animal that may have tougher meat. Choice beef has less marbling than prime, and select beef is leaner still.

Our blind tasting of all three grades of rib-eye steaks produced predictable results: Prime ranked first for its tender, buttery texture and rich, beefy flavor. Next came choice, with good meaty flavor and a little more chew. The tough and stringy select steak followed, with flavor that was barely acceptable. We've found the same to be true for other cuts. Our advice: When you're willing to splurge, go for prime steak, but a choice steak that exhibits a moderate amount of marbling is a fine, affordable option. Just steer clear of select-grade steak.

I assume "grass-fed" and "grain-fed" refer to what an animal ate, but what do these labels actually mean for the quality and taste of the meat?

Grain-fed beef has long been promoted as richer and fattier, while grass-fed beef has gotten a bad rap as lean and chewy, with an overly gamy taste, but we didn't find that in our taste tests.

Picking out a steak is no longer as simple as choosing the cut, the grade, and whether the beef has been aged. Now there's another consideration: the cow's diet. While most American beef is grain-fed, many supermarkets are starting to carry grass-fed options as well.

To judge the difference between the two types for ourselves, we went to the supermarket and bought 16 grass-fed and 16 grain-fed rib-eye and strip steaks. Because the grass-fed steaks were dry-aged for 21 days, we bought the same in the grain-fed meat. When we seared the steaks to medium-rare and tasted them side by side, the results surprised us: With strip steaks, our tasters could not distinguish between grass-fed and grain-fed meat. Tasters did, however, notice a difference in the fattier rib eyes, but their preferences were split: Some preferred the "mild" flavor of grain-fed beef; others favored the stronger, more complex, "nutty" undertones of grass-fed steaks. None of the tasters noticed problems with texture in either cut.

What accounts for the apparent turnaround in meat that's often maligned? The answer may lie in new measures introduced in recent years that have made grass-fed beef taste more appealing, including "finishing" the beef on forage like clover that imparts a sweeter profile. Perhaps even more significant is that an increasing number of producers have decided to dry-age. This process concentrates beefy flavor and dramatically increases tenderness.

Our conclusion: For non-dry-aged grass-fed beef, the jury is still out over whether it tastes any better (or worse) than grain-fed. But if your grass-fed beef is dry-aged—and if you're OK with fattier cuts like rib eye that taste a little gamy—you'll likely find the meat as buttery and richly flavored as regular grain-fed dry-aged beef.

What does it mean when beef is labeled "blade tenderized"?

Blade-tenderizing is a process used to minimize toughness in chewy cuts of meat.

Blade-tenderized (also known as "mechanically tenderized" or "needled") meat has been passed through a machine that punctures it with small, sharp blades or needles to break up the connective tissue and muscle fibers with the aim of making a potentially chewy cut more palatable (or an already tender cut more so). But because the blades can potentially transfer illness-causing bacteria from the surface of the meat into the interior, the USDA recommends that all mechanically tenderized meat be labeled as such and accompanied by a reminder to cook the meat to 145 degrees with a resting time of 3 minutes (or 160 degrees with no resting time).

A handful of retailers label their tenderized beef, but if you're concerned, you can ask your supermarket butcher to confirm whether the meat has been processed in this way. As for the effectiveness of blade tenderizing, we compared tenderized top sirloin steaks and rib-eye steaks with traditional steaks and found that the blade-tenderized steaks were indeed more tender when all the steaks were cooked to a safe 160 degrees. But we prefer our steaks cooked to medium-rare, and since that isn't advisable with blade-tenderized beef, we'll stick with traditional meat.

What do the terms "Kobe," "Wagyu," and "American Wagyu" beef mean?

Kobe and Wagyu refer to a particular breed of cattle from Japan. American Wagyu is a hybrid breed from the United States.

Wagyu is a breed of cattle originally raised in Kobe, the capital city of Japan's Hyogo prefecture. Wagyu have been bred for centuries for their rich intramuscular fat, the source of the buttery-tasting, supremely tender meat. Wagyu cattle boast extra fat since they spend an average of one year longer in the feedlot than regular cattle, and end up weighing between 200 and 400 pounds more at slaughter. What's more, the fat in Wagyu beef is genetically predisposed to be about 70 percent desirable unsaturated fat and about 30 percent saturated fat, while the reverse is true for conventional American cattle.

In order to earn the designation "Kobe beef," the Wagyu must come from Kobe and meet strict production standards that govern that appellation. The "American Wagyu" or "American-Style Kobe Beef" that appears on some restaurant menus is usually a cross between Wagyu and Angus, but the USDA requires that the animal be at least 50 percent Wagyu and remain in the feedlot for at least 350 days to receive these designations. In our taste tests, American Wagyu proved itself a delicacy worthy of an occasional splurge: It was strikingly rich, juicy, and tender.

I sometimes see meat at the supermarket labeled "lean" or "extra lean." What do these terms mean?

These designations have pretty specific meanings, but this labeling isn't required, so some very lean meat may not be labeled as such.

According to the USDA's Food Safety and Inspection Service, the terms "lean" and "extra lean" are used not only on beef but also on pork, poultry, and seafood to convey information about fat content, including the amount of total fat, saturated fat, and cholesterol per 100-gram serving (about 3½ ounces). A "lean" designation means that the product contains fewer than 10 grams of total fat, 4.5 grams of saturated fat, and 95 milligrams of cholesterol per serving. "Extra lean" indicates fewer than 5 grams of total fat, 2 grams of saturated fat, and 95 milligrams of cholesterol per serving. (Following these rules, 93 percent lean ground beef would technically be considered "lean," while "extra lean" beef would have to be more than 95 percent lean.) These designations can be used for any cut of meat as long as the packer includes nutritional information on the label. Whether they appear at all, however, is up to the individual packing company.

I just bought ham, and its label says, "water added." What does that mean, and why am I paying for added water?

The label stems from a process called "wet curing," in which ham is treated with a brining solution, affecting both its water and protein contents.

The USDA grades cooked ham products. "Ham, Water Added" is one of the four categories used in classifying ham. The others are "Ham," "Ham with Natural Juices," and "Ham and Water Product."

Cooked ham is commonly wet-cured with a brining solution (often water, salt, phosphates or nitrates, and sugar). This makes the meat more seasoned and less likely to dry out when reheated at home. However, it also allows the producer to make more money by increasing the weight of the ham with water.

Officially, a cooked ham product is labeled by the percentage of protein by weight: The more water you add, the lower the percentage of protein in the meat. The USDA bases its grading scale on this protein percentage. Water-added ham has 17 to 18.5 percent protein by weight. We prefer ham with natural juices, which is 18.5 to 20.5 percent protein by weight and has good flavor and moisture when cooked.

What is "enhanced" pork enhanced with? Is it better than regular pork?

We prefer natural pork to enhanced pork,
which has been injected with a saline solution.

More than half of the fresh pork sold in supermarkets is now "enhanced." Enhanced pork is injected with a salt solution to make lean cuts, such as center-cut roasts and chops, seem moister. But we think natural pork has a better flavor, and a quick 1-hour brine adds plenty of moisture. We recommend buying natural pork.

Manufacturers don't use the terms "enhanced" or "natural" on package labels, but if the pork has been enhanced it will have an ingredient list. Natural pork contains just pork and thus doesn't need an ingredient list.

What are nitrites, and why should I avoid them?

This additive can lead to the formation
of carcinogenic compounds.

Cured pork products, such as bacon, often contain nitrite, a food additive that has been shown to form carcinogenic compounds when heated. So should you buy "nitrite-free" bacon? The problem is that while technically these products have no added nitrites, some of the ingredients used to brine them actually form the same problematic compounds during production. In fact, regular bacon contains lower levels of nitrites than some brands labeled "no nitrites or nitrates added" once the products are cooked. All the bacons we tested fell well within federal standards, but if you want to avoid nitrites you need to avoid bacon and other processed pork products altogether.

When shopping for whole chicken, I've seen "broilers," "roasters," and "stewing" birds. Can I really use them only for their assigned purpose?

*Those labels give you some useful information, but that doesn't
mean that you have to do exactly as they tell you to.*

These terms refer to the age of the bird—an important factor, since as chickens mature, they develop connective tissue that turns their meat tough. The older the bird, the more substantial the tissue, and the longer it takes to break down during cooking. However, since these terms are not widely used or understood, we call for poultry by weight, which is typically a good indicator of age.

Broilers (or fryers) are younger chickens: The USDA requires that the birds be slaughtered when they are around 7 weeks old and weigh 2½ to 4½ pounds. Next come roasters, processed at 8 to 12 weeks and weighing 5 pounds or more. Stewing chickens aren't slaughtered until 10 months or older and typically weigh at least 6 pounds.

When we roasted and stewed each type, the mature hens were undeniably tough and chewy compared with the tender broilers and roasters. But after three hours of stewing, the stewing birds tasted even richer and were just as tender as the broilers and roasters, since their connective tissue had enough time to transform into gelatin, which lubricated and flavored the meat. Our recommendation: If you're roasting, broiling, or frying, stick with a younger, more tender broiler or roaster. For a long-simmered stew or soup, it's worth seeking out a stewing chicken (which, unlike broilers or roasters, may require special ordering).

What makes a "kosher" chicken kosher?

The process of koshering a chicken involves soaking, salting, and washing the chicken, as does brining; they just happen in a different order and for different reasons.

In accordance with the dietary laws that govern the selection and preparation of foods eaten by observant Jews, chicken is processed in a prescribed manner to make it kosher, or fit to eat. The primary function of koshering chicken (as well as other meats) is to remove blood, the consumption of which is prohibited by the dietary laws.

After slaughter, inspection, and butchering, kosher chickens are soaked in cool, constantly replenished water for a half hour and then set out to dry before being covered entirely—inside and out—with coarse kosher salt. The chicken is left to sit and drain for an hour, at which point it is rinsed three times to remove the salt. According to Dr. Joe Regenstein, professor of food science at Cornell University, when salt is applied to the surface of the chicken, the free-flowing liquid within the proteins is drawn out. The salt, in turn, is absorbed back into the proteins. The salt denatures, or unwinds, the coiled strands of proteins, thereby priming them for the absorption of more liquid when the salt is rinsed off. The water and salt molecules, tangled in the web of protein strands, are what make the koshered chicken moist and flavorful.

Brining essentially combines all these steps into one. Immersed in a large container of salt and water, the chicken (or turkey) goes through much the same process as a koshered bird. Liquid rushes out of the proteins to dilute the solution of salt, which is then absorbed back into the meat, causing the protein strands to unravel and eventually absorb and trap additional moisture. This moisture retention is the primary function of brining.

The chicken I buy is labeled "natural," but what does that mean? Is it the same as "organic"?

❧

"Natural" and "organic" are not the same. If you see the word "natural" on a poultry or meat label, take it with a grain of salt: The term has very little meaning.

While the term "natural" sounds nice, it doesn't have much meaning on food packaging. The USDA stipulates that meat or poultry labeled "natural" can have no artificial ingredients added to the raw meat. It doesn't cover how a chicken was raised, however, so a producer can tack the label on a package even if the animal was fed an unnatural diet, pumped with antibiotics, and/or injected with broth or brine during processing.

On the other hand, "USDA Organic" is a tightly regulated term. It applies not only to the meat itself but also to how the animal was raised. To earn this label, the animals must eat organic feed not containing animal byproducts, be raised without antibiotics, and have access to the outdoors.

What is the difference between "air-chilled" and "water-chilled" chicken?

❧

As the names suggest, one is chilled in cold air and the other in cold water—and which process is used can have serious repercussions for the chicken's flavor and texture.

When working on chicken recipes, we almost always use a high-quality bird from one of our favorite brands, Bell & Evans. One morning when these chickens weren't available, we tested a recipe for roast chicken using a regular supermarket brand instead. The chicken behaved completely differently—the skin did not brown as much, and the meat tasted bland and washed-out. When we read the fine print on the label—"Contains up to 4% retained water"—we understood why.

Unlike Bell & Evans chickens, which are air-chilled soon after slaughtering in order to cool to a safe temperature, most supermarket birds are submerged in a 34-degree water bath. According to the USDA's Agricultural Research Service, chickens can absorb up to 12 percent of their body weight in moisture during this process; the amount drops down to about 4 percent by the time they are sold. Air-chilled chickens, on the other hand, are not exposed to water and thus do not absorb additional moisture, which helps account for the more concentrated flavor of their meat and better browning of their skin.

My grocery store sells frozen "Atlantic salmon," but the package says "product of Chile." What gives?

"Atlantic salmon" refers to a species of salmon, not to the ocean where it was caught.

Atlantic salmon did originate in the Atlantic Ocean, but nowadays most Atlantic salmon sold in the United States is raised on farms in Norway, Scotland, Chile, and Canada. Similarly, Pacific salmon—which includes sockeye, coho, and Chinook (also called king)—originated in the north Pacific Ocean. Most Pacific salmon sold in this country is wild-caught in the American northwest, British Columbia, and Alaska and has a more assertive flavor and a lower fat content than farmed Atlantic salmon.

Cheat Sheet

🍶

La Cuisine Française:
Commonly Misunderstood
(and Mispronounced)
French Food Terms

BECAUSE OF FRANCE'S RICH AND INFLUENTIAL CULINARY CULTURE, you will encounter a lot of French terms at restaurants, in cookbooks, and on food packaging. This handy guide will help you avoid confusion and embarrassment the next time you're out to eat with your foodie friends or navigating the gourmet market.

Word/Pronunciation	What It Is
aïoli *aye-OH-lee*	Aïoli is a rich mayonnaise sauce infused with garlic, although other flavorings are sometimes used. It is served as a condiment for meats, fish, and vegetables or spread on sandwiches.
à la mode *ah luh MOHD*	Literally translated, this phrase means "in the latest style or fashion." It usually refers to a dessert served with ice cream.
aperitif *uh-pair-ih-TEEF*	An aperitif is an alcoholic drink that you have before the meal to stimulate the appetite. The opposite of an aperitif is a digestif, which you drink after the meal to aid in digestion.
bain-marie *bayn-muh-REE*	A hot water bath called a bain-marie is used to gently cook delicate foods like custard by modulating the heat of the oven.

Word/Pronunciation	What It Is
béarnaise *bare-NAYS*	This classic French sauce is a variation on hollandaise. Both are buttery, creamy emulsified sauces, but béarnaise has a slightly more savory flavor profile due to the addition of white wine and tarragon. It is frequently paired with steaks, chops, and fish.
béchamel *BAY-sha-mell*	The classic French white sauce is traditionally made by stirring milk into a cooked mixture of butter and flour, or roux (see page 241). It serves as the base for numerous dishes such as lasagna and creamed spinach.
confit *kon-FEE*	The confit cooking method involves slow-cooking food in abundant fat until the food is completely tender. Traditionally used for duck and other meats, this method can also be applied to ingredients such as garlic or mushrooms.
crème Anglaise *krem ahn-GLAYS*	This velvety custard sauce is served with fruit, fruit desserts, cakes, and puddings, including sticky toffee pudding.
croquette *kro-KET*	A croquette consists of food (such as minced meat, fish, or vegetables) shaped into a small ball. Croquettes are often breaded and deep-fried.
dacquoise *da-KWAZ*	A dacquoise is a multilayered pastry dessert made from meringue, buttercream, and chocolate ganache. Its name means "of Dax," the town in southwestern France where the dessert was first made.

continued on next page

Word/Pronunciation	What It Is
demi-glace *DEH-mee-glahss*	Demi-glace is a highly reduced sauce base with rich, concentrated flavor and glossy texture.
en papillote *enh pah-pee-YOTE*	This cooking method is characterized by enclosing the food in a parchment paper packet before cooking. The food steams in its own juices for pure, clean flavors.
fleur de sel *fluhr deh SELL*	This flaky, crunchy sea salt (literally "flower of salt") is made by skimming off the thin film of salt that forms on seawater. It is often used as a finishing salt.
haricots verts *AH-ree-coe vair*	While the literal translation of haricots verts is just "green beans," this name refers to a particular type of thin French green beans.
hors d'oeuvre *or DERV*	Literally translated, this phrase means "outside the work"—it refers to food that is "outside" the main meal, or food served before the meal. These small appetizers, often finger foods, are usually savory.
mille-feuille *meel-FWEE*	A mille-feuille is a type of dish made by layering puff pastry and filling. It can be savory or sweet. The name literally means "thousand sheets," although most recipes do not actually have a thousand layers.
mirepoix *meer-PWAH*	*Mirepoix* is a mixture of onions, carrots, and celery that serves as a flavor base for stocks, broths, sauces, and braises. The classic ratio is 2 parts onions, 1 part carrots, and 1 part celery.

Word/Pronunciation	What It Is
mise en place *meez uhn PLASS*	This term for the process of preparing and measuring out all the ingredients for a dish before you begin to cook means "putting in place" in French.
pâte à choux *pat ah SHOO*	This light, basic pastry dough is used to make the base of profiteroles, eclairs, cream puffs, and gougères. You may also see the terms *pâte brisée* (shortcrust pastry, as used in a pie) or *pâte sucrée* (sweet pastry, as used in a tart).
persillade *pur-see-YAD*	*Persillade* refers to a mixture of finely chopped parsley and garlic that is commonly used to garnish meat or vegetables.
rémoulade *ray-moo-LAHD*	This creamy, tangy sauce usually contains capers and herbs and is traditionally paired with fish and shellfish.
sablé *sah-BLAY*	*Sablés* are French butter cookies similar to shortbread.
sous vide *soo VEED*	During *sous vide* cooking, vacuum-sealed food (the name literally means "under vacuum") is cooked in a water bath that is heated to the food's final serving temperature (e.g., 125 degrees for salmon).
terroir *tehr-WAHR*	*Terroir* describes the way that the unique place in which a food was grown can affect its flavors. It is frequently used to describe wine but can apply to many other kinds of natural products.
velouté *veh-loo-TAY*	This classic, rich French sauce is made from stock, cream, butter, and flour.

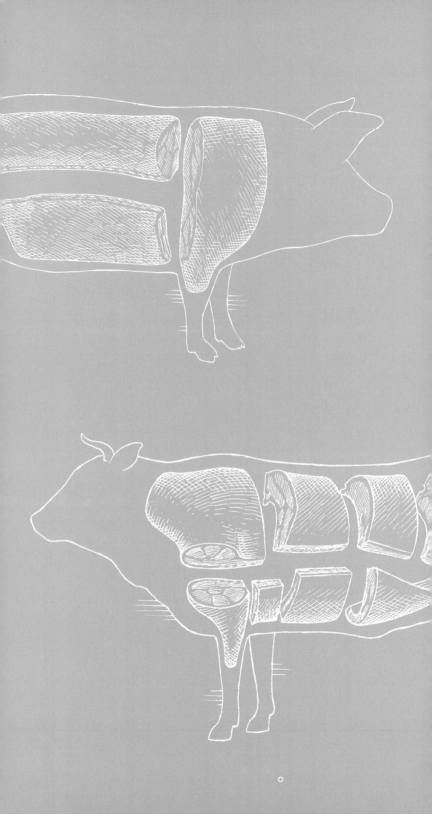

Index

A

Adsorption, 189
Agave nectar, 74
Aïoli, 282
Air-chilled chicken, 280–81
À la mode, 282
Alcohol
    evaporation of, during
        cooking, 39
    flambéing with, 39,
        186–87
Al dente, 22, 270
Alliinases, 192
All-purpose flour
    measuring, 53
    protein content of, 63
    substitutions and, 63, 64
Almond butter, as peanut
    butter substitute, 81
Aluminum foil, tenting
    meat with, 158
American Wagyu
    beef, 274–75
Amylopectin, 243
Amylose, 68, 243
Anchovies
    freezing, 220
    substitutes for, 60

Angel food cakes
    as cupcakes, 134
    egg temperature and, 18
    pans for, 133
Anthocyanins, 234–35
Aperitifs, 282
Apple cider vs. apple
    juice, 126–27
Apples
    browning of, 232–33
    pureeing, 142
    ripening, 223
Apricots, 223
Arugula
    measuring, 163
    wilted, reviving, 154
Asparagus
    thickness of, 28
    white vs. green, 102
    wilted, reviving, 154
Atlantic salmon, 62, 281
Avocados
    freezing, 220
    ripening, 34, 223
    selecting ripe, 34
    varieties of, 34

B

Bacon
fat, vegetarian substitute
for, 59
freezing, 220
nitrites in, 277
as pancetta substitute, 58
Bain-marie, 282
Baked goods
butter temperature
and, 201
butter type and, 90–91, 131
cocoa powder in, 78
cooling, 139–40
crumb of, 259
in disposable pans, 138
eggs in, 18–19, 84
espresso powder in, 79
gluten and, 239
humidity and, 216–17
rotating, in oven, 17
stale, 218
substitutions in, 82–83
whole-wheat flour in, 64
see also specific types
Baking powder
baking soda vs., 71
substitute for, 83
Baking soda
baking powder vs., 71
cleaning wooden spoons
with, 169

Baking soda *(cont.)*
with peroxide,
for lessening chile
burn, 156
as refrigerator
deodorizer, 46
Banana bread, 212
Bananas
freezing, 220
other fruit ripened
with, 222–23
ripening, 33, 223
roasting green, 33
Basil
frozen, 109
Thai, 145
in a tube, 108
Basting, 226–27
Beans
green vs. wax, 101
haricots verts, 284
Béarnaise, 283
Béchamel, 241, 283
Beef
American Wagyu, 274–75
blade-tenderized, 274
choice, 272
color changes in, 10, 236
doneness temperatures
for, 178
dry-aged, 215, 273
extra lean, 275